REVOLUTION

Volume 24

PROFIT AND POVERTY
IN RURAL VIETNAM

PROFIT AND POVERTY IN RURAL VIETNAM

Winners and Losers of a Dismantled Revolution

RITA LILJESTRÖM,
EVA LINDSKOG,
NGUYEN VAN ANG and
VUONG XUAN TINH

LONDON AND NEW YORK

First published in 1998 by Curzon Press

This edition first published in 2022
by Routledge
4 Park Square, Milton Park, Abingdon, Oxon OX14 4RN

and by Routledge
605 Third Avenue, New York, NY 10158

Routledge is an imprint of the Taylor & Francis Group, an informa business

© 1998 Rita Liljeström, Eva Lindskog, Nguyen Van Ang and Vuong Xuan Tinh

All rights reserved. No part of this book may be reprinted or reproduced or utilised in any form or by any electronic, mechanical, or other means, now known or hereafter invented, including photocopying and recording, or in any information storage or retrieval system, without permission in writing from the publishers.

Trademark notice: Product or corporate names may be trademarks or registered trademarks, and are used only for identification and explanation without intent to infringe.

British Library Cataloguing in Publication Data
A catalogue record for this book is available from the British Library

ISBN: 978-1-032-12623-4 (Set)
ISBN: 978-1-003-26095-0 (Set) (ebk)
ISBN: 978-1-032-19074-7 (Volume 24) (hbk)
ISBN: 978-1-032-19080-8 (Volume 24) (pbk)
ISBN: 978-1-003-25756-1 (Volume 24) (ebk)

DOI: 10.4324/9781003257561

Publisher's Note
The publisher has gone to great lengths to ensure the quality of this reprint but points out that some imperfections in the original copies may be apparent.

Disclaimer
The publisher has made every effort to trace copyright holders and would welcome correspondence from those they have been unable to trace.

PROFIT AND POVERTY
IN RURAL VIETNAM

Winners and Losers of a Dismantled Revolution

Rita Liljeström, Eva Lindskog,
Nguyen Van Ang and Vuong Xuan Tinh

CURZON

Nordic Institute of Asian Studies
Democracy in Asia Series, No. 3

First published in 1998
by Curzon Press
15 The Quadrant, Richmond
Surrey TW9 1BP

Typesetting by the Nordic Institute of Asian Studies
Printed and bound in Great Britain by
Biddles Ltd, Guildford and King's Lynn

Copyright © 1998 by Rita Liljeström, Eva Lindskog,
Nguyen Van Ang and Vuong Xuan Tinh

British Library Catalogue in Publication Data
A CIP catalogue record for this book
is available from the British Library

ISBN 0-7007-0987-8

Publication of this work was assisted by a grant from the
Swedish International Development Cooperation Agency (Sida)

Contents

List of Figures vi

List of Tables viii

Preface ix

Acknowledgements xi

List of Abbreviations xiii

List of Weights and Measures xiv

List of Terms xv

1. Introduction: Winners and Losers of a Dismantled Revolution 1

Case 1: Standing on Two Feet
    2. Land and People 17
    3. The Shift to a Commodity Economy 29
    4. Restructuring of Tan Thanh Forest Enterprise 42
    5. Redivided Responsibilities 59

Case 2: Two Models of Modernization
    6. Custom and Commerce in Phuc Tam Village 75
    7. Substitution of a Failing Management Model 95
    8. Modernization by the Market 102

Case 3: "Neither Bat nor Rat"
    9. Advancement and Deprivation in Khuoi Nieng 133
    10. Reconciliation of Hardships in the Past 151
    11. Current Ambiguities 167

Case 4: "All Have to Eat Rice"
    12. Poverty and Environmental Degradation 177
    13. Customary and Modern Approaches to Forest Protection 200
    14. An Unequal Struggle for a Better Future 210

15. Summary: The Impact of Doi Moi 237

Epilogue 258

References 259

Index 263

List of Figures

Note that photographs marked with "[EL]" in the caption were taken by Eva Lindskog and those marked "[RL]" by Rita Liljeström.

1. Location of the four case-study areas in the provinces of Tuyen Quang and Ha Giang. xvi
2–5. Many different ethnic groups live with one another within the same territory. 4
6. Local (Tay) leader in Lam Tien with family. 21
7. Local (Kinh) leader of the forestry workers with family. 21
8. Tay farmer coming back from the wet-rice field. 28
9. Dao woman bringing hill rice back home. 33
10. Enterprising forestry worker. 35
11. Tobacco for sale at the market in Phu Luu. 36
12. A typical Tay house on poles. 38
13. A typical Kinh house in brick. 38
14. Minh Dan Brigade in 1987. 46
15. Minh Dan Brigade in 1994. 46
16. Household structure in Minh Dan in 1987 and 1994. 49
17. A family planning to return to the Delta does not invest in housing, 1994. 54
18. In 1989 we met this family who had already started to invest in a brick house. 54
19. Kindergarten in Minh Dan Brigade in 1994. 56
20. Vaccination of a young mother, 1994. 67
21. One of the classes in Lam Tien, 1994. 68
22. Mrs Luong and Mr Chi have worked for many years as forestry workers. 71
23. Households with rice husking machines serve families in the village and Brigade 481. 85
24. Director Dien at Chiem Hoa forest enterprise, 1994. 96
25. A row of collective houses at Brigade 481, 1989. 103
26. State employees had access to nursery and kindergarten. 106

LIST OF FIGURES

vii

27. A planting group in action. 107
28. Sau was cheerful and lively and had an impressive capacity to do household chores and gardening with her single arm. 112
29. The key to economic success is diversification. Burning bricks is a common source of extra income. 119
30. Some husbands had engaged in gold digging in the Lo River – a dangerous and risky activity. 121
31. The parents have sacrificed everything, sold what they had and put themselves in debt to save their daughter. 124
32. A planting group at rest. 129
33. Mr Hien and Mrs Huan became forestry workers in 1972. 129
34. Dao farmers at the village tea house. 135
35. Although there are many new jobs and goods in Khuoi Nieng, cutting bamboo for use as ropes is still a necessity. 145
36. Father and son in Area II. 149
37. Collective house in Brigade 5 in 1987. 159
38. The same house in 1995 – cut into pieces to serve as private houses. 159
39. Dao woman in Area 11, Khuoi Nieng village. 169
40. Mrs Luong, a forestry worker in Brigade 5B. 173
41. After unloading the horses, the men take them to the stream that runs at the bottom of a ravine. 178
42. Nung woman selling alcohol at the market. 179
43. Small children wear lovely headgear, often decorated with silver coins. 181
44. All daughters, even when married, live in their parents' home until they are about to give birth. 187
45. Mr Si makes horse bridles during the annual hunger-months in order to feed his large family. 193
46. Mr Vinh and his month-old daughter. 197
47. The workers are engaged in the nursery caring for pine seedlings. 218
48. "Our children do rather well at school. We hope that they will get stable jobs in the future." 224
49–50. The village school and one of its two classes. 225
51. Mrs Su, a teacher, is married to an employee at the forest enterprise. They are both Kinh. 228
52. Dao mother with her child. 232
53. H'Mong mother with her child. 233

viii   PROFIT AND POVERTY IN RURAL VIETNAM

54.   Only a decade ago many daily necessities were rationed. Now they are displayed in shops and stalls along the roads. 240
55.   A well-off family. 248
56.   A poor family with a sick child. 249
57.   Young Dao woman. 254
58.   Dao youth. 255
59–60. All children are eager to learn. 256

Colour plates: Hoang Su Phi Sunday market. *between 174 and 175*

List of Tables

1.   Population of ethnic groups in northern Vietnam. 6
2.   Ratio of children per couple in Lam Tien village, 1994. 66
3.   Family size of Tay and Kinh households in Phuc Tam, 1994. 78
4.   Land allocation per capita in Phuc Thinh commune, Nov. 1994. 82
5.   Employee numbers at Chiem Hoa forest enterprise, 1970–94. 113
6.   Employee statistics for Brigade 481, 1987–94. 113
7.   Reasons for retirement in Brigade 481, 1987–93. 114
8.   Land area of households interviewed in Khuoi Nieng. 137
9.   Garden land ownership in Khuoi Nieng. 143
10.   Area of household fields in Po Lung, 1995. 189
11.   Incentive payment rates given to peasant household by Hoang Su Phi forest enterprise, 1995. 208
12.   Categorization of marital alliances within the Hoang Su Phi forest enterprise, 1995. 212
13.   Teacher/pupil statistics for Hoang Su Phi district, 1995. 228
14.   Number of forestry enterprise employees, pre-1987 to 1994–95. 245

Preface

The present study is a follow-up of a study on the living conditions in state forest enterprises and agricultural cooperatives in northern Vietnam in 1987. It coincided with the initial stages of Doi Moi, the new policy of economic renovation. We encountered a collectivistic order hit by the insolvency of the state and people, who attempted to find means for survival without regard to their political correctness. Actually, Doi Moi had then adopted those means that proved to be viable.

In 1993 the Swedish International Development Cooperation Agency (Sida) commissioned us to study the social impact of the new economic policy in Vietnam on rural households in those areas where we had made our previous studies. The overall aim was to return to selected brigades and households and establish what the new economic policies have meant for the workers. We could then compare their present living conditions (demographic structure, housing, source and level of income, access to land, etc.) with those of 1987 and 1989.

The fieldwork was carried out by a team of four. In this volume, Mr Vuong Xuan Tinh (a researcher working at the Institute of Ethnography in Hanoi) is responsible for the presentation on the villages, their history and population, the ongoing socioeconomic changes, and the relationships between the main ethnic groups. As he is presently engaged on a thesis about food habits in the mountain region, Mr Tinh here also pays attention to the survival strategies of families.

Dr Nguyen Van Ang (an economist working at the National Economic University in Hanoi) gives an account of the spread of the contractual systems that opened up as a result of the land reforms in 1988 and 1993. He follows the local implementation of these reforms and the conflicts in their wake.

Eva Lindskog and Rita Liljeström investigate how the state forest enterprises reorganized their production, and what it meant for the workers in the selected brigades.

Eva Lindskog is a sociologist working as consultant at Jaakko Pöyry Consulting AB, Stockholm, on socioeconomic and cultural changes in rural areas in developing countries. Her main experience is from Vietnam. She is fluent in Vietnamese.

Rita Liljeström is a professor emerita at the Swedish Council of Social Sciences and Humanities. She is a sociologist with a special interest in the impact of modernization on gender and family relationships.

PROFIT AND POVERTY IN RURAL VIETNAM

The contributions by the Vietnamese team members have been decisive. They provided the foreign team members with basic knowledge about Vietnamese institutions and structural changes, thus enabling them to place the interviews on a household level within the broad framework of transition to a market economy.

In a sense, the Vietnamese colleagues were insiders, while the Swedes were clearly outsiders. However, this distinction is relative. As university-educated and urbane Kinh men, they were also outsiders in the villages. Being non-Vietnamese has certain advantages. It is possible to ask questions that the Vietnamese could not ask. A foreigner is naïve and does not know the restrictions that govern insiders. In this way foreigners can be more intrusive and touch upon sensitive issues, hopefully without causing offence.

The Vietnamese team members seemed to possess a respectful directness and discretion. They reported the full names of their respondents. When the issue of confidentiality was raised, they said:

> People are not so foolish as to say anything that could be used against them. Why should people reveal things that will harm them if they appear in print? On the contrary, credit should be given to the person who informs us.

The two team members seemed to assume that people knew the rules of separating public and private opinions.

We intended to conserve the individual authorship of each team member. Our styles of writing differed and besides, we wanted to give the credit to each author for his or her own work. However, in the end we had a fragmented manuscript with undue repetition and inconsistency. Indeed, the authors expended much effort in writing their own part of the study, but less in reading each other's texts.

Therefore it fell to Rita Liljeström to integrate all the contributions into a readable and coherent whole. By reorganizing and mixing, by adding and omitting text, the editor pieced parts together, while at the same time shifting meanings and changing values by creating new contexts. The editor pulled together the testimonies of four pairs of eyes into a "common" outlook.

She also wrote a general introduction into the case studies and a summary to tie up all the results. It should be mentioned that while the introduction was written in mid-1997, data in the case studies were assembled in report form back in 1994 and 1995, which explains the use of present tense when describing the observations in a given situation. It is the editor's hope that the gains outweigh the losses, and that the reader thereby feels part of the team.

Acknowledgements

The authors of the present book would like to express their heartful thanks to the Swedish International Development Cooperation Agency (Sida) for the generous contribution which made the fieldwork possible. We also thank Sida for the financial support to facilitate the editing and publication of the work.

We feel grateful to Ambassador Börje Ljunggren, Hanoi, who came up with the idea of the study. The fieldwork proved to be a powerful and provoking experience of the people and their conditions.

The late Ms. Susanne Rubin took part in the preparatory field work in Ha Tuyen province in the Spring of 1987. Her notes from fieldwork in Chiem Hoa have been of great value to the present study. We owe her memory our appreciation and gratitude.

We had several meetings at the Research Centre for Gender, Family and Environment in Development (CGFED) in Hanoi. The director, Professor Le Thi Nham Tuyet, had set up her centre when Doi Moi made it possible in 1992. She took part in the preparations of the study, and followed us on our first visit to Tuyen Quang province. Professor Nham Tuyet acted as our local professional counterpart. She introduced us to our Vietnamese co-workers, Mr Vuong Xuan Tinh and Dr Nguyen Van Ang. She generously lent her services and those of the centre to us. We owe a debt to Professor Nham Tuyet for all her support.

Rita Liljeström had to rely on a Vietnamese interpreter, while Vuong Xuan Tinh and Nguyen Van Ang needed interpretation into English. Professor Nham Tuyet provided us with three interpreters: Ms Nguyen Thi Hue from the Voice of Vietnam who assisted us in Hanoi and during preparatory visits to the provinces; Mr Nguyen Dai Phuong and Mr Tran Ngoc Tien, both journalists at Vietnam News Agency in Hanoi, who took part in fieldwork in Tuyeng Quang province and Ha Giang province respectively. We wish to express our appreciation for the way they all cooperated and developed empathy with the people we met. In spite of the considerable language barriers, the team was able to share views and opinions. We mutually gained from the days of reporting, discussing and comparing, which followed each period of fieldwork.

The fact that none of us has English as our mother tongue made us dependent upon translations and skilful editing. The Vietnamese manu-

xii   PROFIT AND POVERTY IN RURAL VIETNAM

scripts were translated into English by the late Mr Nguyen Van Hop of the Vietnam Confederation of Labour, and Mr Peter Colenbrander from Vancouver, Canada did the copy editing of the first full draft of the report. Subsequently, Ms Leena Höskuldsson of NIAS Publications demonstrated her skills in editing the revised and integrated manuscript.

List of Abbreviations

AFD	Agriculture and Forestry Department
CEMMA	Committee for Ethnic Minorities and Mountainous Areas
CGFED	Research Centre for Gender, Family and Environment in Development
FE	Forest Enterprise
GDLA	General Department for Land Administration
IUD	Intra-uterine Device
PC	People's Committee
Sida	Swedish International Development Cooperation Agency
VPSU	Vinh Phu Service Union

List of Weights and Measures

bo ma	Traditional measure, equivalent to 22 square metres
bung	Traditional Tay measure, equivalent to 1,000 square metres
cum	Traditional Dao measure, equivalent to 2.5 kilograms of paddy
dong	About 11,000 dong = US$1 (mid 1997)
mau	3,600 square metres
sao	360 square metres
thuoc	36 square metres

List of Terms

Association of Tay peers (*Tung Khoa*)
This is a voluntary association of male peers born in the same year in Lam Tien village. They pledge to maintain close relations with one another for their entire lives and to help one another in whatever ways they can.

Decree 100 (*Chi thi 100*)
Management system of the cooperatives introduced in 1981 that defined eight work links (see below) in rice production. Some links were contracted directly to the farmers and some links were managed by the cooperative.

Eight work links (*8 khau cong viec*)
1) production of seeds
2) preparation of land
3) sowing/transplanting
4) irrigation
5) fertilization
6) tending
7) pest control
8) harvesting

Family economy (*Kinh te gia dinh*)
Diverse economic activities – including farming, livestock breeding and small-scale industries – mainly done by the members of a household. The concept emerged spontaneously when the state and the cooperatives were no longer able to supply employees and farmers with sufficient salaries in cash and in kind. Later with Doi Moi it became officially encouraged.

Farmer/peasant (*Nong dan*)
In this study farmer and peasant are used as synonyms.

Farm/estate (*Trang trai, trai*)
This Vietnamese expression is usually translated as farm. However, in the area where this study has taken place it is normally understood

xvi   PROFIT AND POVERTY IN RURAL VIETNAM

as a piece of land at some distance from the living quarters and home gardens, where rice and cash-crops are grown.

Five land-use rights (*5 quyen su dung dat dai*)
These are the right to:

1) inherit allocated land
2) transfer land
3) change the land use
4) use land as collateral
5) lend land

Forest garden (*Vuon rung*)
Originally this is a piece of land with natural forest close to the living quarters that the ethnic groups in northern Vietnam used as their "private" forest.

Forest protection/control station (*Hat kiem lam*)
A state body at provincial and district level whose main duty is to police a forest area against illegal intrusion.

Land Law 1988 (*Luat Dat Dai 1988*)
Land belongs to the public under the sole management of the state. The state entrusts land to organizations and individuals for long term use. Beneficiaries of land may sell the fruits of their investment in the entrusted land.

Land Law 1993 (*Luat Dat Dai 1993*)
The five land-use rights (see above) are promulgated.

New Economic Zone (*Vung kinh te moi*)
Policy emerging during the 1960s to move people from the densely populated Red River delta to the mountain areas of northern Vietnam. Two main occupations were offered: opening up of new areas for farming in cooperatives and employment at state enterprises (forestry and agriculture).

Project 327 (*Du an 327*)
State-funded project aiming at reforestation of land suitable for forestry.

Regulation 176 (*Nghi che do 176*)
Provisional regulation (October 1989–December 1991) on retirement, which allowed forestry workers to leave their employment with an one-time lump sum of money.

LIST OF TERMS xvii

Resolution 10 (*Nghi quyet 10*)
Decision in 1988 by the Politburo of the Vietnamese Communist
Party to hand over (at least) five of the eight work links to the
farming household. This meant that the so-called family economy
was established as the main motor of rural production.

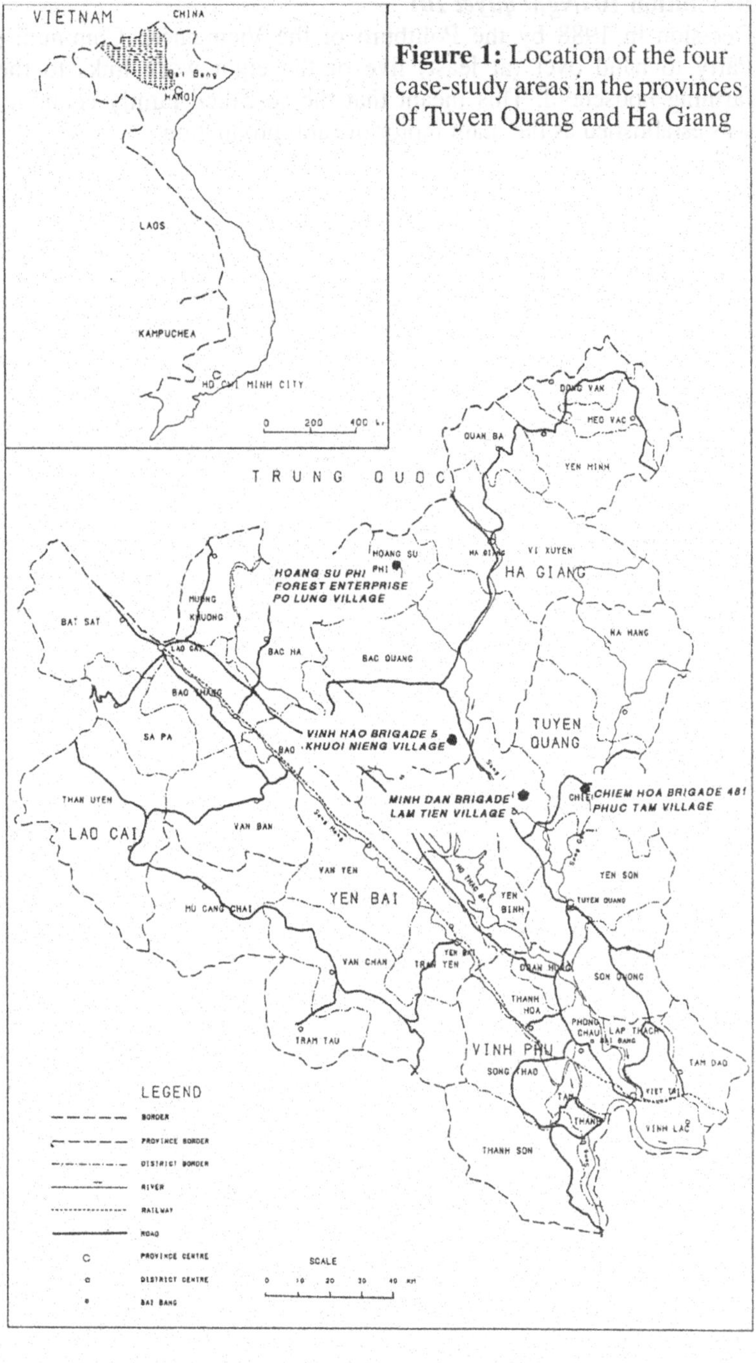

xviii   PROFIT AND POVERTY IN RURAL VIETNAM

Figure 1: Location of the four case-study areas in the provinces of Tuyen Quang and Ha Giang

ONE

Introduction: Winners and Losers of a Dismantled Revolution

BACKGROUND

In 1993, Börje Ljunggren, the then head of the Swedish International Development Agency's (SIDA) Asian section, suggested that Eva Lindskog and I should return to the areas where our 1987 study on the living conditions in state forest enterprises and agricultural cooperatives was conducted (Liljeström et al. 1987, 1988). The aim, to try to assess the impact of Doi Moi on rural households, we could not have approved more. The market-oriented economic reforms are known as Doi Moi. Literally *doi* means change and *moi* means new.

The 1987 study was motivated by an alarming report by Katarina Larsson and Lars-Erik Birgegård (1985) about the forestry workers' deplorable working and living conditions, and furthermore, the authors suspected the state enterprises of using forced labour. According to them, "Some workers felt that their recruitment had contained elements of subtle coercion or that they had been cheated; others had the sense of being compelled to stay in the forest while wanting to leave" (from Liljeström et al. 1987: 3).

The 1987 study had the broad goal of "analysing the recruitment and living conditions of the forestry workers in the light of the cultural, social and economic conditions prevailing in Vietnam" (Terms of Reference). Contrary to earlier on-the-spot evaluations, the Liljeström team tried to set the conditions of forestry workers in a wider context. We found no evidence of institutionalized "forced" labour. However, we were able to identify two exceptional instances where the usual regulations of labour recruitment were clearly violated (Liljeström et al. 1987). In 1987, it was unique for a team of foreign

2   PROFIT AND POVERTY IN RURAL VIETNAM

social scientists to be allowed to conduct fieldwork in rural northern Vietnam, especially as economic conditions were at a very low point. The state was bankrupt and the mass of people were extremely poor. Consequently, local state enterprises and cooperatives used unofficial methods to overcome their stagnation and lack of basic means. These solutions proved more productive than the formal system, and they were successively accepted officially and eventually adopted, thus opening the way for market economy.

While the economic changes in Vietnam have been rapid and impressive, one keeps wondering how they have affected employees in the state forestry and members of the agricultural cooperatives whom we met in 1987. Börje Ljunggren knew of our vantage point for comparing the present conditions with our field notes and interviews from 1987.

The investigation took place in a fluid and rapidly shifting situation. The ongoing changes meant that we could not even be sure that the brigades were still organized as such or that the agricultural co-operatives of the late 1980s still existed. However, we intended to discover what had happened to previous structures and, as far as possible, to describe what had replaced them. Particular attention was to be paid to the consequences of Doi Moi for women and men, for local ethnic groups and for the Kinh, who have migrated into the region.

PREPARATIONS IN HANOI AND SELECTION OF STUDY LOCALES

In December 1993 we went to Hanoi in order to prepare for our study on the impact of Doi Moi. The institutions we visited had all come into being in the wake of Doi Moi.

We were briefed by Mr Doan Trung My, land and law inspector at the Land Use and Management Department. He was involved in the 1988 Land Law and the 1993 Amendment of the Land Law. He made an excellent presentation of the land-user's five rights (exchange, transfer, lease, inheritance, and mortgage of land use), which aim to make land available to 70–80 per cent of the rural population and to encourage investment of labour and money in land.

In 1993, the Committee of Ethnic Minorities and Mountainous Areas had been set up. We introduced ourselves to Dr Vu Quang Dinh, the international relations officer, who told us about the committee and its task as an advisory body to government on shaping policies towards ethnic minorities.

Our fieldwork in Ha Tuyen province in the spring of 1987 had left a lasting impression on us. This was our very first sojourn among the forest brigades. Today, Ha Tuyen is divided into two provinces, Tuyen

INTRODUCTION: WINNERS AND LOSERS 3

Quang and Ha Giang. We decided to return to the southern and northern parts of the former Ha Tuyen. In Tuyen Quang we chose Minh Dan brigade, Tan Thanh forest enterprise, as one case, remembering the discontent that prevailed in 1987, the extreme poverty, the weeping infants in the nursery, the nocturnal rats, the powerful nurse Mrs Bun, and the workers sneaking to us behind her back. In May 1987, we had spent a week in Brigade 481, Chiem Hoa forest enterprise. In spite of the extremely hot and humid weather our notes and memories were vivid, and we included Brigade 481 among our cases. The adjacent villages of Lam Tien and Phuc Tam were also chosen.

In Ha Giang province, we selected Brigade 5, Vinh Hao forest enterprise, because we wanted to see how far the aspirations to turn it into a forest village had succeeded. The neighbouring village of Khuoi Nieng was also included. We believed that in all these places people would recognize us, and we would enjoy the trust given to caring visitors who returned, especially as we had visited those brigades in both 1988 and 1989.

During our previous fieldwork we had been intrigued by the minority people, but not able to understand the relationship between them and the majority Kinh. At that time, ethnicity was not recognized as an issue; nor did the Swedish aid consider the presence of ethnic minorities. By choosing a remote district where minorities were a majority, we intended to learn more about them. Besides, we wanted to compare the three familiar areas with one that was untouched by Swedish aid. That is why we chose Hoang Su Phi forest enterprise and Po Lung mountain village as our fourth case.

THE KINH AND ETHNIC MINORITIES

The mountain area of northern Vietnam contains great cultural diversity. Historically, the population consists of native people such as the Muong, Tay, and Thai, as well as ethnic migrants, mainly from China, including the Dao, H'Mong, Ha Nhi, and Lo Lo. There were large migrations to northern Vietnam thousands of years ago (e.g. the Thai) and more recently, in the past 200–300 years (such as the H'Mong). Additionally, sporadic clandestine migration of families and clans across the Vietnam–China and Vietnam–Laos borders has occurred. It is difficult to gather and validate statistics about these movements. At present there are thirty-one officially recognized ethnic groups which speak languages belonging to seven distinct linguistic groups. A ranking by size is given in Table 1.

Of the thirty-one ethnic groups, seventeen have populations under 10,000, and a few under 1,000 (Rambo and Cuc 1996). Their ethnic territories comprise three ecological zones: the low-lying valley

Figures 2–5: Many different ethnic groups live with one another within the same territory [RL].

region at about 400 metres above sea level; the intermediate region from 400 to 800 metres; and the upper region above 800 metres. If the Red River is held to divide northern Vietnam, then the valley region to the east is the home of the Tay and the Nung ethnic groups, while

the west is home to the Muong and the Thai. Living near and occasionally intermingling with ethnic groups in the low-lying region, there are ethnic groups from the intermediate region, such as the Dao, the Giay, the San Chi, the Kho Mu, and the Xinh Mun. The H'Mong,

6   PROFIT AND POVERTY IN RURAL VIETNAM

Table 1: Population of ethnic groups in northern Vietnam

Ethnic Group	Population
Kinh	2,500,000
Tay	1,000,000
Nung	600,000
Thai	600,000
H'Mong	530,000
Muong	460,000
Dao	440,000

Ha Chi, and Lo Lo live in the upper region. However, the classification is relative because in some places the majority of a group lives in a low-lying region, while a minority of the same group lives in the highlands, as for instance the Nung. Some ethnic groups in the intermediate region, like the Dao, settle in the valleys. Indeed, according to Rambo and Cuc (1996), a distinctive feature of the northern mountain region is that many different ethnic groups live with one another within the same territory

For example, out of the 109 districts and towns in the eleven northern provinces, more than half (fifty-nine) have ten or more ethnic groups present, with nine having fifteen or even more. There is not a single jurisdiction with an area exceeding 300 square kilometres that comprises only one ethnic group. Only 3 per cent of the villages are mono-cultural, the vast majority having three or more ethnic groups.

From time immemorial ethnic groups in northern Vietnam have lived by agriculture and animal husbandry. Many ethnic valley dwellers such as the Tay, Muong, Thai and Nung have practised an advanced wet-rice cultivation. Ethnic groups living in the intermediate and high regions cultivate terraced fields or hilly land. They also raise several kinds of fowl and cattle.

Of the four villages in our study, three are situated in the valley region and one in the high mountain region. Although these villages are different, the ethnic groups living in them share general historical, economic and social characteristics common to other ethnic groups in the northern mountain region. In this region, the Kinh account for a large percentage of the population, especially after 1954 when North Vietnam was liberated from French rule. With the state's policy of

INTRODUCTION: WINNERS AND LOSERS 7

placing key officials in the mountain region and of reclaiming wasteland, the number of Kinh people in the valleys increased.

In the 1960s it became government policy to establish state forest
enterprises in the northern provinces. The majority of the workers were
recruited from the delta. The state also encouraged farmers to migrate
and open up new land in the mountain regions. The Kinh believed that
they had a mission to civilize ethnic minorities.

The migration fundamentally altered the upland demographic balance.
In the years between the 1969 and 1989 censuses, the Kinh population in
Ha Tuyen province increased by 426 per cent. In the northern region as
a whole, the number of Kinh rose from 640,000 to almost 2.6 million.

The massive Kinh migration, combined with high rates of population growth among indigenous minorities, resulted in a tripling of the
region's population density between 1960 and 1989. Thus, average
densities increased in former Ha Tuyen province from twenty-six to
seventy-five per square kilometre. This increased pressure on rural
resources has had a devastating effect on the environment (Rambo
and Cuc 1996).

To sum up, the population consists of diverse ethnic minorities as
well as the Kinh, the Vietnamese majority. The state forestry recruited
mainly Kinh workers, while members of the agricultural cooperatives
are both Kinh and from local ethnic groups.

MILESTONES IN THE RENOVATION OF THE LAND RELATIONSHIP

The land relationship should here be understood as the relationships
between men in regard to land. These relationships have been expressed
as the rights of government, of cooperatives, of farmers, and of the state
forestry over land, and as the obligations of each land-user towards
society.

Early years

The land relationships of Vietnamese farmers have undergone remarkable changes over the past half-century. Before 1953, the peasants
had no land: they were employees of landlords through the system of
tenancy. Land renting was common in northern Vietnam from feudal
times until 1954.

In May 1954, the French colonial regime in Vietnam collapsed,
and in the same year the Geneva Agreement was signed. Since then,
northern Vietnam has followed a socialist path. Land reform began as
early as 1953 and was eventually executed in 1957. Most of the arable
land was confiscated and distributed to the landless peasants. The
yield from the land increased rapidly and the growth in agriculture

8 PROFIT AND POVERTY IN RURAL VIETNAM

was higher than during the previous decades. This continued in the early years of land collectivization. The revolutionary ardour of the masses rose, and they were ready to follow the party in building socialism.

Collectivization of the land relationship established public ownership of the means of production. The political leaders and intellectuals had been convinced that private property was the main obstacle to equality and social justice. The Communist Party had great ambitions to secure rapid economic growth for the good of the people. However, regarding the land relationship, the objectives of collectivization were almost the opposite of those of the land reform between 1953 and 1957.

Unfortunately, the economy did not unfold as planned. It can be said that in the years between 1978 and 1980 the economy of Vietnam fell into a deep recession, the ultimate cause of which was low agricultural productivity. The manner in which the cooperatives applied equal distribution during wartime deprived farmers of their initiative and incentive. Sluggishness and torpor were widespread. The rice yield fell and the peasants faced a permanent shortage of food. The target of 21 million tonnes of food was set up for 1980, but only 14 million tonnes were produced. Cooperative management deprived the farmers of their role as managers of the land. The predominance of the cooperatives actually amounted to an ownerless regime over land and the other means of production. The consequences only became fully apparent when the cooperatives no longer received subsidies from the state, and when the spirit of permanent self-sacrifice had gone.

Vietnam's agriculture in that period was essentially wet-rice growing. The whole rice cultivation process has eight steps: seed supply, ploughing, sowing, transplanting, tending, fertilizing/manuring, irrigating the land and draining surplus water, pest prevention and eradication, and harvesting. All eight links were affected by the collectivization in the period prior to 1981. The payment to the farmers was calculated on the number of workdays without regard to quantity or quality of the accomplished work.

Decree 100 by the Party Central Committee

Faced with severe economic crises, many agricultural cooperatives began to devise schemes for survival. Instead of fully assuming the "Eight Work Links", cooperatives began to assign farmwork on a contractual basis to member families, who would take total charge of a number of links. They were entrusted with completing the links within a fixed quota of workdays. The number of work links entrusted to households differed from one cooperative to another: four links in one, five in another, and maybe only three links in some. The remaining links were performed collectively.

INTRODUCTION: WINNERS AND LOSERS 9

Thus compensation to farmers was calculated on the number of workdays they put in for the collective, plus the workdays needed for the contracted work links. These changes came from the grassroots level. Some cooperatives in Vinh Phu province, and later in some other regions, adopted this new management approach in order to solve their economic problems. Some work links were entrusted as a package. The families implemented this approach all by themselves. It was no longer compulsory to work collectively according to an administrative time schedule.

Initially, the innovations were implemented secretly. However, their impact attracted researchers as well as political leaders. The farmers could now use their initiative in performing a number of work links, and they strove to benefit themselves. The land relationship remained the same. However, the contract work was a foundation for the development of the farmers' right to be active and creative in the use of land.

In January 1981, the Central Committee promulgated Decree 100 on the improvement of agricultural management in Vietnam. Contract work was officially approved and permission was granted for it to be applied on a larger scale. It is noteworthy that Decree 100 did not urge different cooperatives to entrust the same amount of work to households: this was to depend on the local situation and the amount of available work. Later, the Central Committee officially permitted packages of all eight links to be entrusted to households.

The contract system recognized by Decree 100 in 1981 resulted in a rapid increase in paddy yields: the yield had decreased from 22.2 tonnes per hectare in 1976 to 20.8 in 1980, but it rose to 27.8 in 1985 when the eight links contract was being applied. Food shortages were basically eradicated. More important still, the Decree created the prerequisites for Vietnam to reform the management of agricultural production. The work-package contract was the beginning of a new mode of management. Land was given to households for their own production. The farmers paid taxes for the operation of the cooperative, and a proportion of the material investments made by the cooperative. The more land was given to households to work on contract, the more land disputes arose in the countryside, because farmers soon realized the practical significance of receiving land from the cooperatives.

The 1988 Land Law

The complex changes in land management that followed in the wake of Decree 100 compelled the state to adopt a land law. The 1988 Land Law emphasized the following principles:

- Land belongs to the public under the sole management of the state. The state entrusts land to organizations and individuals for longterm use.

10 PROFIT AND POVERTY IN RURAL VIETNAM

- Beneficiaries of land may sell the fruits of their investment in the entrusted land.
- All buying and selling of land is forbidden.
- Rules and regulations are set out for settling land disputes and conflicts.

Contrary to the socialist view, this law allows the state to entrust land not only to organizations but also to individuals. The right to sell and buy the fruits of investments in land was an innovation in Vietnam.

Resolution 10 of the Party Central Committee

Following the 1988 Land Law, the Central Committee adopted Resolution 10 on the renewal of the management of the agricultural economy in June 1988. The Central Committee's sixth session asserted that a farmer's household is the primary unit of production, where earlier the production brigade in a cooperative held this position. Formerly, only state enterprises and collective sectors were regarded as the main economic components by the socialist regime. Other economic units were seen as vestiges of the former regime, to be transformed and gradually eliminated. The Central Committee stated the goal of shifting Vietnamese agriculture from subsistence to commodity production.

Resolution 10 officially recognized the package contract for the eight work links and instructed cooperatives to allocate land to households along the following lines:

- According to the investment capacity of the cooperative it may keep some work links for collective work, and households may or may not be entrusted with some or all the links for rice production.
- The level of the farmers' contribution to the cooperative must be proportional to the investment level of the cooperative.
- The land must be entrusted to families that receive the whole package of eight rice production links. Besides the investment made by the cooperative, the households may make an additional investment and they will retain 100 per cent of what they produce above their predetermined quota. (This is the prime stimulus for farmers to make their own investment in intensive cultivation.) In addition households will receive the products of the crop according to the calculated workdays on each land unit as contained in the contract. The source of products for distribution to households in proportion to the number of workdays contributed by them derives from the contractual quota of products delivered by households to the cooperative.

In fact, many cooperatives had no means to invest money for the benefit of peasant households. For that reason, the products that house-

INTRODUCTION: WINNERS AND LOSERS 11

holds delivered to cooperatives were just enough to pay state taxes, for social support within the cooperative (subsidies to the elderly, family survivors of war casualties, and war invalids), and for salaries to its management body. In the process of implementing Resolution 10, the managerial body has dwindled simply because it no longer plays a role beneficial to farmers' households. In fact, that management became parasitical, hindering the progress of agricultural production.

Decree 100, the 1988 Land Law, and Resolution 10 were intended to create a combined stimulus for farmers to make additional investments in intensive cultivation. However, the 1988 Land Law contained some obsolete stipulations. For example, while the party shifted from subsistence to commodity production, the law did not consider land as a commodity, but did consider the products of investments in land as commodities. Article 5 of the law banned renting of land in any form and it forbade the use of agricultural land for any other than the prescribed purpose.

The 1993 Land Law

Given the theoretical premises and the actual practices in the 1980s and in the early 1990s, a new Land Law was adopted in July 1993. Its significance may be summed up as follows.

First, the state recognizes the five rights of the persons entrusted with the use of land, namely the right to:

1. transfer land as inheritance to their successors
2. transfer land to other persons if they so wish
3. change the purpose of the use of the land
4. use land as security for a mortgage
5. rent land.

Second, the period during which a peasant household may use land runs for twenty years where the cultivation is of plants with a short period of growth (one year at most), and for fifty years for perennial plants. After this period, if the need arises, the household may request more time to use the land.

Third, the amount of land to be handed over is clearly determined: in northern Vietnam's plains, no more than 2 hectares with annual plants and no more than 10 hectares with perennial plants. With regard to the central highlands and the provinces of the Mekong River, the corresponding sizes of land are 3 and 30 hectares respectively (Article 5, Decree 64, September 1993).

The 1993 Land Law shows a marked shift from centralized economic planning to the market economy in comparison with the 1988 Law. The law created a basis for turning land into a commodity. This

12   PROFIT AND POVERTY IN RURAL VIETNAM

was strictly forbidden prior to 1988 and was very restricted from 1988 to 1993.

The provision authorizing the selling and buying of land creates a legal base for land concentration in agriculture. Since 1993, peasant households are entitled to buy more land to increase the acreage under cultivation. This was also forbidden, albeit unofficially, in the period of central economic planning in Vietnam.

Apart from the progressive items oriented towards an agricultural market economy in the 1993 Land Law, it also contains several neutral solutions. On the one hand, it avoids the tendency towards privatization of land that prevailed prior to collectivization and land reform. This would disturb sociopolitical stability in the countryside. On the other hand, this law has created new conditions for land ownership in agriculture.

However, the application of the 1993 Land Law varies greatly from one rural area to another. That is precisely what we intend to illuminate by studying changes in the land relationship in four villages.

OUR METHODS OF WORK

During the research process we were all briefed by central and local authorities at different levels, as well as by forest enterprise managers and brigade leaders. We were thus able to obtain general information and general understanding. In the village and household studies we observed living and working conditions and interviewed between fifteen and twenty forestry workers' households at each place, and at least ten households in the villages. In addition, between twelve and fourteen village households were interviewed about land issues. In total there were about forty interviews per case study.

In all four cases, team members exchanged roles for a day. When the Vietnamese interviewed the forestry workers, we foreigners went to the villages to meet the farmers' families and vice versa. The change in roles was made to gain insight into the workers' as well as the farmers' living conditions, and thus enable us to discuss and compare our experiences.

We did not use a questionnaire. We structured our themes in an open and flexible way and adapted the interviews to the particular people and settings. Some people were interviewed alone; some with their spouses or other family members; sometimes even neighbours dropped in. We looked for forestry workers we knew from previous visits, and we selected households of single women and couples. We went to poor, average, and wealthy households; to Kinh and to local ethnic people.

We built much of our understanding on interviews, on what people told us, their perceptions, and the meaning that the changes have had

INTRODUCTION: WINNERS AND LOSERS 13

for them. Life in rural Vietnam is undisguised and visible. Generally our observations confirmed what people said. It was surprising how rapidly people reconstructed their social realities when old economic institutions eroded. They soon took advantage of the new institutions as these replaced the previous ones.

Generally we were well received. People willingly discussed the changes since 1987 and they often seemed to enjoy being interviewed. However, it would be illusory to believe that they disclosed confidential personal or political information. Besides, whether we liked it or not, we became associated with Swedish aid, and although we explained our limited aims, we were doomed to raise hopes.

People showed great hospitality and curiosity, and many were obviously pleased at getting attention. Yet, did people participate voluntarily? Could they refuse being interviewed? We were supported by higher echelons and the rules of politeness made it difficult to refuse. To be frank, it was pure ritual when we informed them about the voluntariness of participation. However, to our surprise, two interviewees showed their dislike of being questioned, although they did not feel free to speak out. Both were single mothers cohabiting with new men. Since SIDA has been involved in assisting single mothers, visitors from Sweden, consultants, and journalists have often interviewed such women over the years, and they were as fed up as single mothers in the suburbs of Stockholm about repeatedly disclosing their circumstances. As soon as I understood their feelings, I broke off the interviewing.

We were very well received in the place we visited for the first time: the remote Hoang Su Phi people still welcome visitors who show genuine interest in their difficult circumstances and their efforts to overcome food shortage and severe ecological deterioration. We awakened their hopes for aid from the outside world. Why should we otherwise sit with them for hours and listen to their suffering?

Hierarchy and isolation

Research institutions in northern Vietnam are hierarchically organized. People at the lower levels are not entitled to express their opinions. At the top level, opinions tended to be coloured more by ideology than by analysis. Generally only professors draw conclusions while subordinates provide data. The belief in a strict age hierarchy assumes that younger researchers respect and learn from those who are senior.

No wonder, then, that Vietnamese researchers hesitate to put into print views that they have stated in private discussions. They are very helpful in explaining pre-revolutionary Vietnam, whereas they tend to be cautious, self-censoring and reluctant to write their opinions about ongoing social and political issues. There are several reason for this.

14   PROFIT AND POVERTY IN RURAL VIETNAM

Presumably, the Vietnamese assume that a foreigner will not grasp the full meaning of what they say, since things are too complex to be easily explained. Moreover, they do not have the habit of airing their opinions in the sceptical and speculative way that is common in the West. The custom of giving normative answers, of differentiating a public view from a personal one, and the emphasis on consensus and social harmony make it embarrassing to criticize unless the criticism is generally accepted.

Moreover, Vietnamese researchers have long been isolated from international debate and literature. They are not used to explaining themselves to foreigners. Whereas, for instance, Japanese intellectuals have written books comparing themselves to the West, analysing their institutional peculiarities and cultural key concepts, it seems that the Vietnamese take themselves for granted, or our questions might have been projections that did not make sense to them.

Clearly, some of the restrictions that apply to the researchers apply to workers and farmers as well. People know the rules for separating public and private opinions. It is not easy to look behind the screen. Not even foreigners fluent in Vietnamese seem to step over this threshold. We have a Western habit of exploring personal issues, and feel deprived when the respondents prove evasive. My point is that even two or three follow-up interviews with the same households would probably not generate deeper insights, only more data.

Below we shall present our study case by case, emphasizing their specific features and we shall conclude our investigations by summarizing the effects of Doi Moi. The main themes of the present study are:

- the 1988 and 1993 Land Law reforms and their local application
- institutional changes: the decline of cooperatives and the emergence of new village organizations
- restructuring of state forest enterprises, their management and workforce
- the emergence of a commodity economy and the diversification of household economies
- the social differentiation and the processes that cause poverty and wealth
- the state and the family network as providers of social support
- cultural encounters between Kinh migrants and local ethnic groups.

Basically, the study tries to highlight the farmers' and the forest workers' perception and understanding of their experiences of central economic planning and of open-market models of modernization.

CASE ONE

Standing on Two Feet

TWO

Land and People

BACKGROUND

The main theme in this case is social integration in the midst of an evolving commodity economy. Integration here encompasses two kinds of encounters: one between farmers and workers who have coexisted for decades without much intermingling, and another between the Tay ethnic group and the Kinh newcomers from the Red River delta. Most of the workers in Minh Dan brigade, Tan Thanh forestry enterprise, and half of the farmers' households in Lam Tien village, Minh Dan commune, are Kinh migrants.

Minh Dan commune is located in the northwest of Ham Yen district, Tuyen Quang province. The commune has 3,197 inhabitants divided in three ethnic groups: 1,424 Dao, 1,013 Kinh, and 760 Tay.

An ethnological sub-theme here as in all the other cases is the delineation of customs and institutions that either facilitate or counteract the commodification processes, such as the Tay labour exchange and the lifelong mutual support in Tay peer associations. We explore human bonds as support and insurance systems on the one hand, and market forces that build on economic profit on the other. We do not assert that these are incompatible: we merely expose the psychological and political tensions of modernization.

POLICY IMPACT ON LAND MANAGEMENT

Tuyen Quang province lies in the northern mountain region of Vietnam. The region has small wet-rice-fields. The plots of land are terraced, and are thus less suitable for intensive production. For centuries wet-rice land in the mountain provinces has been insufficient to feed the local ethnic groups. Therefore, they have also made their living from products extracted from the natural forest. Their custom of slash-and-burn

18   PROFIT AND POVERTY IN RURAL VIETNAM

cultivation arose from scarcity of land and the difficulty of hillside cultivation.

From the early 1960s four important sociopolitical events have had an impact on land relationships in this highland area:

- *The collectivization movement* meant that people of different ethnic groups contributed their land, their draft animals, and other important means of production to the cooperatives. Having witnessed the land reform in 1953–57, the ethnic groups had gained more confidence in the new regime. Thus, people were well disposed towards collective production.

- *The fixed cultivation and settlement programme* aimed at preventing forest destruction through swidden farming by persuading nomadic people to come down from the mountains to grow wet-rice. As a result, households that had wet-rice land had to share small plots with former nomads.

- *The new economic zones movement* mobilized people in the densely populated delta provinces to migrate and build new economic zones in the mountainous regions. The Kinh people moved to the highlands, but continued to grow wet-rice. This automatically reduced the average area per capita.

- *The proclamation of the Socialist Republic of Vietnam* led to a declaration by the state that all the land, including forest and water, belonged to the people (i.e. the state). This meant that ethnic minorities were no longer free to use forest resources. This limitation of their previous rights came at a time when there was not enough wet-rice land, and the conditions of cultivation were beset with difficulties.

The political declaration that all land belonged to the whole people made farmers think that it "belonged to the pagoda". By that the Vietnamese mean that just as the pagoda is open to all, so is the forest resource. Thus, forest growing on such land belongs to the pagoda and everyone can cut it.

Consequently, later land relationships were more likely to become tense. Even during the period of collectivization (1960–1980) there were conflicts between state-run farms and state forestry enterprises on the one hand, and indigenous people on the other. Many conflicts were prolonged and insoluble.

LOCAL HISTORY AND ETHNIC DIVISIONS

Landscape and history

Lam Tien village is located in a small valley intersected by low hills. The dwellings are on both sides of the intercommunal road, a forestry

LAND AND PEOPLE 19

track large enough for timber lorries. The distance from the village centre to the commune headquarters is only 1 kilometre, to the Phu Luu market it is 4, and to Ham Yen district town 30 kilometres. The distance is not great but the road is so bad that it takes at least two hours by car as the travellers must cross the Lo River using an old ferry. Compared with many other remote mountain areas, Lam Tien enjoys an advantageous location.

The wet-rice-fields lie mostly in the valley, near the dwellings. Two streams, the Bau and the Khang, which rise in the Da Trang (White Rock) mountain range, converge at the village and supply fresh water to the fields and water power for all the micro-hydroelectric stations for household use. Further towards the northern part of the village is the Go Meo mountain range. Several households live at its foot. At the top and on the slopes there are terraced fields, trees and bushes. Some natural forest remains for logging, cattle grazing, and for the collection of fuelwood and bamboo shoots. The forest near the Minh Dan brigade of Tan Thanh forest enterprise is in the southern part. The distance from Lam Tien village to the big Lo River is only about 4 kilometres.

The households of Lam Tien are scattered at the foot of the hill and have a large piece of land and a garden, an orchard, and even a fish-pond near the houses. Some of the dwellings are on stilts, others are on the ground. They are separated from each other by animal sties.

Lam Tien village does not have a long history. Only two ethnic groups live in the village area, the Kinh and the Tay. The opening of virgin lands and their conversion into arable use are associated with the Tay. We met Mr Ly Van Tuong. He is an 82-two-year-old Tay who continues to garden and graze his buffaloes. Recently he even attended the wedding of his close relatives who live 20 kilometres' walk away. Mr Tuong recounted his history of Lam Tien: his paternal grandfather was one of the three founders of Khang mountain village, the predecessor of Lam Tien. By conventional calculation, based on a twenty-year span for each generation, Ly Van Tuong's paternal grandfather would have been about 122 years old in 1994. Thus, Khang mountain village came into being about 100 years ago.

Prior to 1954, northern Vietnam was still under French occupation. Between 1954 and 1994, Khang mountain village underwent significant name changes, such as Khang Thuong village and Thuong Lam cooperative. In 1994, this cooperative was split into three villages, one of them Lam Tien.

The Kinh people who live in Lam Tien village originate in the delta plains. Their home is in Hung Ha district, Thai Binh province, the most densely populated province in northern Vietnam's plain, which has a population density of 1,200 per square kilometre. The

20   PROFIT AND POVERTY IN RURAL VIETNAM

migration of the Kinh has taken place since 1973. In that year eleven families arrived comprising seventy-nine members. Nine of the families remain in Lam Tien.

The distinguishing trait of these migrants was that they were not organized by the local authorities in their native homes. Instead they contacted Minh Dan commune administration and other relevant authorities in Tuyen Quang province about relocation. After being accepted by the new commune administration, they sold everything, houses, furniture, utensils, etc., and hired a bus. All seventy-nine members together with their belongings travelled along a road of 300 kilometres. At that time, there was no road for cars from Tan Thanh forest enterprise to Minh Dan commune, as there is today. The migrants had to carry their possessions up hill and down dale to the spot where they desired to settle.

From the outset, the Kinh newcomers received local assistance, such as support in the construction of makeshift houses. They were incorporated into production teams in Thuong Lam agricultural cooperative. The Tuyen Quang provincial authorities allocated food for six months at subsidized prices.

The ethnic relationship between the Kinh and the Tay in Lam Tien has now existed for more than twenty years and found expression in many respects, first and foremost in the land relationships. Up to now the Tay had twice shared their patches of land with the Kinh. The first time had been in 1973, when the Kinh had just migrated to Lam Tien. The land had still been extensive and lain idle. The rice-fields could not be used by the cooperative. Thus it had been easy to share land with the migrant Kinh. The second time was in 1994.

By November 1994, there were altogether sixty-eight households in Lam Tien village: thirty-four are Tay and thirty-four Kinh. They are all farmers. In addition, there are two retired forestry workers and their families, not to mention a teacher and his family, thus bringing the total number of inhabitants registered in Lam Tien village to 340. Of these, 201 are Tay and 139 Kinh.

Taking a general view of the whole residential area, it is apparent that the eastern part is inhabited by Kinh and the western part by Tay. The Kinh households are near or even intermingled with the families of forestry workers of Minh Dan brigade. The residential area occupied by the Kinh families is still called "Minh Tien residential area". It has been called this right from the time of their arrival. *Minh* means enlightenment, *Tien* implies progress.

Family structure and ancestry

In the past few years, family structure has changed radically. The nuclear family is becoming common. Family size has tended to decrease, especially among young families. When the Kinh families first migrated

Figure 6: Local (Tay) leader in Lam Tien with family [EL].
Figure 7: Local (Kinh) leader of the forestry workers with family [EL].

to this upland area, five of the eleven families comprised three generations, and seven of the eleven families had seven or more members each. Indeed, one household had ten members, another eleven. At present only three out of thirty-four Kinh agricultural families span three generations and nine have as many as six to nine members each. All the others have two to five family members.

22   PROFIT AND POVERTY IN RURAL VIETNAM

Compared with the Kinh, Tay families are much bigger. At present ten of thirty-four Tay households are three generational and seventeen families have from six to eleven members.

One reason for the smaller Kinh households is that newly married couples prefer to have a separate home, and their parents like them to become self-supporting. Kinh families make careful preparations for their children to live separately. They allot them of a piece of land big enough to build a house on. Many families prepare for the formation of separate homes when each of their children is still young. For instance, if a couple has three sons, they open at least two patches of land near the village. They grow trees and make gardens on that land. When the sons marry, they build houses on the land.

Among the Tay, the married couple usually lives in the parents' home for about five to six years. Then they are asked to build a separate home for themselves. This custom is no longer as rigid as it used to be: the young married couple would today ask to make a separate home after only one or two years.

Several of the Kinh households that moved to the uplands in Lam Tien in 1973 belonged to the same family lineage or were related through marital alliances. A particular feature of those households is that they keep close contact with their native land. They pay frequent visits to their native village for *Tet* (New Year) and death anniversaries. Mr Tan Van Y revealed that every year he or his wife return to the native village on the anniversary of his father's death or his wife's father's death. Mr Y's family has a genealogical register. When a grandchild is born, he will have the name recorded in the family genealogy when he visits his home village. The head of the family lineage will then hold a registration ceremony.

Association of Tay peers

In Lam Tien there still exists a form of voluntary association initiated by the members themselves. This is the Tay *Tung Khoa*, an association of male peers born in the same year. These men commit themselves to maintain close relationships with one another for the whole of their lives. Besides mutual visits and gift-giving, the members help each other's families with big projects like house construction, wedding parties, and funerals. The members offer their labour and even money, rice and alcohol. The roots of this association stretch back into the past. The membership is confined to the Tay in Lam Tien, but extends to the Tay in the territory formerly covered by Khang mountain village.

Because of the improved economic conditions, members of the association now make bigger monetary and material contributions for the celebration of weddings and funerals. For instance, each member of the *Tung Khoa* association of Mr Au Trung Dam contributed a gift

LAND AND PEOPLE

worth 50,000 dong when one member of his family celebrated a wedding. The usual gift for such an occasion is between 10,000 and 20,000 dong.

Tay and Kinh – keeping apart and coming together

Mixed marriages between different ethnic groups are an indicator of relationships between those groups. Despite living in the same village for over twenty years, marriages between Tay and Kinh are still rare. So far there have been only four cases of mixed marriages in the whole village.

One case was between a Tay man and a Kinh woman. Of the three cases of marriages between Kinh men and Tay women, two involve Tay women from the district. The two couples were either students or workers when they fell in love somewhere away from Lam Tien.

The villagers explain the few mixed marriages by referring to different customs and manners. We heard an interesting remark about men who live in other areas and come to Lam Tien to marry. I discovered that twelve men, either forestry workers or carpenters from the delta, or men coming from other villages in Ham Yen district, had married Kinh women and established their permanent dwellings in the village of their wives.

This contrasts sharply with Kinh customs and values in the rural plains of north Vietnam. For a Kinh man to live with his wife's family is seen as shameful and to be avoided at all costs. According to a Kinh saying, "Living with one's wife's family is like a dog creeping under the kitchen cupboard." There are several explanations as to why men marry and stay in Lam Tien. First, there are extensive virgin lands for cultivation (according to the rules and regulations in Minh Dan commune, such sons-in-law are not allowed to have rice-fields). Second, the prejudice against living with one's wife's family is not as rigid as in the plains. Last but not least, ethnic unity is achieved through marriage.

The relationship between Tay and Kinh in Lam Tien finds expression in contact and communication, especially when it comes to collective occasions such as funerals and wedding ceremonies, and death anniversaries. When there is a death in a family, it has become common practice for people from other households to offer ritual objects to the deceased, to condole with the bereaved family, and offer their services to the latter during the funeral. Here, ethnic groups who live together respect each other's customs and values and behave accordingly.

However, there are some differences in commitment. The head of a Kinh family must invite guests to the party. In Lam Tien, with a total of sixty-eight households, the organizer usually invites them all. But

24   PROFIT AND POVERTY IN RURAL VIETNAM

distinctions are made in terms of money offerings. Mr Tran Van Y noted that if he attends a Kinh wedding party he offers a gift of 20,000 dong. In the case of a Tay wedding, his gift would be only 10,000–15,000 dong. The differing amount arises from his affinity with his fellow Kinh compatriots.

Another relationship that has changed is that between the workers in the forestry enterprise and the village households. Mr Chuan, the leader of Minh Dan brigade, explained how workers formerly lived in collective quarters. They had very few contacts with local people. Since the time when workers married village women and built their own houses in the village, the relationship between workers and villagers has become closer. When there are weddings, funerals, or other ceremonial occasions, the workers go there and share the joy or sorrow with the families concerned.

THE LAND RELATIONSHIP IN LAM TIEN VILLAGE

The situation in Lam Tien is similar to that in many other places in the northern mountain region: wet-rice was limited, and local ethnic groups had to share land with the newcomers from the delta who came to build new economic zones. Compared with many other places, there were fewer nomadic people living by swidden cultivation in Lam Tien. However, the wet-rice land was shared with those nomads who had come down from the mountains.

Against that background, one would expect conflicts when the 1993 Land Law was implemented. We learned that such conflicts were common in northern regions. According to Mr Tran Cuoc Toan, general editor of the *Thong tin ly luan* magazine, from 1988 to 1992 there were about 30,000 conflicts over land in the mountain region between settlers from the delta and local people. There were even cases where newcomers had to return to their native land or go elsewhere because there was simply no more land.

Evolution of the wet-rice management

According to Mr Tu Quang Thich, the party secretary of Minh Dan commune, before 1981 most families in the commune suffered from hunger. They had to mix rice with cassava and maize all year round. Collective farming led to a situation where "no one weeps for a father to all when he dies", as commented by Mr Thich.

When the Central Committee in 1981 issued its famous Decree 100, cooperatives were instructed to sign contracts with groups of people or individual households. In fact, in Minh Dan commune, the people wanted to work on household contracts while nobody wanted to work collectively any longer.

LAND AND PEOPLE   25

In the early 1980s the Minh Dan cooperative entrusted three work links to the households, namely sowing/transplanting, tending, and harvesting. The contract system was introduced gradually, and not in the whole village at the same time. But by 1986–87 Lam Tien obtained the full work contract. Thus, although Lam Tien is in the mountainous periphery, the implementation of the package of the eight links began relatively early, simultaneously with many places in the delta.

In April 1988, the Central Committee's Resolution 10 came into effect. It laid the legal basis for Lam Tien to entrust land to households. Now the whole process of rice production is organized and implemented by the family households themselves. The role of the cooperatives has been gradually reduced; by the end of 1993, they had almost no effect on household production. In fact, by the beginning of 1994 the cooperative no longer existed, not even in appearance. The cooperative's former functions were now taken over by the commune and village authorities. These functions included, for example, the distribution of water for the common irrigation system, the announcement of production seasons, and information about pests.

Due to the implementation of the Decree 100 and the Resolution 10 contract system in Lam Tien, and the 1988 Land Law, households had the right to use land but not the right to own it. However, the reality was that the households had the virtual right of land ownership.

Allocation of land

The smooth process of land allocation resulted from a combination of initiatives by the cooperative in Minh Dan commune and the decisions and directives of the Vietnamese Communist Party and the authorities on various levels. The guiding principles followed by the party were:

- To respect the current situation for land which has been entrusted to family households while the cooperative still exists.
- To ensure solidarity and political stability in economic development.

The policy of Minh Dan commune was to readjust the wet-rice land within each village and not on an average basis throughout the whole commune. Water conservancy works in any area would be under the management of and for the use of that area. Its value would be converted into money to be paid back to the cooperative. After that, such works would finally be entrusted to the villages. Other fixed properties have also been reassessed.

The manner of dividing the properties of the former cooperative for the villages in Minh Dan was discussed in an open and democratic

26   PROFIT AND POVERTY IN RURAL VIETNAM

way. That is why there were no unclear issues among the villagers before the disbandment of the cooperative. Actually, there was no announcement about the disbandment at all, the division of the properties indirectly demonstrated the fact.

Complaints and conflicts

The family of Mr Nguyen Van Hanh was the only one to complain. This household has five members. The total area they received was 840 square metres or 168 square metres per capita. This was equivalent to only one-third of the average in Lam Tien. When we asked the family about the issue, the wife answered that at the time when the co-operative had already divided the fields, they were newly retired due to bad health. We asked if they had claimed more land and she said they had. The village head had told them that by next season they would receive one *sao* and four *thuoc* more, totalling 480 square metres.

When we saw the village head again, we brought up the case of Mr Hanh. He informed us of other cases where the number of family members had grown after the cooperative had finished allocating land. These cases were being considered. The village had land in reserve to divide further among people whose families had increased in number. However, the additional land would be less than the earlier average. After 1993, they could not consider more cases as all the land would be divided then.

When the formalities to issue land certificates recognizing the household's right to own land were completed, Mr Lap, the commune chairman, told us that in the whole Minh Dan commune there was only one claim to have land returned from the time before the co-operative was established.

In Lam Tien alone there was no case of conflict. Why was this? As the village head explained,

> It was because the allocation of land was made in a fair and open way. If there were any unclear issues, the authorities would explain, and the people would have to follow. That is all.

We think that this answer reflects the reality of Lam Tien. The best thing for an ordinary person is to accept fate because, even if he raises problems, they will not be solved. Even in the case of Mr Hanh, we felt that there was not a strong claim for land, although he had the smallest wet-rice-field per household and per capita.

Norms for land allocation

All the ten interviewed households, except Mr Hanh's, had an average land area per capita higher than the average land allotted by the co-operative in 1993. The average for rice land is 569 square metres. We

LAND AND PEOPLE   27

later realized that, besides the land allotted by the cooperative, there was land that people cleared themselves during the period of collective work or after the land division of 1993. In reality, the authorities respected the land situation prior to the Resolution 10 contract system and accepted the private land that households already had. While people were still doing work collectively, all families had land of their own.

We made comparisons between five Tay and five Kinh households. Among the five Kinh, the average land per capita was 576 square metres of rice land, and 563 square metres among the five Tay households. One could expect a bigger gap in favour of the Kinh as the majority of the local commune officials are Kinh. This proves that land allocation in Lam Tiem has by and large been fair.

If a comparison is made between the size of land allocated in Minh Dan and the amount specified in legal documents, the land distributed to families is far from the maximum. According to a decision of the People's Council in Tuyen Quang in April 1994, Decree 64 of the government on the implementation of the Land Law is embodied at the provincial level as follows. Limits of the size of land allocated to households is to be determined thus:

- annual plants: up to 1 hectare
- long-term crops: up to 5 hectares
- forest land: up to 10 hectares

Natural forest, protected forest, and forest formerly grown with government money will be allocated to state-run organizations or to households for conservation and management. However, if the beneficiaries misuse forest land or do not use it for twelve months, the land is to be withdrawn.

Forest gardens

This concept is common among the ethnic groups in the northern mountain region. The Tay have farmed forest gardens since time immemorial. In essence they occupied large areas of forest land propitious for farming in the vicinity of their houses. This land became their property through this practice. The late-coming Kinh have by all ways and means sought to secure forest gardens of their own.

The customary rights are practices that the local people adhere to as a law. In Lam Tien village every Tay household we met had a forest garden. Actually, the trees in the garden were not cultivated by the owner, but had grown naturally.

In Lam Tien, each Tay household has a natural stretch of forest around its house. The local community recognizes that and nobody violates the forest garden of others. When the forest enterprise was

Figure 8: Tay farmer coming back from the wet-rice field [EL].

established, these areas were considered to belong to it. But in reality the managers were the family households.

The official reallocation of forest gardens from the enterprise to the communes and the commune's handing of the users' rights back to households has legalized local people's customary rights to forest land.

THREE

The Shift to a Commodity Economy

RENEWALS IN LAM TIEN VILLAGE

One of our deepest impressions of Lam Tien village is that the former perennial food shortages have definitely ended. The per capita average of wet-rice land in this village is lower than in many regions of northern Vietnam's plains (about 720 square metres per person). In addition to wet-rice, the farmers grow other food plants such as maize, sweet potatoes, and cassava on the terraced fields, on the banks of waterways along Bau and Khang streams, on burnt lands on the tops of hills, and on Go Meo and Da Trang mountains. They mainly use newly opened land for subsidiary crops in the first years after breaking the ground.

How is it, then, that the farmers using such lands now enjoy self-sufficiency in food and even produce some surplus for sale where before there was a permanent food shortage? The fundamental cause lies in the change of the land ownership, in replacing the agricultural cooperative with farmers' households.

In the past few years the paddy yields have risen higher and higher. In the opinion of Mr Tran Ngoc Sy, the secretary of the village party cell, before 1981 (that is before the implementation of Decree 100) the paddy yield obtained by the cooperative was about 40 to 50 kilograms per *sao* (360 square metres) of rice-field. This corresponded to a payment for one workday of 0.6 kilograms of paddy.

After 1981, the cooperative raised its paddy yield to about 80 to 90 kilograms per *sao*. In 1989, when the contract system was put into practice (Resolution 10), paddy yields went even higher. Since the implementation of the renovation policy, the paddy yield has at least doubled.

30 PROFIT AND POVERTY IN RURAL VIETNAM

The basic reason for increasing paddy yields is that farmers have been using available funds to invest in intensive cultivation. However, the Tay people have less experience of intensive farming than the Kinh. Mr Au Van Hien, a 34-year-old Tay farmer, told us with evident pride, that he has the highest paddy yield among the Tay community. On the other hand, he openly confessed that his paddy yield is only 80–85 per cent of that of Kinh farmers. Mr Tran Van Y (63 years old) is one of the richest heads of Kinh households in the village. His household has a record of high paddy yield. He manures his rice-fields as follows: 500 kilograms of cattle dung, 5 kilograms of nitrogenous fertilizer, 15 kilograms of phosphorous fertilizer, and 30 kilograms of potash fertilizer per *sao*.

If people know how to be good farmers, they can be self-sufficient in food grains. On average, each person needs annually about 300 kilograms of paddy. Except from the rice-fields, villagers harvest more grains from their burnt lands and terrace fields on the mountain slopes and on the stream and river banks. Mr Ma Van Cao (56) is a Tay. His family is composed of seven members. He revealed that in 1994, with only one *mau* (3,600 square metres) of rice-field, his family had harvested 2,400 kilograms of paddy, 300 kilograms of maize grown on burnt lands on the Go Meo mountain slope, not to mention some 3,000 cassava plants. In the farmer's family economy, different food grains are important to their livelihood.

In Lam Tien village, where the commodity economy has not yet developed, subsistence food production is a matter of prime importance. Animal husbandry, gardening, and other occupations are only supplementary in character. Nevertheless, the peasant household economy is an interrelated entity. Thus, many activities will supplement the main ones, and help to raise the family's living standards.

Currently in Lam Tien, nearly all secondary crops such as maize, sweet potato, and cassava, have been mainly reserved for livestock feed. This is quite different from the period prior to 1989, when secondary crops were mostly used to feed people. Only one household in the village does not raise pigs. Many Tay families are engaged in diversified livestock breeding. The family of Mr Au Van Hien has four buffaloes, thirteen goats, and seven pigs (excluding the two pigs that were slaughtered for the funeral of his father). This family does not neglect poultry either: they have thirty-two chickens, eight ducks, not to mention a pond with 4,000 fish of different kinds. Livestock breeding also provides dung for manuring the rice-field. However, cattle breeding has caused much damage to plants on burnt lands, terraced fields, and to stream and river banks.

The products of livestock breeding (chicken, duck, fish) have been used to improve the daily fare of the family, to supply provisions for *Tet* (the Vietnamese New Year festival), funerals, weddings, and other

THE SHIFT TO A COMMODITY ECONOMY 31

ceremonial occasions. Some products have been sold on the market. Like farmers in many other areas, the inhabitants in Lam Tien regard pig rearing as a sort of saving. They make the fullest use of all the food remnants for feeding poultry. When they sell pigs, they will obtain money for family necessities, such as more rice.

Gardening also supplements food production for daily use and for sale. Gardening is not only much cherished among the Kinh, but also of great interest to the Tay. They grow all kinds of fruit trees such as orange and tangerine, and vegetables of all sorts for daily use and for pig fodder. In fact, self-sufficiency in food and other provisions from intensive farming, livestock breeding, and gardening has made it unnecessary for the inhabitants of Lam Tien to burn forest to clear new land. Before 1989, almost all households had some patches of burnt land on the mountain slopes for producing more food. Now this practice is dwindling. In the whole village, there are about ten Tay families who still till fields on the mountain slopes. Kinh households are not engaged in this kind of activity at all. Mrs Tu Thi Lien says, "To do burning one has to go far. It takes time and is very tiresome and after all we do not harvest very much. The products are not worth our efforts."

Introduction of orange *trais*

People call the place where the orange trees grow *trai* in Vietnamese (in translation, orange farm or orange estate). The word *trai* as used here originates from the Kinh language and has existed for a long time. Historically, the Kinh people living on the plains usually called the land used for agriculture and husbandry (or any cultivated place located at some distance from their dwellings) a *trai*. Makeshift huts for guards to secure the place were erected on such lands. There are many kinds of *trai*: guava, sugar-cane, duck, and fish *trais*. Where several households live together in a cluster of those lands, the dwelling is called a zone of *trais*.

The expansion of the *trai* economy in Vietnam is widely debated. Though having different views, the experts agree that the *trai* economy consists of agriculture and husbandry or in a combination of agriculture and forestry. However, its aim is to produce commodities. Here, we want to focus on the economic aspect of the *trai* in Lam Tien village. The *trai* has become a very common phenomenon over the last few years. Many households have selected land for planting oranges. The land is located far away from their dwellings, usually in another village or even commune. The reason for this is that there is no longer an area suitable for oranges available in Lam Tien.

Before the migration of the Kinh, orange trees were grown everywhere, albeit in a scattered way, and were mainly used to produce fruit for home consumption. In 1974, a number of Kinh realized that

32   PROFIT AND POVERTY IN RURAL VIETNAM

the sale of oranges would be profitable and they started to cultivate orange trees. Many Tay households followed suit. Orange trees bear fruit after four or five years and cease to produce after a further ten years. Now almost all the orange gardens in Lam Tien have ceased yielding fruit. People have to cut them down and plant other trees instead, because replanting orange trees would not yield sweet fruit. But during several years, the produce from orange orchards created good conditions for many households.

Even now oranges remain a fruit of some economic value. In 1994, the people could sell oranges wholesale for 4,000–5,000 dong per kilogram. For that reason, many households want to continue growing oranges. Lam Tien people now make their orange gardens on lands stretching along the shores of Lo River. These are extensive grasslands with low hills.

What have orange gardens to do with the problem of farm/estate economy? The details of the activities on these orange farm/ estates must be explored to see whether they conform to a rational understanding of *trai* economy. The nearest orange *trai* in Lam Tien is at least 2 kilometres from the farmer's dwelling. To cultivate the *trai*, the owner must register his possession with the local administration (village, commune) and pay taxes calculated on the cultivated area. Once the orange trees are planted, the owner can grow other crops between the rows of trees, depending upon the soil conditions and availability of manpower.

If the soil is fertile, the owner will usually grow a crop of upland rice in the first year. In the second year, he will grow maize, and in the third year beans or groundnuts. If the land is poor, the owner will grow one or two bean or groundnut crops. The owner must erect a makeshift hut at the *trai* and place one person there to tend the farm and care for the young plants. All the households possessing orange *trais* are engaged in commercial orange cultivation.

Thus, the orange *trai* has emerged as a new phenomenon in Lam Tien village since 1989. The history of the Kinh people reveals that the *trai* has existed since feudal times. However, it was not instituted for commodity production, but more often to secure land. The whole concept of growing for a market is completely new to the Tay in Lam Tien. And even more so for the Dao.

These localities along the shores of Lo River are mostly inhabited by the Dao people. From time immemorial, the Dao have tilled burnt fields that they cleared on the mountain slopes, because there are few wet-rice-fields. Nearly all the Dao are engaged in clearing the forest, and many trees have been burnt. They regard the burnt land as more fertile than the grassland below. The grassland needs a large amount of manure, and the Dao do not customarily use dung. They have moved

THE SHIFT TO A COMMODITY ECONOMY

Figure 9: Dao woman bringing hill rice back home [EL].

far beyond the areas inhabited by Tay and Kinh to reach the Go Meo and Da Trang mountain ranges. They have to cover a distance of 10–15 kilometres to reach their areas of cultivation.

The constituent elements of commodity production

We shall dwell on the constituent elements of commodity production so as to highlight the changes in comparison with a predominantly subsistence economy. The emergence of orange *trai* is a living expression of the elements of the commodity economy in Lam Tien village.

First and foremost, labour has become a commodity, though it is not yet a common commodity. This means that farmers in Lam Tien hire labour. Many Kinh villagers earn wages by tilling other farmers' lands in Minh Thai village and Minh Khuong commune where buffaloes are scarce.

In Lam Tien, several households have buffalo-drawn carts. They use them as family transport and to transport goods for money: timber, oranges, building materials, bricks, tiles, cement. When interviewed about incomes, Mr Tran Ngoc Sy indicated that in 1993 his son earned as much as 800,000 dong merely by hiring out his labour and the family's buffalo cart to carry materials.

At present human labour is badly needed by several households. However, the latter prefer to hire labourers from the plains, mostly migrants from Vinh Phu province. The labourers are hired to dig, weed, etc. For instance, in June and July 1994 Mr Khai hired three people to

34   PROFIT AND POVERTY IN RURAL VIETNAM

weed the orange *trai*. Thus, hired labour, unknown five to seven years ago, has become familiar. Usually, people still exchange work and assist one another, for instance in house construction, in transplanting seedlings, and in harvesting the rice crop.

It is noteworthy that farmers in Lam Tien tend to engage in business and commodity production. Before the period of renewal, they mostly carried out subsistence farming for themselves and their families with only a small surplus for sale. They might sell only a few kilograms of pork, a small amount of bamboo shoot, wood collected from the forest, and only rarely rice. They were not concerned about market fluctuations, nor were they willing to produce for the market.

Now the situation has changed radically. Farmers see that marketable products are mostly derived from animal husbandry and gardening. The Tay people breed buffaloes. Many households rear more than ten goats apiece. Mr Au Van Hien says that it is more profitable to rear goats than pigs, but it takes more effort to tend them. In 1993, he sold twelve goats, each of them bringing him 150,000 dong. The grazing grounds are located in a large area at the foot of the Go Meo mountain and in the wasteland of the forestry enterprise.

The Tay are more inclined to rear the local pigs than the commonly used crossbred hogs. They contend that although the local pigs fatten more slowly, they need less food. The Kinh breed fewer buffaloes than the Tay, each household keeping only one or two animals for draught purposes. They rear pigs for the market. In order to crossbreed hogs, the Kinh buy semen pills from the breeding farm in the district. Mr Tran Van Y is well known for rearing good strains of pig and has profited considerably from this business. In 1993, he sold 300 kilograms of live weight. He related that prior to 1989, no other families could sell as many kilograms as he did. He could do this because he husked the rice for the villagers and made use of the waste bran to feed his pigs. According to his calculations, the profit from rice husking was insignificant, but the bran enabled him to make much more profit from his pigs.

Fish breeding has brought no less profit. Twenty-seven households in the village have their own fishponds, among them Mr Hung Van Chang, a Tay. He possesses up to five fishponds with a total surface area of 8,672 square metres. New, faster-growing breeds of fish are cultivated and are in great demand. Among the new species are African carp, dory, and even local carp. Other breeds of carp must be bought from the district fish-farm while local carp can be obtained from Tay locals for 50 dong per fish.

In gardening, many households have turned to commodity production. Oranges bring profit. In 1989–91, when the orange trees still bore good fruit and were not stunted, a number of families each collected

Figure 10: Enterprising forestry worker [EL].

as much as 3 to 4 tonnes per year. At present, the old orange trees are being gradually replaced by new ones that will yield high economic returns. Mr Au Van Hien grows apricot trees which are quite popular in the region. This species of apricot is very sweet smelling and tasty and surpasses the crossbred apricots now sold at the market. In addition, he succeeded in grafting this variety of apricot on to another and obtained a high-yielding variety which has brought high profits to the growers. Calculated at 1994 market prices, 1 kilogram of apricots is worth 5,000 dong, equivalent to 5 kilograms of paddy. An apricot tree will yield fruit after three years. Thus apricot trees formerly planted for home consumption are now yielding a marketable product.

By contrast, Mr Tran Ngoc Sy's family does not grow apricots. He prefers planting other marketable fruit trees, such as longan, on an area of 1,500 square metres of land. Cinnamon was introduced in Lam Tien in 1991 and many households have planted this high-value tree.

Trades and occupations have only been practised for some years. In the whole village, there is only one household in the business of mechanical rice plucking and husking and of making and selling soya cakes locally. One household husks rice and runs a small restaurant concurrently.

Three households are carpenters by trade. Additionally, one household, that of Mr Tu Quang Thich, party secretary of Minh Dan commune, has bought a generator to sell electricity to nine households and to the office of Minh Dan brigade. Each household has to pay at least 20,000 dong per month to use a 60 watt bulb and one television set. The generator runs from 6pm until the TV programmes have finished.

The goods exchange in Lam Tien can be used as a yardstick for the market economy. We have interviewed households about how and where they sell their farm produce such as pork, poultry, oranges, rice, maize, sweet potato, cassava, etc. Almost all of them used to sell to each other in the village. However, since 1989 private traders have come to every home to buy surplus farm produce. Several residents took their surplus to Phu Luu market for sale. However, they were generally intercepted halfway by traders who bought what the people wanted to sell at the market.

Where do people buy the necessities of life? Over the past three years they would buy them in the village. Necessities like breeding fish, plant species, fish sauce, etc., are brought there by private traders. Other consumer goods are purchased at Phu Luu market, where goods

Figure 11: Tobacco for sale at the market in Phu Luu [EL].

THE SHIFT TO A COMMODITY ECONOMY 37

are conveyed by car from the provincial district towns. On both sides of the road, a variety of shops sell all the necessities of daily life like cloth, soap, cigarettes, batteries, needles and threads, cakes, sweets, sodium glutamate, dry fish, salt, fish sauce, etc. People in Lam Tien now joke: "We are afraid of having no money; if we have it, we can buy everything we need without difficulty".

This situation utterly contrasts with that prevailing before the renewal period. Because of shortages of goods and necessities, the Minh Dan marketing cooperative had to sell everything down to matches, soap, needles and thread by ration card according to the system of state distribution, the so-called subsidized system.

Improvements in the living standard

According to the people in Lam Tien and to people in Vietnam in general, when assessing if the living standard has increased or not, one should first look at people's housing and everyday comfort.

The Tay people in Lam Tien mostly live in houses on stilts. There are two types of such houses: those with their poles set in the ground and those with their poles resting above the ground on foundation stones. The latter houses are always bigger than the former. A building of the larger type usually has five rooms, each measuring 2.6 x 6.8 metres and with a total floor-space of 95.8 square metres.

For that reason this type of house requires a lot of building materials: about 10 cubic metres of timber, 100 bamboo trees, and 7,000 palm leaves. What is most important are the poles for the stilts. A house with five rooms needs twenty poles. The stilt poles at the house of Mr Ly Van Tuong have a circumference of 1.04 metres.

The floor-space of a house with stilts set in the ground is smaller. Mr Hoang Van Tang's house has only three rooms. Its poles have a circumference of 0.54 metres. Before 1954, almost all Tay people in Lam Tien built their houses on stilts set in the ground. At that time, the forest still had numerous big trees, but the war and poor conditions prevented people from constructing big houses. The houses with stilts on stones have been built since 1960.

In five to seven years' time new houses will nearly always be constructed with buried poles, due to the scarcity of big trees. Moreover, the cost of a house with stilts supported by stones has been calculated as similar to that of a house with a flat concrete roof, like those of the Kinh people. At present, in the Tay community, only one family has built a brick-walled concrete roofed house in Kinh style, and another family is preparing to construct a Kinh-style house.

The Kinh people in Lam Tien live in brick houses. Yet it is interesting to note that prior to 1954, many Kinh migrants from the plains to

Figure 12: A typical Tay house on poles [EL].
Figure 13: A typical Kinh house in brick [EL].

Minh Dan commune lived in stilt houses. At present, the Kinh people commonly regard a concrete-roofed house as the embodiment of wealth and many families aspire to this type of house. So far, five Kinh families live in ferroconcrete-roofed houses. They were built after 1989.

THE SHIFT TO A COMMODITY ECONOMY   39

Improved living standards also find expression in the possession of a television set and a motorbike, items first introduced to Lam Tien village only three or four years ago. Thirty-five families (twenty-eight of them being of Kinh origin and seven of Tay origin) in the village have a television set. All the television sets are monochrome. Several people assert that they could afford colour TV sets, but in the uplands a colour TV set does not receive broadcasts as well as a black-and-white set. Five families have motorbikes: one Tay and four Kinh households. Besides the above articles, radio-cassette recorders, modern beds, and elegant wardrobes are considered to be signs of prosperity. These items are commonly found in Kinh families. Wardrobes are not constructed for stilt houses, yet they are found in a number of Tay homes.

Electricity is a visible proof of improved living standards. In the past three or four years, micro-hydroelectric power stations have spread to the highlands. In addition to the households using electricity produced by Mr Thich's generator, nearly all the remaining houses enjoy a supply of hydroelectricity for lighting and for TV sets, radio-cassette recorders, and other electrical appliances. Owing to the availability of electricity, more and more families want to buy TV sets.

Differentiation between rich and poor

Recent socioeconomic changes have led to sharp differentiation between rich and poor in Lam Tien village. We discussed the subject with both officials and ordinary villagers. By and large their opinions coincide about who has become richer and who the poor are, but they differ in their views about the causes of wealth and poverty.

The village party secretary indicated that one should consider ethnic background. Wealthy Tay households are at the same level as upper-middle level Kinh households. Poor Tay households are much poorer than the poor among the Kinh. Mr Au Trung Dam, the village chief, was of the same opinion. The income of wealthy Kinh households ranges from 12 to 15 million dong per year, while the annual income of wealthy Tay households ranges from 8 to 10 million dong. Poor households have no valuable assets and they lack food for one or two months per year. Mr Hoang Van Ly still has a debt of 100 kilograms of paddy to settle with the former cooperative.

Why have the wealthy households become wealthy? According to Mr Tran Ngoc Sy, it is because they are fortunate. They reside in a fertile area from which they always harvest bumper orange crops, and this enables them to become rich. As for Tay households, their wealth derives from their opening of new patches of virgin land and their inheritance from their parents of major assets, such as a house, buffaloes, and other items.

40   PROFIT AND POVERTY IN RURAL VIETNAM

According to Mr Tran Van Y, himself a Kinh, he became rich through hard work. Yet he expects that the wealthy Kinh households will cease to be rich in future when their children grow up, get married, and settle in a separate house, because this will lead to a lack of labour. However, in the coming years, many households will establish large orange *trais*, and they will certainly be richer than the wealthy households of today.

Why have a number of families become poor? Almost all the wealthy families interviewed attributed poverty to laziness. In their opinion, the poor want to spend money, even though their earnings are too low to meet their needs. Alternatively the poor do not know how to manage and improve their lives.

We were also interested in the actual relationship between poor and rich families in the village. People unanimously agreed that there was no dismissive behaviour towards or contempt for the poor. The rich have little to do with the poor. The poor usually hire out their labour to those who need it. Social oppositions between poor and rich in Lam Tien are not yet acute.

From cooperatives to villages

The shift to a market economy is accompanied by reconstruction of social institutions. One of the major changes since 1989 has been the gradual dwindling of the cooperatives. In Minh Dan commune the cooperative simply disappeared when the village was set up.

While the cooperative had nominally been a production organization for the farmers, it actually assumed administrative functions such as mobilizing labour for communal work, collecting taxes, managing land, etc. After the implementation of the agricultural contract system in 1989, farmers' households took the initiative to make the best use of land entrusted to them. The role of the cooperative became more limited. While earlier it had controlled all the production links, its responsibility was now reduced to irrigating the cultivated fields.

Until now the administrative apparatus of the state comprised four echelons: central, provincial, district, and commune. In earlier times, there was hardly any administrative machinery below the commune. That was why the cooperative was called upon to assume an administrative function.

When the cooperative of Minh Dan commune dissolved itself automatically, the villages were set up. The administration of the territory fell under the jurisdiction of the villages. Here, village is defined as an administrative level below the commune. It is a community of people living together as a social group, sharing habits, customs, and even beliefs.

The village administration in Lam Tien is composed of the village chief, responsible for general affairs, a policeman responsible for civil

THE SHIFT TO A COMMODITY ECONOMY 41

status and population registration, and three militiamen to maintain order and security. This village body is entrusted with the task of managing land, upholding procedures for population registration, maintaining order and security, collecting taxes, mobilizing the population for public works, and last but not least, seeing to the irrigation and hydraulic work, formerly assigned to the cooperative.

What is the advantage of the village and its organization as compared to former practices? I asked Mr Au Trung Dam, chief of Lam Tiem village, for his views.

> This new organization has proven to be much more advantageous than the past one, especially in the administrative field. For instance, formerly, if thefts and robberies happened in the village, the leader of the production brigade or the chairman of the cooperative had to go to the commune's headquarters to report the incident and ask the commune officials to visit the area to investigate and solve the case. Now village officials are fully authorized to solve such questions themselves.

The village chief receives a monthly allowance of 20,000 dong from the state, while the police and the militia are paid from the village fund, to which each household must pay 12 per cent of the crop yield. In addition to the village administration, Lam Tien still has several organizations like the party cell, the Women's Union branch, the Youth League branch, and the Association of Village Elders. Each of these assumes functions related to its membership. Such organizations have been systematically formed throughout Vietnam.

FOUR

Restructuring of Tan Thanh Forest Enterprise and Minh Dan Brigade

MANAGEMENT OF FOREST LAND

To deal with the land relationships regarding forest and forest land, it is impossible to ignore the land relationships of Tan Thanh forest enterprise and Minh Dan commune as well as the ongoing change in management system within Tan Thanh enterprise.

Tan Thanh forest enterprise was established in the mid-1960s. Before 1986 the enterprise covered all eight communes in Ham Yen district, comprising 26,711 hectares of forests and forest land. This huge area extended over a large mountainous region. However, this was only on paper. In reality, it was impossible for the enterprise effectively to manage such a large area.

As the resources of the enterprise were limited, the land was not used effectively and was even left fallow. At the same time, local people lacked land for their livelihoods. Consequently, the wave of free cultivation of and living in the enterprise area was difficult to stop. The forest plantations of the enterprise have been regularly logged by local people and damaged by untended animals. We think that the underlying cause is the land management system. State forest is perceived as no man's land, common to all.

The second important cause is the management itself. Actually, the forestry workers are only employees. The forest belongs to the enterprise but the enterprise is the same as the state and government, implying that it does not belong to anyone. So the forestry workers' responsibility to protect forest is limited. They had no interest to do so and thus planted forest was often lost.

The third cause is that the protection department of the enterprise was poorly staffed. It was impossible to increase the personnel to an extent where there would be enough guards for the whole area. The solution to that problem was to hand over the enterprise's land to local people. In Vietnam at the time this was not limited to Tan Thanh, but was common to state-run farms and forest enterprises in other districts and provinces. There was great pressure from many directions to claim land back for the people.

Between 1987 and 1989, the enterprise revised its land area and transferred land to the local community. Towards the end of 1989, the Tan Thanh enterprise still managed 12,036 hectares of forest and forest land. By 1990, according to Instruction 5 of the Ha Tuyen provincial people's committee, the enterprise revised its area once more, and kept only forest and forest land that it could manage and efficiently exploit. At present, the area of forest and forest land under Tan Thanh management has been reduced to 5,000 hectares.

Therefore, in the space of four years, Tan Thanh handed back to eight communes, including Minh Dan, about 22,000 hectares of forest and forest land. This area was then allocated by the communes to the farmers for management. This is a striking feature of the relationships between the enterprise and the adjacent communes in the late 1980s. This transfer of land had the aim of ensuring that all forest land would be managed by a real person, and gradually erased the farmers' belief that the forest and forest land could be exploited freely because it belonged to the state.

By the end of November 1994, Minh Dan commune had received 450 hectares of forest and forest land from the enterprise. In addition, there were another 400 hectares under the management of Tan Thanh enterprise and under the administration of the commune.

Of the forest land that the enterprise handed to the commune, Minh Dan commune officially allocated 196 hectares to various households. These were mainly forest gardens, as already mentioned. The rest, over 200 hectares of forest land according to the chairman of the commune's people's committee, would be fully allocated to households during 1995. All this means that the farmers work not only in agriculture but also in forestry. In fact, two distinct processes are going on: the farmers are becoming forestry workers and vice versa. This change is to the benefit of the forest and the environment.

Contracts for forest land
The current renovation in Tan Thanh forest enterprise has a direct impact on forest and forest land management by forestry workers and local

44   PROFIT AND POVERTY IN RURAL VIETNAM

farmers. According to the director of Tan Thanh forest enterprise, before 1989 the enterprise only contracted forest planting to regular staff workers, according to workdays. This contract system was similar to that of the cooperative. In Tan Thanh workers were paid according to the given quota of work that was fulfilled, for example, the numbers of hectares cleared, holes dug, or seedlings transplanted. This meant that the workers did not need to concern themselves with the final result, i.e. the survival of the trees.

From 1991, the contracts were signed for set periods. The people who received contracts were still only workers of the enterprise. For example, they were given contracts for the period of planting (including clearing, digging holes, transportation and planting seedlings), or for the tending and protecting period. In 1992–93 the contract for the whole growth cycle was instituted.

In 1994, the enterprise started to manage the forest according to the investment contract. This contract is for the whole growth cycle, and it is clearly stated in the deed between the contractor and the enterprise. The latter makes investment for the contractor and can obtain products proportionately. Excess products belong to the contractor. If there is no investment by the enterprise, the contractor only has to pay land-use taxes and the whole product belongs to him or her. Now, contractors are not only workers but also local farmers. This contract system helped turn farmers into forestry workers as it attracted farmers to work on enterprise land.

According to Mr Tho, the acting director, the contracted land still belongs to the enterprise. The contractors own the product equivalent to the norm set by the enterprise and the excess output. This form of contract according to the ratio of investment is similar to the agricultural cooperative contract existing at the end of the Decree 100 period and during the transition to Resolution 10.

Among the three different contracts mentioned above, only the third attracted farmers to work on enterprise land. Since 1994, there has been another form of forest land management contract, namely the joint venture by households and the enterprise. The partners of the enterprise are both workers' and farmers' households. The land area of the joint venture is not only on enterprise property land, but also on land belonging to local people. This is forest land allocated to these people during the past few years. This is probably the most flexible management form both for the partners and the area forestation. The joint venture is similar to the third management form mentioned above. It covers land owned by local people. They are able to implement the five rights defined by the 1993 Land Law for joint venture forests.

Farmers and forestry workers are of the same opinion: households with little capital prefer to contract forest land according to the third

RESTRUCTURING OF TAN THANH FOREST ENTERPRISE   45

management form. Those with more capital prefer joint venture contracts. Farmers who have joint ventures with the enterprise are now working land that is gradually transferred from the enterprise to the farmers, because they have the right to the joint venture for cycle after cycle.

What then is the picture as seen from the forestry workers' perspective?

THE FORESTRY WORKERS IN MINH DAN BRIGADE

It takes about forty minutes by car to reach Minh Dan brigade from the enterprise headquarters on the eastern side of the Lo River. In bad weather the brigade is accessible only by bike or on foot as the road is bumpy and full of potholes.

We pass a hilly landscape, just at boundary between the rice-fields and the lemon grass; there are houses surrounded by gardens. The houses are on stilts and have wooden or straw walls and thatched roofs. Among these dwellings there are one- or two-storey stone houses, indicating that both minority people and Kinh live here.

Revisiting the brigade after seven years, we immediately notice that the long collective houses are no longer there. Something has obviously happened since we first came to this brigade in early 1987. We shall highlight these changes from different angles, the reasons for and the effects on the workers and their families. We shall also examine the workers' understanding of what is happening, how they deal with it, and their hopes for future.

Life in the brigade in 1987

Minh Dan is one of eight brigades belonging to the Tan Thanh forest enterprise. These units were not only a method of production management, but also a way to arrange housing and social conditions for employees. Thus, the brigade was a physical place, a centre for working and social activities. It had rooms for offices, daycare and kindergarten for children, school and health services. The workers did not pay for the services, including housing. Around the central yard there were long row-houses where the forestry workers lived. The collective houses were simple and some were nearly collapsing; they were classified as temporary. They consisted of six rooms in a row where the workers lived in one room, either singly in groups, or in families.

Since it was formed the brigade has moved twice. This partly explains why the housing conditions were not good. More than half of the workers lived in such collective houses, while the rest had already moved out into private houses. Some private houses were even simpler. They were more like camps, and some were still under construction.

Figure 14: Minh Dan Brigade in 1987. No collective house of this type exists any more [EL].
Figure 15: Minh Dan Brigade in 1994. Two collective houses made in brick. They are mainly used as a brigade centre [EL].

Our interviews revealed that the worst hardship the workers faced was the shortage of food. The following quotations are from our 1987 field notes:

RESTRUCTURING OF TAN THANH FOREST ENTERPRISE 47

We found it difficult to form an opinion about the supply of food. When we put questions to the workers, the common answers were: "as usual" and "enough". On the other hand, when we asked them about the most urgent improvements, they mentioned food production, supply of rice, more pigs, etc. A young mother we met several times ended up by saying, "To be honest, we do not have enough to eat. The work is heavy and the food is scarce."

To support its workers, the enterprise encouraged families to develop their own economy to supplement forest work. All the workers receive 0.5 hectares of forest land for private hill-rice cultivation, in combination with the first year on a newly planted area. Families in the collective quarters get 30–40 square metres for a garden close to the home. Families in private houses get 120–130 square metres for garden plots. They grow rice, cassava, peanuts, soya beans, and fruit trees for their own consumption, to exchange for consumer goods, or for sale on the local market. The distance to the market is 4 kilometres.

To summarize the situation in 1987, the most striking impressions were the appalling poverty, seemingly equally distributed, and the great number of women and small children. In fact, 70 per cent of workers were women. Some of them were married and lived with their husbands in the brigade; some husbands were absent, working elsewhere. Some married men had wives who stayed in their native villages and waited for them to return upon retirement. Then there were the single women, some of them with children.

The isolation of forestry work had cut off young women (and men) from social and cultural contact. Many women were deprived of an opportunity to marry because of the absence of men. When this problem became publicly acknowledged, it was argued that they should still have the right to become mothers provided that certain conditions were satisfied. This explains the relatively high number of unmarried mothers, sometimes up to 20 per cent of the women with children.

In everyday life, the women who had their husbands working elsewhere shared the fate of unmarried mothers of being alone. After work in the forest, the women had to rush home to take care of children, do the household chores, and find time for some extra work in the so-called family economy.

We looked for explanations for the large numbers of married couples living apart, and the striking gender imbalance, and reached the following conclusions (Liljeström 1987: 68–70):

> The job opportunities were primarily created in state employment. Living conditions for the new workers did not encourage them to take the families with them. Furthermore, in what remained a poor and risky environment, families could ensure against unforeseen

48 PROFIT AND POVERTY IN RURAL VIETNAM

difficulties by spreading their options, keeping access to land and subsistence in their home village for absent state employees.

Therefore, the separation between couples is often an expression of a long-term family strategy that sacrifices the couple's immediate gratification in the name of investment in the future of the children and the wider family group, and which also minimizes the risk created by "putting all your eggs in one basket".

A family member may work outside the home village for years, [even] decades and finally return home when he retires. While he is away the wife takes care of the children and if she, as often is the case, lives with her parents in law, she might look after them as well.

The custom that men should leave their home village dates back long in history. Furthermore, split families were part of daily life during the long wars. But what is new in the situation, is that today women also are employed as individuals.

State forestry work was seen as an opening for daughters from poor families to state employment. But this emancipation occurred in specific historic circumstances, in the shadow of wars, with gender imbalance between regions and occupations. It took place in forestry, an occupation where unmarried women could find themselves isolated in remote areas and deprived of opportunities to marry, and where mothers would be left alone with their children far from their native villages and their close kin. Paradoxically, those who are most badly hit are the women who should be liberated.

The single mothers and the wives with absentee husbands made up more than half the women in Minh Dan brigade. The dominant image from 1987 is of all women and their small children living in poor housing conditions and being short of food. Seven years later, one of our first issues was to see what had happened to them.

Household structure in 1994

The first inhabitants to meet the visitors are the children. Over the following days, they hang outside our rooms, watchful and curious. The children are older now and less shy than when they were small. In fact, we see no infants and no mothers carrying them. Many children have reached school age. We learn that the number of children has increased from forty-nine in 1987 to sixty-four in 1994. The reason for this is that workers from other brigades arrived to join Minh Dan brigade in 1988 and 1989, after three brigades at Tan Thanh forest enterprise had been disbanded. There are, however, fewer children aged under 4 years than before: eleven as compared to twenty-three in 1987. Most children, thirty-three out of sixty-four to be exact, are now aged between 6 and 10.

RESTRUCTURING OF TAN THANH FOREST ENTERPRISE 49

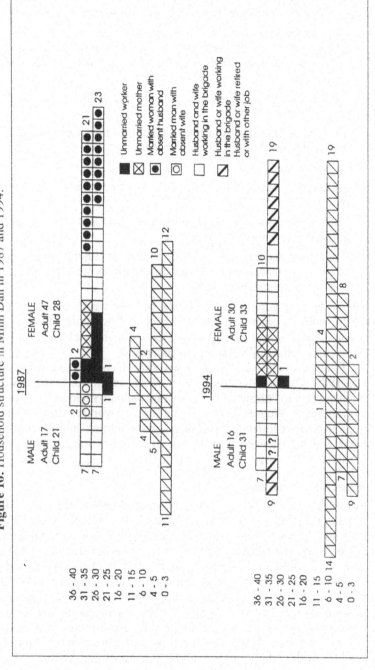

Figure 16: Household structure in Minh Dan in 1987 and 1994.

50   PROFIT AND POVERTY IN RURAL VIETNAM

The majority of the adults are in their forties. Mr Chuan, the brigade leader, draws our attention to the following changes:

The unmarried women have either married in the brigade or elsewhere, or they have become single mothers. In addition, there has been a reunification of split families. A few of them have stayed in the brigade, while most of them have left for the delta.

The predominance of women is still high, although it has decreased from 70 to 65 per cent.

The number of unmarried women has declined from ten to two, and thereby the surplus of women is smaller.

In 1987, there were six single mothers, now in 1994 there are ten.

Previously, there were many wives with absent husbands. In 1994 there are none.

There are eleven couples where both husband and wife are employed in the forest enterprise.

Ten couples have found it more profitable for either the husband or wife to remain as workers while their partners are either retired or are doing some other work.

There are some gaps in the 1994 data, because we are unable to trace all the workers. However, the trend is clear. The family situation has become more stable. The previous isolation has lessened and the interaction with local villagers has increased.

The figures indicate that no new workers have moved in after 1988 and 1989. On the contrary, when workers reach 40, both men and women seem to "disappear". At any rate they are no longer registered as employees. We met former female forestry workers who now have became farmers following their marriages to farmers in the neighbourhood. Still others live in the brigade as retired people. A third group consists of those who have returned to their native homes in the delta.

Rules for retirement

Since 1987, forty-three people have retired. There are mainly two ways to retire. One is when the worker reaches retirement age, 55 for men and 50 for women. This has recently been raised to 60 and 55 respectively. The second possibility is to retire after completing twenty years of continuous work. As many forestry workers started in their late teens and as most of them are more or less worn out at 50, they prefer to retire after fulfilling a certain number of years of work. If the pension begins after twenty years of work, it will amount to the salary during the last ten years, and the gratuity corresponds to the salary for twenty months. If the worker reaches full retirement age, up to 100 per cent of the salary will be paid for the rest of that worker's life.

RESTRUCTURING OF TAN THANH FOREST ENTERPRISE 51

Workers feel uncertain about the current retirement regulations, especially about the number of years that have to be completed before the full retirement age. A female worker has been employed for sixteen years and needs four more years to achieve "sufficient years", but for a pension she will still not have attained retirement. Thus, she does not know exactly when she can retire.

The *mat suc* retirement (i.e. retirement due to bad health, or literally "lost force") is generally more common. This gives some indication of the health of workers. The principle is that the pension is paid for half the number of years worked. The risk here is that if a medical check establishes that a worker has recovered, at the end of that period she or he must resume work, but if the worker does not recover, there will be no further pension payment.

A new termination system called Regulation 176 was introduced and put into effect between October 1989 and December 1991. This temporary regulation allowed workers to leave with a lump-sum payment so that they could devote time to other work. Thus the enterprise could shed their surplus labour. During this period most enterprises reduced their workforce by up to 40 per cent. In fact the reductions had started before 1989 and have continued since 1991. The Tan Thanh forest enterprise, for example, had more than 800 employees in 1987 and only 230 in June 1994.

A common strategy among households has been to let one spouse leave under Regulation 176 and keep the other as worker. All benefits can then be combined. The next most popular solution among the workers' families is to take advantage of the opportunity to return to the delta since Doi Moi made possible favourable loans. Most workers who left did have land and sometimes even a house to go back to.

Nearly half (twenty-one) out of the forty-three who have retired from Minh Dan brigade since 1987, have done so under Regulation 176. The other half have reached full retirement age or have retired because of ill health. Of the forty-three people, seventeen have returned to their native homes in the delta.

We probed deeper the identity of those who retired, those who left the brigade and their reasons for doing so. A worker explained:

> There are several reasons to return. Some faced economic difficulties, having old parents waiting for them. Some workers suffered from poor health. As it is easy to make money from the family economy, quite a few became farmers. There was no need to be forestry worker any longer. Other workers left because policy changes made life unpredictable; for instance, the increased age of retirement. There are cases where husband and wife regret that they did not retire earlier, while the old policy still held.

52   PROFIT AND POVERTY IN RURAL VIETNAM

Phuong says of her motives:

> There was a campaign in the brigade for family planning. I was pregnant with my fourth child, I was under pressure. Besides, I wanted to join my husband who is a farmer, when the village was allocating land to farmers. My husband told me that we needed more land because of all the children. And I could invest in the family economy. So I quit the forestry by the end of 1990. Then, 710 square metres of paddy land was allotted to me.

Those who move back to their native villages

Although the workers in Minh Dan brigade have been able to improve their lives in comparison to 1987, some still plan to return to the delta. We were invited to the house of Mrs Lien and Mr Thuy by their 10-year-old daughter who recognized us. The house is on the other side of a small stream. To get there, we have to wade across the stream, which was quite high on the day of our visit. For a girl of 10, the water reaches her waist. After climbing up a steep hill we arrive at a small, very simple house. It is made of bamboo and has an earthen floor.

It is Wednesday morning and both Mrs Lien and her husband are at home. The paternal grandmother is here to assist occasionally. In a simple house like this, there is only one room and everything is visible. While the grandmother serves tea, we look around: there are two wooden beds with mosquito nets. A big wooden box is at the spot where the family altar is usually placed. We are sitting at a small table. There are no pictures on the walls.

Thuy is 36 years old. He does not look well, he does not know for sure if he is suffering from a particular illness. Anyhow, he feels weak. Actually, he retired last year because of ill health. He had been logging for almost twenty years. He will receive a pension for a further ten years. It is about 146,000 dong per month.

Lien is two years younger than her husband. She too came here from Vinh Phu in 1978. They met here in the brigade. They emphasize that they are from the same native land although from different hamlets.

The custom of marrying within the same commune is still very strong in the Red River delta (Pham Van Bich 1997). According to a Vietnamese saying, it is "Better to get married to a fellow villager, who may be as lowly as a dog, than a person of high social status outside your village." In this way the young couple will live near both sets of parents. None the less, patri-local tradition and filial piety encourage sons to live near their parents. This facilitates mutual help and makes it easier for sons to assume the cult of ancestors when their father passes away. Interestingly, the strong preference for marrying

RESTRUCTURING OF TAN THANH FOREST ENTERPRISE 53

people from the same neighbourhood exists even among people who have moved from their native land. As we observed in 1987, the workers' relationships with their families in the delta are quite solid. We asked our hosts, "How come you left your homeland?"

People from the forest enterprise went there and recruited workers. We were young and came from poor families. We did not have any choice. And anyway, the stint in the forest would be limited. In fact, we plan to move back to the delta in five years when Lien has completed her "term of work". You know, when our daughter was born in 1983, we sent our 2-year-old son back to Thuy's mother. We have a piece of land and a small house there. And besides, Thuy has the obligations because he is the eldest son.

All sons have obligations towards their ageing parents, particularly the eldest (or the youngest). This is partly due to the tradition of ancestor worship. It is the eldest son who normally conducts the rituals for the spirits of dead parents. Without these rituals, their souls would wander forever. Contact with the spirits is upheld through anniversaries of death. The family altar is the centre of the ceremony. The cult of ancestors has undergone a marked revival in contemporary Vietnam (Hy Van Luong 1993).

Because they intend to return to the delta, Lien and Thuy do not invest in their house; instead they save everything in a big wooden box. Another family explains that they plan to return to the delta to secure the education of their children. Besides, the husband is the eldest son. They have a piece of land back home but no house waiting for them. Since they started to work at an early age, they hope to retire from the forest brigade according to the age rule. However, as the age of retirement has been postponed by five years, they do not know when they will be able to leave.

A couple who have been forestry workers for sixteen years have no idea about their future. In fact, they would like to return to the delta, but they have no savings and they have no land back in Vinh Phu. They worry about their ageing parents, especially as the husband is the oldest son.

We ask a healthy couple who are both engaged in many economic activities why they work so hard. They respond: "We want to earn a lot of money to be able to return to our native land. All our relatives live in the delta."

Single mothers
In Minh Dan brigade there stand two stone buildings at right angles to each other set about an open place that was previously a courtyard. The stone houses are of typical design with a single storey and pillars

Figure 17: A family planning to return to the Delta does not invest in housing, 1994 [EL].

Figure 18: In 1989 we met this family who had already started to invest in a brick house [EL].

on a cement base. The tiled roof reaches down to the pillars, creating a shelter from rain and sunshine outside the four or five rooms. The rooms have a direct entrance to the sheltered area.

The two houses have replaced the former bamboo and clay houses. They have been built by Swedish aid. They are used for the public business of the brigade, such as the brigade office, the nursery and the kindergarten, and as rooms for the brigade leader and one cadre. These two men have families living in another place. Two rooms are for two single mothers and their children, and one room is for a young single woman. They all live collectively, while most of the workers have left the common quarters. The main problem with this kind of house is the lack of space for gardens and pig rearing.

In 1990, the brigade started to mark out land for private housing. Today, almost all households in Minh Dan, including those of the single mothers, have their own houses. Some private houses are quite close to the centre of the brigade. Others are scattered on the other bank of a small river.

There are two types of private house. The simpler ones have bamboo walls with or without clay, wood and a thatched or tiled roof and an earthen floor. A good house is made of bricks and lime with either a thatched or tiled roof. The floor is earthen, cement or painted tile. The quality of the house often reveals the general standard of living, although some families do not invest in housing since they plan to return to the delta after their full period of service.

As we live in the centre of the brigade, it is from here that we hear the first sounds of morning chores. Women sitting on their heels prepare breakfast, cooking rice in a pot on an iron tripod right at the floor level. The open flames are nice and hot in the chilly morning but the smoke dirties anyone who comes too close.

In front of the stone houses, at the other corner, there is a simple house of bamboo and clay with some rooms that are used as kitchens by the small households in the collective houses. In the countryside, Kinh kitchens have traditionally been located in a separate house.

At the centre of the brigade we hear the familiar sounds of children playing and crying in the nursery, and the talking and singing of the staff. There are eight or nine children. No child is less than 1 year old and all are free to move about as they like. The equipment is very limited, almost non-existent: just a few beds and sleeping mats. In this regard, nothing has changed since 1987.

The kindergarten is more crowded with about twenty children aged 4 to 5. Some of them are children of nearby farmers. The kindergarten is regarded as a pre-school activity and is compulsory for all children. For this reason the farmers' children are welcome.

While it is a cultural norm that all women should marry and have children, in remote state farms and enterprises there are not enough men. When a woman has passed the age of 30 it is very difficult for a

Figure 19: Kindergarten in Minh Dan Brigade in 1994 [EL].

Vietnamese woman to get married. Many of these unmarried women still want to have a child. This issue was discussed in the press as well as in Women's Union:

> On the one hand, it is important to respect women's right to have children, not to force them to have abortions, or deny their children rations. However, both married women and the Women's Union were afraid that a more liberal view on extra-marital relationships and unwed mothers would undermine the very recently established principle that men should not have more than one wife. The traditional cultural pattern of "main wife" and a "little wife" could reoccur.
> (Colloquium on "Women, Employment and the Family", 1983)

This is why the identity of the father of a single mother's child had to be kept secret. Otherwise, the second wife would have been reinstated. In 1987 the brigade nurse, Mrs Bun had argued: "The right to be a mother has recently been written in our constitution. The way she takes advantage of this right is not our concern." Asked whether the fathers did not have any obligations she replied, "Nobody knows who the father is. The woman raises the child herself. She alone takes all the responsibility." That is ideology; as usual, real life is more complicated.

Half of the ten single mothers in Minh Dan brigade do in fact cohabit with the father of their children. None of the fathers works in the brigade. Four of them are from the delta, but come to Ham Yen district to work. Because they already have a wife and children in

RESTRUCTURING OF TAN THANH FOREST ENTERPRISE   57

their native place, the mothers in the brigade are classified as single. Sometimes the men cohabit with the "single mothers", each of them being a father of two or three children in the brigade. Sometimes they stay with their wife in the delta. According to the brigade leader, Mr Chuan, the same situation prevails in the other brigades, too.

One single mother met a demobilized soldier who had retired after sixteen years in the army. Having been in the South, in Laos and Cambodia, he was injured during the war against China: his leg was broken, his hearing and sight impaired. Today, they have a 3-year-old daughter. The couple has recently built a new house and acquired 4,000 square metres of *trai* land. She has both an investment and joint venture contract. His pension from the army adds 2.7 million dong to their yearly income. One hopes that these two, who now have passed 40, may succeed in making life easier for each other.

In five cases the identities of the fathers are hidden. The following two examples illustrate how the prospects of single mothers vary depending on their access to help from their families.

After three years' training in forestry, Ms Cai came to the Minh Dan brigade in 1989–90. About two years later she followed a carpenter from the delta to another brigade. There they built a house on his relative's land. However, after a year or two the mobile carpenter abandoned her and their son.

> Actually, we did not have a wedding. He cheated me and told that he was single, but he was already married to another woman. He then returned to her. There is no support from the father of the son.

Cai returned to her former brigade. She was afraid of staying alone in the house. She felt threatened by minority people around; maybe it was in someone's interest to get rid of her. Anyhow, Minh Dan brigade provided her a sleeping place in a storage room. Cai is no longer a member of the brigade. Her former workmates give her and her son leftover food. Cai is girlish. She has an unsuspecting smile, disarming and defenceless. She lost her mother while still a child. There was no one to protect her then as there is no one to support her now. Her father has passed away, and she cannot go back to her native land in her "special condition".

The prospects of Ms Nghi look better. She worked at the enterprise headquarters for about ten years and probably would have still been there if she had not became pregnant. She had a relationship with a married man living nearby. In 1992, Nghi came to Minh Dan brigade. She bought a house for 2 million dong. She saved 1 million and she borrowed the rest. She still has a debt of 400,000 dong. In fact, Nghi is able to pay it back, but as the workers have not received salaries

58   PROFIT AND POVERTY IN RURAL VIETNAM

since August (now it is November), she has to hold on to her money. Nghi possesses 1,000 square metres of garden land around the house. In addition she has a *trai* of 2,500 square metres. She has been raising pigs for a long time and has earned 1.3 million per year. That is why she had savings.

Nghi looks graceful and serious, nearly stern. She suffers from heart disease. Now and then she has to take a fortnight or so off work because of her poor health. Kien, her son, is 3 years old. Nghi worries about his frequent respiratory troubles. Nghi comes from a poor farming family in Vinh Phu. She is the second of ten children. Now, her economic prospects are promising due to the supportive labour of her brothers.

> During the harvesting season or whenever there is heavy work my brother comes to help me. He came to assist me when I got my child. He moves back and forth. He is not married yet. Another brother too is willing to come. Last harvest two of my brothers came. I do not need help from the brigade since I have my brothers. So far we have planted 250 oranges trees on my *trai*. My younger brother stays there and tends the oranges.

The sister and her brothers work for their mutual benefit. The brothers are poor and underemployed; Nghi provides them with a job. Nghi does not receive any support from her son's father. However, he once came to see his son.

Single mothers without relatives or cohabiting partners to assist them are the worst off, according to the brigade leader. Now that the number of labouring hands matters more than before, there is not much scope for single mothers. Yet, the enterprise provides credits of little or no interest. Even single mothers have been able to save for investing, although this places great demands on them.

At the end of the day, we walk back to the brigade centre. During the twilight, some of the single mothers living nearby prepare an evening meal. The children are playing, sometimes too close to an open fire. Some women pass the big yard carrying water and firewood. A little further away, on the small road leading to the river, some Dao women and men return from the forest after working with their dry rice. The pigs are grunting, the chicken clucking. Somewhere, a cock is trying to drown out everything with his crowing. The darkness is now settling so that the surrounding mountains appear to have come closer. The kerosene lamps look like stars. For the passing visitor this is an idyllic spot.

FIVE

Redivided Responsibilities

FORESTRY WORKERS BECOME PART-TIME FARMERS

In the late 1980s the Tan Thanh forest enterprise faced two vast problems: the continuing destruction of the forest, and the deterioration in the forestry workers' economic and social lives. In early 1988, the enterprise undertook a survey which revealed that only 50 per cent of planted areas of forest still have trees. The same year there was a general improvement in management and other activities under the leadership of the newly-appointed director, Mr Hung. He decided to restructure the enterprise and concentrate on three issues: reorganize forest production, reduce staff, and improve the workers' living conditions.

From paternal provider to employer

In 1987, the state was still supposed to supply the forest enterprises with salaries and certain goods as payment for the workers who logged, planted, tended, and protected the forest. The enterprise was also responsible for educating children and for health services for all inhabitants of the brigade.

Dilemmas arose when the state could no longer afford to pay the salaries in time or deliver the supplies such as sugar, fish sauce, bicycle tyres, etc. Soon salaries were paid in rice, and sometimes this was the only remuneration the workers received. Furthermore, workers often received only 70 per cent or even less of the rice ration. The brigade began to set aside land for the collective production of staples like rice, maize, cassava and sugar-cane. The workers were totally dependent on the enterprise for their physical survival.

Years before official policy had sanctioned and later supported privatization of social life by allowing workers to build their own houses and have their own gardens, some families had already taken

60   PROFIT AND POVERTY IN RURAL VIETNAM

the steps out of necessity. A separate house and particularly a garden, was the first impressive stepping stone for a family to start accumulating to improve their living conditions. Having gardens meant food, not least pig fodder. Breeding pigs is a way to save money for future investments. In 1987 the workers grew rice in between the newly planted forest. This was a measure to alleviate the scarcity of food. Later, in 1991, the enterprise set up forest *trais*.

Essentially, the forest enterprise has now reduced its responsibility as an employer, and left each family to cope more or less by themselves. This corresponds with developments in the agricultural cooperative in Lam Tien. The former cooperative used to control and manage both the production and social life of its members. As a worker puts it: "The period from 1960 to 1993 was under the state and cooperative rule; now we are back under the authority of the village."

A major problem for the forest enterprises in Tuyen Quang province is the continuing logging ban. Since May 1992, the forest gate is closed (*dong cua rung*). The ban has placed high demands on each enterprise to find temporary means for the workers to survive. In Tan Thanh, except for afforestation, the strengthening of the family economy has assumed increasing importance.

The significance of the family economy

In line with the new economic policy, workers take increasing responsibility for their lives outside the sphere of contracted work. Tan Thanh supports this process. As early as 1987, the enterprise allowed fifteen days off per year to enable them to work in the so-called family economy. This period was extended to three months in 1989.

The workers tell us about other measures to stimulate supplementary activities:

> We borrowed 500,000 dong from the enterprise to build our house in 1991. Since 1993, we have about 0.6 hectares of forest *trai* where we grow oranges. We borrowed money for our house and for the forest *trai* from the enterprise. We pay 3 per cent in interest. The enterprise borrows from the bank at 2.7 per cent of interest. The difference covers the administrative costs.

The leadership of Tan Thanh acts as the intermediary between the bank and the workers to secure favourable loans. Workers cannot borrow directly from the bank as they normally do not have any assets that can be used as collateral.

The forest *trais* are a new phenomenon that did not exist in 1987. These areas, identified by the enterprise, are bare and are intended for tree planting. A family gets 2 to 5 hectares. Workers can dispose of them as long as their action is in harmony with the plans of the

REDIVIDED RESPONSIBILITIES 61

enterprise. Most families grow different fruit trees, particularly oranges. The area is considered suitable for this fruit. It is also common to grow rice and other crops between the trees during the first years of the orange tree cycle. Fourteen out of thirty families have such forest *trais*.

According to the brigade leader, Mr Chuan, only the wealthiest families have a *trai*. To be profitable, the *trai* needs a labour input. The richest families hire labour. The labour capacity is decisive. Actually, all the households have labour support from their relatives in the delta. After rice planting, when it is idle time for the farmer, then they have time to help their *trai* relatives. The same pattern occurs amongst the villagers, except the very rich farmers who hire local labourers, Mr Chuan adds.

Salaries and total income

In reckoning their total income, workers add the salary from the enterprise to the revenues from family economy.

Generally, the conditions for growing food and cash-crops are favourable. The soil is fertile. However, hills are more common than level land. The land is divided into three categories: home garden land, rice cultivation land, and cash-crop land. Dry-rice cultivation is practised by everyone during the first years of tree plantations. Some people even have land for wet-rice.

In Minh Dan brigade the salary and the revenues from the family economy each account for half of the total income. Not all workers regard this as an ideal situation:

> We are forced to use the family economy for our survival, because forestry fails to provide our living. But my identity is as a forestry worker. With 300,000 dong per month, I would do only forestry work.

A family explains that even if the family economy is important for both immediate survival and accumulation, family members regard the forestry work as their main occupation. Another family was asked about their main occupational identity:

> It depends on how many labourers there are in a household. If family members have poor access to work, they prefer monocultural work. In our case, we prefer a combination. We are both strong and do not suffer from disease.

Other families saw only advantages:

> In the garden of 1,300 square kilometres we first grew oranges, but this did not work. Now we have planted cinnamon and apricots. It is too early to predict the outcome. When we still lived col-

62 PROFIT AND POVERTY IN RURAL VIETNAM

lectively, we had chickens and pigs. The difference now is that the numbers have increased. Since the end of 1993, we have a forest *trai*. It is 2,500 square metres and it is located about 3 kilometres from here. We grow oranges and cinnamon. It takes four and ten years respectively for the first harvest. We have been able to harvest rice from the forest *trai*. The first time we got 400 kilograms of paddy. This is a relatively good yield.

Since forestry work is seasonal, monthly earnings vary. The range in Minh Dan was 160,000–260,000 dong, that is about US$12–20. Based on the current rice price (about 3,500 dong per kilogram) it should be possible to get 45–75 kilograms of rice.

The corresponding figure for 1987 differs markedly, because of the double price system. At that time, one kilogram of rice on the free market cost 100 dong, while the state-subsidized price was 5.2 dong. The lowest salary at that time was 400 dong, the equivalent of either 4 kilograms of rice on the open market or 77 kilograms at state-subsidized price. But the state rice supply was only theoretical, since the enterprise never succeeded in supplying 100 per cent of the salary. In fact, there were times when a worker received only 6 kilograms of rice per month. It is estimated that a hard-working labourer needs at least 20 kilograms a month.

The workload of women has always been heavy; adding to their forestry work and motherhood duties the burden of responsibility for the family economy has made it even heavier.

The initiatives taken by the Tan Thanh forest enterprise in 1988 have been largely successful. Both the contract system and the support to the family are generally welcomed by workers, whatever their family status.

Reorganization of forestry work

In its general pursuit of alternative working relationships, the enterprise started to lease out forest land to both its workers and to neighbouring farmers. Starting in 1988, contracts with workers and farmers took different forms over time.

In regard to the investment contract the family, families, or a group of workers get paid according to how much work they have invested. The work is measured in a unit called *cong*. Each *cong* is worth about 4,000–7,000 dongs. The number of *congs* depends of the kind of work done, such as clearing land, planting, tending, and protecting.

The size of the forest land is different, depending on access and the labour capacity of each family. In Minh Dan brigade, two to three families have chosen to collaborate to take care of 15 to 30 hectares. Single mothers, two or three to a group, can take care of 3–30 hectares.

REDIVIDED RESPONSIBILITIES 63

The more the workers invest in labour, the more they will gain. All the other investments are made by the enterprise. If the enterprise cannot pay a salary, the worker will take the profit at harvest time. In this way, the worker will have an ownership of the trees, while the land is still state land.

What does the forestry work look like nowadays? A male worker explains:

> I began with the investment contract in 1991. We were a group of nine people: two men and seven women. By the end of 1993, the group was dissolved. Many members retired. So I joined three other men for another contract.

> We clear, burn, and prepare land and we dig holes for the trees. We have signed a contract with the brigade for 1995. So far it has not yet been signed by the enterprise. The contract is for planting 1 hectare of cao trees and 1 hectare of styrax. This should mean that we have work to do all the year around. A full cycle of the investment contract is for nine to ten years.

We asked why the enterprise had not yet decided to sow styrax:

> There is the logging ban on mature styrax. As long as there is old styrax, they forbid new planting of trees.

Other workers give an account of their work:

> We share a contract with one family in three different places. The most remote area where we grow acacia and styrax is 3 kilometres away. The techniques are a bit different; acacia is planted while styrax is sown.

> My husband and I work on 2 hectares of forest. My husband is solely responsible for another 30 hectares of forest. I myself work with two other women in the brigade. We are neighbours, so it is easy to call upon each other to work.

Nghi comments on the size of her group:

> I have so far worked on an investment contract. In future, I will also consider the joint venture form. Now there are only three women in the group. In 1991–1992 we worked in a group of eight, including the men. A big group is not efficient. That is why we decided to split in 1993. A group of three women is easy to manage.

We invited the workers to compare the current system to earlier conditions:

> Much has changed since 1987. We eat better. We are able to buy any goods we like. We have better clothes. We work for ourselves. As there is no logging at present, the work is not too hard. However our health has deteriorated over time.

64   PROFIT AND POVERTY IN RURAL VIETNAM

> I think there are pros and cons like between the earlier and the present systems. Now life is more free, but it is also more insecure. We prefer the new system with more responsibility. The economy is better and the work is more independent.

> Of course things are better. We have a house, we can buy things, and we have a TV. For the future, we wish to have a motorbike. We will improve the house and enlarge the forest farm.

Actually, it is the husband who wants the bike whereas the wife prefers to repair the house.

Some single mothers express their opinions:

> It is better now. Previously, we were totally dependent, but now we master things ourselves. The total income is higher because of our own labour.

> Life does not change much. But there are some changes in social security. In the past, I only contributed to the trade union. Today, we have to pay a contribution to an insurance fund. It is made as a salary deduction in the last month of the year.

The differences that the workers consider as significant are obviously not only the rise in the general standard of living. The feeling of independence and of being "master" of the situation are crucial. However, many workers, particularly women, worry that the state is becoming less supportive than before. Seemingly, people are looking for a reasonable balance between being one's own master and intervention by the state. This concern is not unique to Vietnam.

The workers' voice

In Minh Dan brigade there are three forums where workers can discuss matters of social security and services. The sociopolitical organizations include the Communist Party, the trade union and the Women's Union. We talked to their representatives in an attempt to understand the precise roles of these organizations. The workers themselves seem to view them more as formal institutions than as a platform for their own aims and influence.

Mr Tuan has been the party secretary of the brigade since the beginning of 1994. He was elected to this post by the five party members in the brigade. The brigade leader, who is also a party member, and Tuan are responsible for all forestry work. They make and control the work plans, and they report to the next level, the enterprise. Tuan gives the impression that the party is strong here and that is as it should be. The role of the party in Minh Dan brigade has not changed much during the Doi Moi.

REDIVIDED RESPONSIBILITIES 65

The next meeting is with Mr Doanh, chairman of the trade union since 1994. He originates from Thai Binh. Doanh explains the role of trade union in these terms:

All the forty-four workers here are trade union members. The monthly fee is 800 dong and is used for workers in particular need. The main duty of the trade union is to explain the management of work to the workers.

Mrs Khanh has been head of the Women's Union since 1994. She is originally from Vinh Phu. She is responsible for the nursery and the kindergarten of the brigade. The role of the union is described by her in these terms:

First of all, we organize the family planning and increase the political awareness of women. We also ask the forest enterprise to provide loans to women to enable them to develop family economy. Another issue we have raised is to request higher [authority] levels, the enterprise and the district, to intervene and reduce school fees.

Q: What is your own part in this?

A: I attend meetings of different levels, like the enterprise and the district, on women's affairs. Then I bring back the discussion to the brigade.

Q: How often do you have meetings?

A: Since 1993 we have had quarterly meetings at the brigade level.

Q: How many women attend these meetings?

A: Usually only eighteen people take part. After a hard day's work, they have no interests in meetings. Frankly, they are reluctant to participate. However, it depends on the subject of the meeting. When it is about bringing up children or boosting family economy, they attend. I invite the brigade leader, the nurse, or the chairman of the trade union to come and give a speech. The nurse talks about family planning, the brigade leader about forestry work, etc. Then I report to higher levels.

PUBLIC SERVICES

As already indicated, the enterprise and the agricultural cooperatives used to be responsible for all kinds of social services including health services, schools, maternity leave, pensions, etc. At present the state has withdrawn as the guarantor of social security. At Minh Dan brigade we were briefed about the new health system:

An amount corresponding to 15 per cent of the monthly salary is paid to a fund. Of this amount, the enterprise pays 10 per cent and

66 PROFIT AND POVERTY IN RURAL VIETNAM

the employees 5 per cent. Until 1994, regular health checks were carried out at the brigade or the enterprise health stations. There are not any automatic check-ups any longer.

For many years the family planning programme proclaimed two children as the ideal. Nevertheless, the rice rations were distributed to the third child as to any subsequent children. The reason was purely humanitarian as denial of rice rations would have meant starvation. Now that families are supposed to take more responsibility for their living conditions, the sanctions against the state employees for having more than two children are fully applied. No promotion and no increase in salaries for three years are given to those parents.

Since June 1994 activities related to population control and family planning have gained momentum in Minh Dan commune. Lam Tien village now boasts a coordinator for this programme, Mrs Tu Thi Lien. She is also the chairperson of the Women's Union branch. She has executed all the instructions of the Commune Population and Family Planning Commission. Mrs Lien has to report monthly to the commune on family planning and receive contraceptives. She is duty-bound to persuade people to abide by family planning rules and regulations, and to effect their implementation.

Mrs Lien drew examples from her notebook. At present there are fifty-five couples of child-bearing and nurturing age. The distribution of children amongst the couples is given in Table 2.

Table 2: Ratio of children per couple in Lam Tien village, 1994

Number of children	1	2	3	4+
Number of couples	10	20	11	14

Among the fifty-five couples, twenty-seven use IUDs, three use condoms, and six use the rhythm method. So far there has been no case of male or female sterilization in the village. From June 1993 to November 1994, only six children were born. Five of them are first-born children, and one is the third child. A couple with a third child is fined 50 kilograms of paddy. This kind of fine has been applied since 1992.

According to Mrs Tu Thi Lien, there has been a change for the better in birth control, as the women are more inclined to restrict their families to two children. This is owing to radio and TV propaganda and lessons given by the cadres. Villagers are now aware that the arable land area is more and more restricted because of the growing population.

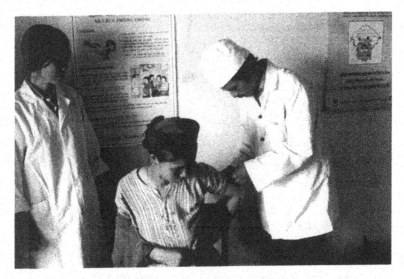

Figure 20: Vaccination of a young mother, 1994 [EL].

In addition to her population and family planning work, Mrs Tu Thi Lien has campaigned against malnutrition in children under the age of 5. There are now fifty-four children of this age group in the village. On the 25th of every month the commune's medical officer cooperates with the village medical offices to vaccinate and weigh the small children. This usually happens in the Minh Dan brigade nursery. Thirty-two of fifty-four pre-school children (59 per cent) suffer from moderate malnutrition, and one from serious malnutrition.

In recent years such common diseases in the mountain region as malaria and goitre have occurred, but only in a few cases. The village has one nurse. If villagers contract a mild disease, they buy medicine from the village nurse and from the village infirmary. If they fall seriously ill, they consult a doctor at the district hospital in Phu Luu village.

The very day that we arrived at the Minh Dan brigade, there was an inoculation campaign for children. Mothers from the brigade and from the villages nearby carried their babies into the nursery. The infants were vaccinated against measles and they also received some drops of vitamin D. The campaign was arranged by the local district. The doctor was from the district, while the nurse was the former brigade nurse, Mrs Bun. The atmosphere was calm and relaxed, and was only interrupted by the cries of the children when they were injected.

Ethnic differentiation in education

Since 1989, farmers' and workers' children have attended the same classes from the first grade. Previously, the forest enterprise was re-

Figure 21: One of the classes in Lam Tien, 1994 [EL].

sponsible for the first years of schooling. Now the district authorities take care of all schooling, although the enterprise assists by supplying labour and construction material for school buildings.

All children over 6 years of age attend school. Moreover, three forestry workers' families have sent their children to the delta for education. Since 1993, there has been a branch of Ham Yen higher secondary school in Phu Luu, 3 kilometres from the brigade.

Education in Lam Tien has changed but generally the improvements are slow and have not kept pace with economic change. The primary and lower secondary schools are located about 1 kilometre from the Lam Tien village, and 3 kilometres from Minh Dan brigade. Consequently, primary school pupils are taught the first two years of school right in the village.

In the past, female pupils, especially Tay girls, frequently left school at lower secondary level. Their reasons for leaving were numerous. Even today there is no purpose in children completing lower secondary school, say their parents, because their future work will be farming and nothing else. In Lam Tien, as in many other upland places, children aged 10 or more, especially the girls, help their parents with many small jobs, such as grazing buffaloes, collecting firewood, and even in transplanting and weeding rice. The children become engaged in farming work as soon as they leave the school.

Ms Sua (39), an unmarried teacher in Minh Dan village, had much to say about the continuing ethnic differentiation in education:

REDIVIDED RESPONSIBILITIES

I have been a primary school teacher in Minh Dan commune for nineteen years. When you were here last time you might have visited the communal school. Since then, we have got a village school. It consists of five grades of primary school and three grades of secondary school. However, a lot of pupils only stay a few years in the school. After four years, less than half of those who began in the first class still remain in grade 4. I myself teach in grade 2 with twenty-five pupils. That is the average size of classes.

Q: Have any changes taken place in the school since 1990?

A: As a village teacher I do not see any changes.

Q: What about the introduction of fees?

A: Only pupils in the secondary school pay tuition fees. When they come to the grade 6 they pay 2,000 dong per month; in grade 7 they pay 2,000 plus 1,000; in grade 8 it is 4,000; and in grade 9 they pay 5,000 per month. The fees were introduced in 1991. During the first years they collected fees in the primary school, but only for one year, because the minorities refused to send their children to school. The local government had to abolish the fees for primary school. It was about 9,000 dong per year from grade 3 on. They collected it for one year only. Minority children do not like to go to school. We have to visit their parents and persuade them to send their children to school. In the grade 1, they do not speak Vietnamese, so we need an interpreter, that is the school has to recruit a bilingual pupil to translate for the minority pupils. They are from Tay and Dao ethnic groups. They make up about half of all pupils.

Q: How do the minority children perform in school compared to Kinh children?

A: In general the quality of education of minority people is lower. It is hard to teach them when they do not speak Vietnamese. In grades 2 and 3 they participate a little more. However, as they reach higher grades they achieve less and less.

Q: What is the proportion of minority pupils in the secondary school?

A: Only 6 to 7 per cent, and only Tay people. I have never seen a Dao pupil in secondary school. Many of them drop out. Usually they are able to follow the first three grades, but they rarely go up to grade 4.

Q: In your opinion, what are the most urgent needs of primary school pupils?

A: There are two main issues. The education service must reduce the contributions other than fees which the pupil's parents must

70 PROFIT AND POVERTY IN RURAL VIETNAM

make, for example, contributions to the construction of the school. In grade 1, the admission grade, everything is free. But in grade 2 they have to pay 12,000 dong per year for the construction of the school. According to the Ministry of Education, every pupil has to contribute four labour days per month as part of their curriculum. But two of the days are compulsory and have to be exercised in the school; the two other are exercised at home. In addition they have to contribute 500 + 500 dong. That is, 1,000 dong per month. Since 1992, they have to pay a compulsory insurance ranging from 3,000 to 9,000 dong per year, depending on liability. Besides, they have to take part in fundraising campaigns for disaster victims (2,000–5,000 dong) or poor disabled students (500 per year), or charities. There are many compulsory funds. Parents complain, and it is necessary to do something about it.

Secondly, the quality of teachers needs to be improved. Measures should be taken to encourage minority pupils to come back to school when they drop out.

Q: Has there been any increase in the teacher salaries in recent years?

A: In 1991 it was increased from 120,000 dong to 260,000. At present a teacher's salary is 265,000 dong per month. The improvements for primary school teachers have been significant, no less than for the forestry workers. Since the reforms, the full salary is paid in cash.

Q: Do you see any other impact of Doi Moi?

A: Last year, 1993, Minh Dan commune was accepted to implement some universal primary schooling. This commune was selected as a pilot commune to adopt compulsory education for all people up to grade 5. The commune has to investigate and establish how many illiterate people remain. Once they know the number, they will prepare a plan to educate them.

The topics that Ms Sua addressed were regularly raised whenever parents or teachers aired their opinions about the school.

SUMMARY

A characteristic feature of Lam Tien village and Minh Dan brigade is the availability of land for both farming and forestry. With the allocation of agricultural and forest land for households, both farmers and forestry workers, the administration and economy are reverting back to a village-like organization based on family farms. Production is not only for self-sufficiency but also for the market. The rise of commodities can be seen in the development of the *trai*, the reappearance

Figure 22: Mrs Luong and Mr Chi have worked for many years as forestry workers. Now they manage 13 ha of forest together with another family [EL].

of hired labour, the raising of livestock, and the cultivation of grains, fruits and trees.

The gap between rich and poor is widening even if the poor have been able to raise their living standards in absolute terms. By and large people do have enough food all year around.

The key to these changes is the new land management system. The land situation of different households was basically stable. There were no serious land conflicts between farmers' households during the course of official land allocation under the 1993 Land Law. The process of renovating the forest and forest land relationship has respected customary rights. All earlier forest gardens of the people have been legalized. All agricultural land has officially been allocated to households. The prospects for handing over forest land for long-term use are good.

With a well-defined owner or manager, people are keen to invest in farming, forestry, or some combination of both. From different starting points, workers and farmers are evidently converging as regards sources of income and interest. It may be that the combination of forestry and farming will reinforce a gender division of labour, with the men taking the lead in forestry, while women develop the household economy based on gardening and rearing animals. On the other hand, the life courses of mothers with only two children deviate from those of previous generations, thus creating new challenges to the old order.

72 PROFIT AND POVERTY IN RURAL VIETNAM

The role of the forest enterprise will probably also change further. At present, the workers in Tan Thanh are still dependent on plans made by the enterprise. They are still paid according to the labour they invest, not according to the result of their work.

The 1992 logging ban causes problems for the forest enterprises in Tuyen Quang province. Tan Thanh enterprise is short of income and cannot therefore invest in the plantations. The enterprises have already reduced their activities and consequently the salaries. The Tan Thanh enterprise has played a vital role in order to create conditions for workers to move into private houses; it has acted as intermediary for low-interest loans, and has provided land for *trai*. It is only because of the family economy that workers can make both ends meet at present.

As most workers see a profitable future in forestry, they are not ready to go over to farming exclusively. Nevertheless, at present they are becoming part-time farmers. This was not the aim of the new economic zones in the 1960s and 1970s. Now, when more forest land is used for agriculture, one wonders whether this trend is sustainable in the long run. Will there be enough land for all the involved groups: the ethnic groups who have lived here for generations, the Kinh migrants, the farmers and forestry workers?

We enquired about changes in the relationship between workers and farmers. In the wake of the economic reforms there are new elements of collaboration, especially in education and health. Because both the state enterprises and the cooperatives have transferred these services to the local districts, both workers and farmers receive the services at the same place. For instance, all the children took part in the vaccination campaign administered by the district inside the Minh Dan brigade. The farmers' children attend the kindergarten in the brigade, while children from the brigade and the surrounding villages go to the same primary and lower secondary schools. However, the early drop-out of minority children will demand imaginative school reforms to counteract ethnic marginalization.

In the future, Minh Dan commune will witness increased production of goods. Land and labour are becoming commodities. Certainly this will mean that workers and farmers will share the benefits and disadvantages of Doi Moi even more closely.

CASE TWO

Two Models of Modernization

SIX

Custom and Commerce in Phuc Tam Village

BACKGROUND

As in several other socialist countries, the Communist Party in Vietnam tried to modernize through collectivization. The old farming family with its age and gender hierarchies, its male lineage, strong blood relationships and cult of ancestors, stood as an obstacle to social progress. Therefore the leadership of the party challenged the power of the old men, the heads of lineages and families. The revolution aimed at eroding the prerogatives of prosperous families that promoted and favoured their own members at the expense of the poor and landless. According to the socialist central planning model, all economic activities should be run by the state or by cooperatives. The establishment of state enterprises and the collectivization of agriculture were tools to overcome the injustices of class. This was an attempt to transmute the cohesion between generations and kin into class consciousness and solidarity between workers.

The collective work was organized in production brigades, and the brigades in their turn were divided into working teams or special task groups. The brigades were not only production units, but embraced the workers' whole lives. They were set up as total environments in an attempt to dissolve the strong community spirit and the lineage-based family. With this intent, the party also restricted and counteracted customary rites and celebrations that upheld family cohesion, like large wedding parties, funerals, burial sites near the farmhouses, death anniversaries, etc. By replacing the bonds of blood with relationships of production, private household with public life in brigades, the party

76   PROFIT AND POVERTY IN RURAL VIETNAM

fought for equality and the universal rights of citizens. The state guaranteed all children the right to education; it provided nurseries and kindergartens, social security and health care. It paid pensions to war veterans and state employees. It constructed a supportive public safety-net to displace family obligations. The establishment of social services was progressive; yet, when the state could no longer afford them, the socialist model of modernization failed.

The second model of modernization had the same aim, whether we call it modernity, progress, or development. However, the means to achieve it were different. Actually, the socialist and capitalist models were mutually hostile to the extent that the global politics were dominated by the Cold War. In Vietnam the war went hot when the US army intervened in 1965–1975. It should be kept in mind that the long wars (the colonial war against the French and the US war) have influenced the choice of the political model and its outcome, although we here restrict ourselves to give evidence on the local level long after the US troops were forced to leave Vietnam. Case Two bears witness to those two models of modernization, both wanting to dissolve bonds of blood and lineage. We begin when the cooperatives already have come to an end or are being called into question. We narrate the evolution of self-management of land and the growth of commerce.

Phuc Tam village and Chiem Hoa forest enterprise Brigade 481 in Phuc Thinh commune had one advantage in the encounter with Doi Moi. They were located on the main district road, which soon became the main road to commodification. The merchandise is for display in the ever-growing number of shops, inns, kiosks, and stalls along both sides of the main road. We shall give an account of how farmers and workers responded to the challenge of profit-making by involving themselves in a variety of trades. How have they managed? What differentiates those who succeed from those who fail?

PHUC TAM VILLAGE: TRANSITION TO A COMMODITY ECONOMY

Phuc Tam and many other villages of Phuc Thinh commune are situated in a large valley stretching from the foot of the Ga mountain pass in the west to Chiem Hoa district town on the Gam River. On the road from Tuyen Quang's provincial town to Chiem Hoa district, the traveller must ascend the Ga mountain pass, about 10 kilometres away from the district town of Chiem Hoa. Standing on the top of this pass, one gets a panoramic view over the valley with its fields and houses stretching into the distance. The Phuc Thinh commune in Chiem Hoa district covers an area of 2,140 hectares with a population of 4,163 (2,135 women and 2,028 men). Besides the two main ethnic groups, the 2,995 Tay

CUSTOM AND COMMERCE IN PHUC TAM VILLAGE 77

and the 1,021 Kinh, there are a number of ethnic migrants whose arrival dates from the border war between Vietnam and China in 1979. These are the Hoa (Vietnamese of Chinese origin), Nung, H'Mong, Dao and Cao Lan. All told they amount to 137 persons. The Kinh migrated to the region in the 1960s.

The complexity of the ethnic structure may complicate the land relationships and influence the land issue in the villages as well. Land conflicts are more likely to arise when the 1993 Land Law is fully implemented. Some conflicts are bound to occur between long-established residents of the village and the newcomers, and also between people of different ethnic groups. When these two dimensions coincide, the conflicts will be more difficult to solve. Also, if the solutions are not frank and fair, an economic problem could become a political one. Phuc Tam village is located near the commune centre, its administrative quarters, the primary and junior secondary schools, the infirmary, and the site of the Chiem Hoa forestry Brigade 481. Here, in the centre of the commune the petty traders have their shops, booths, tea-rooms and kiosks, which stretch along the highway.

On the northern side of the village are the afforested hills held by Brigade 481, and on the south there are extensive cultivated fields of rice and other crops belonging to several villages. The Cau Quang stream flows through the fields to join the Gam River.

The origin of the inhabitants in Phuc Tam

The inhabitants of Phuc Tham belong to only the two main ethnic groups, the Tay and the Kinh. Thus the ethnic composition is less complex than in the commune. Following their custom, the Tay live in houses on stilts and the Kinh in houses on the ground. The majority of households have built their dwellings along the highway. The Tay and the Kinh live together in the same area, and are not separated like in Lam Tien.

The Tay have lived on this land for many generations. In earlier times, Phuc Tam village belonged to Cuong mountain village. At that time, Cuong village covered an extensive area comprising all the land now attached to three villages. The Vietnamese are concerned about ancestry, the family from whom they descend. The Tay family line or lineage (i.e. the series of families from whom they are directly descended) is Ma. Ma is a great lineage whose authority and prestige derive from the large number of its members who were traditional medicine men and shamans. However, there is no Ma family in Phuc Tam any more. None the less, Professor Nham Tuyet took notes from a genealogical register of the Ma descent from its head, Ma Van Tin, in a village adjacent to Phuc Tam. This register contains ten generations. Furthermore, it included the Sino-Vietnamese words *cao, cao*

78   PROFIT AND POVERTY IN RURAL VIETNAM

tang to khao ty, which mean that there were many generations before the given register.

The second family lineage recognized by the Tay is Hoang. Hoang is a Kinh name. The inhabitants bearing the Hoang family name migrated from the plains long ago owing to famine and war. Thereafter, they became Tay through gradual acculturation. The third lineage coming to this village is the Luu. These people migrated from China about 300 years ago. The Kinh in Phuc Tam are mostly people who came to cultivate new land in the early 1960s. They were mainly natives of Ninh Binh province. They came in two waves. The first three households came in 1963 and four more arrived in 1965. In addition, there is a Kinh household whose native home is in Thai Binh province. The husband is a teacher and the wife a farmer. At present, Phuc Tam has a total of thirty-five Tay households comprising 180 persons, and twenty Kinh households with eighty-five persons. Thirteen Tay and three Kinh households consist of three generations. The family size of the Tay and the Kinh people is given in Table 3.

Table 3: Family size of Tay and Kinh households in Phuc Tam, 1994

No. of persons per household	No. of Tay households	No. of Kinh households
From 2–3	5	6
From 4–5	13	12
From 6–9	17	2
Total	**35**	**20**

The old agricultural cooperatives

In 1993, the current names of the villages and their territories were defined. From 1960 to 1992 the inhabitants of Phuc Tam were members of an agricultural cooperative and submitted to its management. This cooperative was first named Na Cuong and considered to be of village size. Then it was renamed An Lac cooperative and it embraced four villages. Later, in 1976, it spanned the whole commune and was called Phuc Thinh cooperative. Thus formally, Phuc Tinh commune consisted of three agricultural cooperatives. However, in 1984 this large cooperative was dissolved. By this time, two cooperatives had dissolved themselves, because their board had no influence on the production and business of members' households. Only An Lac co-operative has continued to operate in some fashion. What kept the

CUSTOM AND COMMERCE IN PHUC TAM VILLAGE 79

management of An Lac cooperative going was the contract system of production. The level of contribution by households is the same as the amount defined by Resolution 10. It is rather high: 12 per cent of the output. In fact, the households in Phuc Tam have to contribute 24 per cent of their income, namely 12 per cent for government taxes and a similar amount for sustaining the cooperative's management, and for the welfare activities of the village and commune.

The contribution to cooperatives was the same as at the early stage of implemention of Resolution 10, although their role was decreasing. Now only two activities remain where the collective has some effect. First, the collective provides credits to members. Households that lack capital can buy materials, fertilizers and insecticides from the cooperative on credit, and pay it back at the end of the harvesting season. By and large, nobody felt that the interest was high. However, such beneficiaries are few. Second, there is the coordination of the irrigation system built during the collectivist era, but the catchment area of this system is not large.

Phuc Tam and An Thinh villages are under the management of Brigade 4. The association of elders in An Thinh village, which in the past was incorporated into agricultural Brigade 4, continues to be managed by the brigade. Mr Hoang Van Thanh, the secretary of the party cell, explained why the elders' association is not yet under the management of the village administration:

> It is because the association's fund is still managed by the brigade. The fund is still governed by general rules of the association and these have applied for many years now: if a member of the association dies, all other members will visit the bereaved family to offer their condolences. They will also be responsible for arranging the funeral. If the association of the elders were placed under village management, the members fear that the material help would be more limited.

Nevertheless, the household contributions are too high in relation to the benefits. That is why there is a smouldering discontent among the peasants. Either they want the cooperative to be dissolved, or the level of contribution to be reconsidered, so that it better matches the present role of the collective. An Lac cooperative will hardly survive for long, and then, its present role will be assumed by the village administration.

Evolution of self-management of land

In early 1980s the contract system was applied in the three co-operatives of Phuc Thinh commune. Three of the eight links in the rice cultivation process were transferred to households. During the

80   PROFIT AND POVERTY IN RURAL VIETNAM

years when the Decree 100 and Resolution 10 were being implemented, many households laboured hard and knew how to organize family members to work most effectively. They received a land allocation and were able to fulfil their contracts. For example, Mr Pham Van Quang was permitted to perform three work links on an area of three *mau* (a *mau* equals 3,600 square metres) and about 500 square metres of land reclaimed by his family. Less productive families contracted for only small areas of land.

In this period there were big differences in access to agricultural land. Only when Resolution 10 had been announced did the latter families realize their mistakes, and they strongly demanded a reallocation of land. Mr Quang and his wife complained that when they had worked collectively, there were many lazy households that didn't want much land to work on. Because Mr Quang and his wife worked hard, they received much cooperative land for a low payment in order to have enough food for their children. Mr Quang thought that the authorities who administered the contracted land were reasonable.

As a result of Decree 100, in Phuc Tam as in other places, the number of contracted work links gradually increased owing to the good results achieved with earlier links. Thus, the possibility of self-managing work in each household increased.

After 1989, the cooperatives in Phuc Thinh commune implemented the package contract system. Then all the cooperatives in Phuc Thinh readjusted the rules for wet-rice fields to contracting households according to following criteria:

* each person of working age was given one quota of land
* two 13 to 15-year-old people qualified for one quota
* three 10 to 12-year-old people for one quota
* the elderly and children under 10 received 200 square metres of land on average.

Each cooperative divided its land by the total number of quotas. By and large, the farmers still regarded the land as belonging to the cooperative and themselves as contractors. Because of the previous manner of work, they did not ask for equal shares of land. Moreover, in reality the division of land did not follow the above principles, because the allocation covered plots of different sizes. All this explains the differences in the size of contracted land between villages and between households in a village.

Reallocation of agricultural land
While studying the land relationships in Phuc Tam village, we interviewed the heads of ten local households, four of them Tay, and six

CUSTOM AND COMMERCE IN PHUC TAM VILLAGE   81

Kinh. Phuc Tam village's location on the road to Chiem Hoa and Ma Hang has an impact on land relationships.

Of the lands of Phuc Thinh commune, 350.7 hectares were for agriculture, including 230 hectares of wet-rice fields. Phuc Thinh is thus a medium-size commune for the northern mountainous region. Nevertheless, Phuc Thinh was one of two pilot communes in Chiem Hoa district for entrusting land to the people according to the 1993 Land Law. This required the commune authorities to review its stock of natural land, including wet- and dry-rice land, forest and forest land.

Even before the new Land Law came into effect, there had been cases in most northern mountain localities where people wanted to get back the land of their ancestors. After the implementation of Resolution 10, the farmers' sense of land ownership began to increase. They realized that the authorities would implement the law according to the party's intentions; namely that farmers would be entrusted with land and forest long term. They now understood this allocation of land; they didn't need legal ownership, only *de facto* ownership. They could keep the land long term and it could be handed on to their children. In the three cooperatives of Phuc Thinh, many households requested that their ancestral land be given back to them.

In preparing to implement the 1993 Land Law, the commune authorities and the mass organizations publicized a decision by the provincial people's council in April 1994, on the principles for entrusting land and forest land to households for long-term use:

- It is important to respect the prevailing state of land relationships.
- Land should not be allocated on the basis of its ownership before collectivization.
- Consideration should be given to ensuring unity in the country-side.
- Conflict resolution should be built into the agreement between the concerned farmers.

In general, conflicts that arose when people claimed back their own land were solved as follows: If the land they demanded was close to their houses, they would obtain that area instead of another area. The newly allocated land was equal to the average area per capita in each village as calculated at the beginning of 1994. If their old area was bigger than average, they would receive the whole area without any reduction. If their old plot of land was smaller than average, they would keep it without any enlargement.

In the case of Mr Ngo Van Tho, the family claimed their old land which was tilled by Mr Ha Phuc Nhu, and this was found to be

82   PROFIT AND POVERTY IN RURAL VIETNAM

reasonable. The plot was near Mr Tho's place so it was returned to him. He had only claimed a plot equal to the average size for Phuc Tam village. Moreover, even after the reallocation of land from Mr Nhu, he still had a considerable amount of land. Mr Nhu himself was pleased with the village's solution. Mr Ha Phuc Nhu is the elder brother of Mrs Ha Thi Khiet, secretary of the party committee in Tuyen Quang district. However, Mr Nhu did not rely on her position to keep his 4,600 square metres of land when Mr Tho claimed it back.

For historical reasons, the average size of land per capita differs between the villages in Phuc Thinh commune, because of different formalities for land allocation. In November 1994 the average areas per capita were calculated as given in Table 4.

Table 4: Land allocation per capita in Phuc Thinh commune, Nov. 1994

Village	Av. area per capita (m^2)	Village	Av. area per capita (m^2)
Na Bo	1,397	Dong Dinh	724
Muc village	1,143	Dong Huong	724
An Quynh	1,047	Dong Lung	724
An Thinh	936	Hoa Da	613
Tan Hoa	901	Tu village	408
Dong Luoc	900	Trung Tam	93
Phuc Tam	817		

It is worth noting that the general policy in Phuc Thinh commune was that the calculation of average land per capita was only a reference for readjusting allocations of land. It was in no way a reallocation by number of household members.

In finalizing the formalities for entrusting land to households according to the 1993 Land Law, land was to be allotted according to the average land per capita of each village, and not to that of the whole area of Phuc Thinh commune. The manner of readjustment at village level was that those households whose land size exceeded the local average by too great a margin would have their land reduced and passed to households who had far less than the average area. Households with little land who did not want more, were not allocated more. In July 1994, the target beneficiaries were members of agricultural households.

CUSTOM AND COMMERCE IN PHUC TAM VILLAGE   83

Unlike the allocation in Lam Tien village, in Phuc Tam the allotted wet-rice areas varied among the ten interviewed households. For example, Mr Ha Phuc Nhu's household had an average per capita of 1.05 *bung*, while Mr Nguyen Minh Sang had only an average of 0.26 *bung* and the average of other households was about 800 square metres. When we asked Mr Sang for an explanation, he commented:

> The quota for 0.7 *bung* is only for my wife, since I have newly been admitted to the household. I am a carpenter and I have only recently come here from the delta. That is why I have no quota, and neither has my newborn daughter.

His life was difficult. Nevertheless he seemed content that a small wet-rice field had been allocated to his family. It was not possible to claim more land since the land fund of the village was already exhausted.

An Thinh was the only village out of thirteen where people divided the land themselves without the intervention of the commune. Moreover, nobody claimed back ancestral land, thanks to the unity of the villagers and the close and concrete leadership of the party. The last statement can be interpreted in different ways.

The implementation of the five rights
By November 1994, the whole area of wet-rice land that previously belonged to the cooperative, had been distributed to the households and a formal declaration was agreed upon. The authorities checked the fields with the purpose of delivering certificates for long-term use of the land. The reserve areas to meet new demands were no longer available. Even the 5 per cent welfare land fund was distributed to households. In Phuc Thinh, the commune authorities raised money for a public fund by urging households to contribute a certain percentage according to their former contracted level of production.

We did not encounter any complaints, confusion or controversy about the manner in which the authorities had conducted the reallocation of land among the ten interviewed households. When we empirically studied the implementation of the five rights (see p. 11) by long-term users of land according to the 1993 Land Law, we found the following:

- There was no case of land inheritance. Perhaps the right to inherit is too new in rural society for any of the interviewed households to have exercised it.
- The right to rent out land had not so far been seen in Phuc Tam.
- The right to use land as collateral for credit has not been exercised in Phuc Tam. Possibly people have another solution. The right to change the purpose of land use was evident in isolated cases. Some low-producing rice plots that used to be flooded in the rainy season

84   PROFIT AND POVERTY IN RURAL VIETNAM

were now used for breeding fish. This was approved by the local authorities.

- The right to sell and buy land was the right that was most clearly expressed. In fact, this was done before the promulgation of the Land Law, even though it was illegal.

Among the ten interviewees, three households expressed their aspirations to buy more land. One of them was Mr Hoang Van Tuyen. He had bought land from a forestry worker. Mr Hoang paid a price equivalent to 2 tonnes of paddy in 1989 and had received 2,000 square metres of residential and garden land as well as a pond. Another inhabitant of Phuc Tam, Mr Hoang Van Phong, bought 400 square metres of land. It can be foreseen that the concentration of land in certain households will happen quite rapidly. This changing tendency in land relationships will permit more efficient use of land in this region. Thus, one of the main objectives of the 1993 Land Law looks likely to be achieved.

Agricultural land, so far the most important for the farmer, has by and large been managed according to the law. However, in Phuc Tam village, relationships between farmers themselves and between farmers and forestry workers have had to be modified.

Profit-making and social support

With agriculture and husbandry the main livelihoods, Phuc Tam already shows signs of transition to the commodity economy. The first impression of Phuc Tam is that market activities are more lively than those in Lam Tien. Only 700 metres from Phuc Tam is the central part of the commune, where trade booms all day long. These businesses actively meet the demand for exchange goods and also cater to different consumer tastes, both inside and outside the village.

A cluster of small shops has existed at the market centre for only three or four years. All kinds of goods and services are found here. They include restaurants, tea-shops, refreshment bars, inns, beer stands, wine shops, news-stalls, dressmakers, tailors, ready-made garment shops, not to mention a sales agent for chemical fertilizers and pesticides. The latter is a service outlet of the cooperative, but is managed privately. The agent sells goods at prices determined by the cooperative, but gets a commission. Since the onset of the contract system, the cooperative is mainly responsible for providing farmers with fertilizers, pesticides, and seeds at reasonable prices. The cooperative does not have its own shop, but buys goods in large quantities from a production enterprise and sells them through this private agent.

Other services needed by village families are rice husking and plucking grain from the rice ears. There are three families in the village

Figure 23: Households with rice husking machines serve families in the village and Brigade 481 [EL].

in charge of mechanical rice husking and they work on commission. Earlier, husking and pounding rice were done by pestle and mortar. The rice-husking machines can also be used to mill fodder. The families with such rice-husking machines still husk rice for peddlers of milled rice.

Another service available is butchery. The butcher slaughters the pigs and sells them to pork retailers who cut the meat in small portions suitable for individual consumption. The household of Mr Pham Van Duong is a typical butcher's household. Mr Duong usually buys pigs from pig-breeding families in different villages. Thanks to his trade, this 38-year-old man is considered to be rich.

Trading in rice is the most advanced business in Phuc Tam. The district town of Chiem Hoa provides a relatively big rice market. Trade in rice is very diversified. If a family has a big sum of money, they spend it by buying paddy during the rice harvest when the price is low and paddy is abundant. Then the paddy has to be stored for the time of scarcity between harvests. Rice dealers may visit remote places to buy rice at a low price to sell it on the open market. Dealers usually have their own rice-husking machines for milling rice. Consequently, they gain a double profit; from the bran obtained through rice husking and milling, and from the milled rice that is more profitable than paddy rice. In Phuc Tam there are dozens of families trading in rice. The rice dealers are mainly women.

86   PROFIT AND POVERTY IN RURAL VIETNAM

Trades and occupations are not yet greatly diversified. The whole village has two families specializing in making bricks for local house construction. The two households each earn about 7 to 8 million dong per year. Mr Hoang Van Thanh, the owner of a brick-kiln, commented:

> I could sell all the bricks that have been produced. The obstacle is coal for burning bricks. The supply of coal is irregular as the dealers must transport it from Quang Ninh coal mine, which is very far from the mountainous region.

A carpenter's household makes furniture: tables, chairs, wardrobes, beds, etc. It should be noted that several Tay do carpentry as a secondary occupation, in addition to rice cultivation. For the Kinh, however, they do not make furniture but build wooden houses. They get about 600,000 dong for building a wooden house frame.

In general, the Kinh are more active in commerce, while the Tay are more inclined to grow rice and subsidiary crops. Those Tay who are semi-professional carpenters are the exception.

A number of households are wholly involved in agriculture to meet consumer demand for grains. The average land allotment in the village is 817 square metres per capita, which includes wet-rice land, alluvial land, a pond, and a garden. But unlike Lam Tien, Phuc Tam village has no cash-crops, although some families have begun to plant cinnamon in their forest gardens. Households grow fruit trees mainly for family consumption. If they sell some of the surplus, the earnings are negligible.

Livestock breeding is a main commercial activity in Phuc Tam. Buffalo breeding is very significant. Buffaloes are bred everywhere, in Tay as well as Kinh households, and they are destined for sale. Mr Pham Van Vang, a Kinh, breeds up to nine buffaloes. He usually lets his animals graze on the village common. Sales of buffaloes have brought him large returns. An average-size buffalo usually fetches 2 million dong.

The family of Mr Vang breeds many pigs. They are able to do it because the family operates a rice-milling machine, and consequently they have a lot of bran. In addition, his household specializes in distilling alcohol, which yields dregs for feeding pigs, in addition to the profits derived from wine sales. In 1993, he sold 400 kilograms of pork. Mr Vang has always made minute calculations about how to raise livestock for maximum profit:

> In early 1994, I had an apricot tree which yielded lots of fruit. I sold apricots for 245,000 dong. Then, with part of this sum, I bought a breeder pig weighing 14 kilograms. This pig rapidly gained in weight and in nine months it had reached nearly 100 kilograms. I

CUSTOM AND COMMERCE IN PHUC TAM VILLAGE 87

sold the pig for 650,000 dong and used the whole sum to buy paddy, as it was the harvest season. I planned to sell the paddy in March 1995, when the price would be high. I would profit much from the sale and buy new pigs for breeding.

He laughed gleefully as he told me how profit would beget profit.

Besides buffaloes and pigs, several households rear goats. Livestock breeding encompasses fish rearing. Thirty-one families in the village have their own fishponds, and the most favoured family possesses 1,980 square metres of water surface. The households usually rear dory, carp, anabas, African carp, etc. Mr Vang's family sold 200 kilograms of fish in 1993 for over 1 million dong.

The existence of an agricultural bank in Phu Thinh commune is further evidence of the relatively advanced state of commodity production and of the role of money. The bank has a direct impact on the process of land use. All the interviewed households in Phuc Tam had borrowed money from the bank at least once. Each loan was for at least 200,000 dong and the largest was 30 million; the shortest term was one year, the longest three years; the lowest interest rate was 1.8 per cent per month, and the highest 2.1 per cent. Among the ten beneficiaries, nine had paid back their loans in time, while one had only managed to pay back the interest. This man intended to breed goats on a large scale (about 200 heads). But he was inexperienced and encountered unexpected problems when the goats were infected by an epidemic.

Thanks to improving commercial, production and service activities, the living conditions in the village are greatly improved. The surplus labourers in the village are hired to do odd jobs by the townspeople, as the village is not far from Chiem Hoa, the district town, where traders need more hands to help them. As already noted, the main trades and occupations are dominated by Kinh people, who often need hired labourers. They prefer to hire Tay people.

In the Tay community, people usually exchange labour and rely on mutual assistance for tasks like house construction and rice harvesting. Unlike Lam Tien, hired labour is quite common in the village. Any family that has no labourer can hire their neighbours' labour or that of other willing people. Rates of hired labour are as follows: soil preparation (tilling, harrowing) costs 50 kilograms of paddy for one *bung* (1,000 square metres); rice harvesting costs 7,000 dong per workday.

Mr Pham To Nga's family possesses 2.4 *bung* of land. In 1994, the family had to hire labourers for soil preparation and for harvesting as Mr Nga is a commune official and is very busy with administrative work. His wife is retired and, owing to bad health, only able to do household chores.

88   PROFIT AND POVERTY IN RURAL VIETNAM

Hired labour has been common in Phuc Tam since 1989. It marks a major change in the thinking of the people and the village authorities.

Family support

Family relationships and social organizations play a significant role in the development of both individuals and households in Phuc Tam. It can be seen in the support parents give to their married children in setting up their own home.

Living in separate households does not mean that the couple's economic ties with their parents are severed, especially in the first years of marriage. In order to help their children set up a home, the parents make all the necessary preparations. They provide residential land, building materials for the house, food for the couple so that they can cope until the harvest, at least a minimum number of utensils like pots, bowls, plates, trays, etc., and usually a breeding pig. Mr Hoang Van Thanh (55) told me that he had three sons and has had to set aside a plot of land and see to the house-building for each of them. Even the youngest daughter, whose husband lives with his parents-in-law, will have a plot of land for a house. The third son, who lives separately, helps his father in making bricks.

In the case of Mr Pham Van Vang and his two sons, he built a house for his younger son when he married. Thus they lived separately from the parents. His eldest son is a forestry official. He married long ago and has four children. Although this eldest son built a house for himself, Mr Vang has expended much effort in clearing a plot of virgin land and digging a pond, since he aims to give the land and the pond to his eldest son and his family once they return to their native village.

However, children also have obligations towards their parents. Both the Tay and the Kinh in Phuc Tam village have the same conception about bringing up and educating children, and accumulating land and other necessities to enable them to make a home of their own. Consequently, parents hope that they can rely on their children, especially their sons, for care in their old age. According to Tay custom, parents who do not have a son marry their daughter to a man who is willing to live permanently in his wife's family. In order to recruit such a son-in-law, parents consent to cover all the wedding expenses. Children of a married couple where the husband lives with his wife's family take the maternal family name. By these means, parents can rely on their son-in-law in old age just like their own son.

This custom has existed since time immemorial. The story of Ma lineage, whose ancestors had founded the Cuong mountain village, is revealing in this regard. The forefather before the ten recorded gen-

CUSTOM AND COMMERCE IN PHUC TAM VILLAGE 89

erations had no son and was obliged to marry his daughter to a man who consented to live with his wife's family. The son-in-law bore his family name of Le. However, his children bore the Ma family name. That happened about 180 years ago. At present there are four sons-in-law consenting to live with the family of their wives. One of them is a young man of 28.

There have been more cases of divorce and separation in Phuc Tam than in Lam Tien village. In the whole village, there are six couples applying for conjugal separation and divorce. Of these, two involve women married to men in other villages. They were ill-treated and abandoned by their husbands and so returned to Phuc Tam to live with their parents. Another two female divorcees have made separate homes where they live on their own, while the remaining two have also returned to their parental homes. Nevertheless, even those two who continue to live separately are assisted by their families and relatives in building their own house, and have received enough food for their subsistence.

Thus, in cases of divorce or separation, the women rely mainly on their parents for lodging and subsistence. If the parents are both dead, the divorced woman relies on other relatives. That is the case with Ngo Thi Nham, who was maltreated and abandoned by her husband and then came to live with the family of her younger brother.

Political and social institutions in Phuc Tam

In Phuc Tam village the organizational structure of the party and the mass organizations, and the administrative apparatus do not differ from those in Lam Tien. The only difference is that the cooperative still exists, although its role has diminished.

One organization that does play a direct role in the development of households is the Women's Union. The village union has fifty members in the age range from 15–45, as is the case in many other localities. The Women's Union here as elsewhere is involved in family planning. There are forty-five couples of reproductive age in the village. One-third of them have at least three children. In 1993, women were still giving birth to a fourth child, since the parents felt better protected against loss by having two sons and two daughters.

Although contraceptives, IUDs and sterilization are given free, the number of women making use of them is still limited: only ten out of forty-five. In addition, five couples resort to the rhythm method. The rest are registered as people who need to be constantly urged to practise effective birth control.

Another task devolving on the Women's Union is assisting members to develop their family economy by lending funds to them. Giving credit has taken shape over the past year. In 1993, the Women's Union stood as guarantor for bank loans of 10.5 million dong with an interest

90   PROFIT AND POVERTY IN RURAL VIETNAM

rate of 2.2 per cent. This sum has then been lent to twenty-one members who did not, therefore, have to mortgage their property for the loan. Nearly all the women have used the money to buy pigs. Up to November 1994, the women had repaid their loans to the bank.

The Women's Union has stipulated that each member should pay a contribution of 5,000 dong per month for the formation of a common fund. This sum is to be used to lend money to needy families and will bear an interest rate of 3 per cent. Any woman who does not want to remain as a member may take back her money, both the capital and the interest. At present the Women's Union in the village has a fund of 1,170,000 dong.

So far we have dealt with the official organizations in Phuc Tam, i.e. those mobilized from the centre down to grassroots level. There are also horizontal organizations consisting of people of the same age. They are called *Tung Khoa* associations.

The Kinh in Phuc Tam also have an association called "fellow villagers". The association was founded in 1982 and includes all the Kinh people who migrated from the Red River delta to this mountain region to reclaim wasteland and clear fresh ground for cultivation. Those migrants now live in two villages in Chiem Hoa district. The members are registered according to their respective production brigades. So far each member family has contributed 10,000 dong to the common fund. The "fellow villagers" hold an annual general meeting. The main function is social, to visit among members, especially to give moral and material support to families with a disabled member.

Another popular organization is the housing construction association, which plays a strong role in the development of Phuc Tam. In fact, the custom of households assisting one another in house building has a long history among the Tay. This longstanding tradition has now spread to the Kinh migrants.

In ancient times, if one Tay household wanted to build a house, other households would give palm leaves for use as roofing material and the members of all of them would work on the task for some days. However, the extent of assistance, both in material and in labour, depended on the goodwill of the person. Five years ago, a housing construction association was founded in Phuc Tam, including An Thinh and Trung Tam villages. The association has a set of strict rules. From the outset it involved over ten households with participants from both the Tay and Kinh populations. The association clearly stipulated that only one or two families could build a house each year. The families had to register their building proposal with the board of the association. If two families both wanted to build a house in the same year, one would have to do it early in the year while the other would have to wait until later.

CUSTOM AND COMMERCE IN PHUC TAM VILLAGE   91

Each member family has to contribute 200 palm leaves, 2 kilograms of chicken, 2 litres of alcohol, and 20 kilograms of rice. In earlier times, the Kinh used to build wooden or brick houses with thatched roofs. In 1993, due to the Kinh-initiated trend towards brick houses with ferro-concrete roofs, several Kinh members withdrew their membership from the association and founded a separate housing construction association of their own. The organization and the activities are similar to those of the earlier association, but the contributions are higher. When a household wants to build a house, other households have to contribute 1 tonne of cement of the type produced by Tuyen Quang cement works. The payment amounts to over 600,000 dong in October 1994 prices. Mr Pham To Nga, a member of this new association, explains:

> Any member who wants to build a house has only to buy iron and steel and bricks and pay the wages of the building workers. The cement is supplied free. If the cement exceeds the amount needed, the other members may be asked to pay their cement contribution in cash.

As for the Tay housing construction association, although members' contributions are much smaller than those of the Kinh, the material assistance given by the association is crucial. According to a Vietnamese saying, the Kinh regard house building as one of the three major events of life, the two others being buying a buffalo and getting married. The Tay hold the view that building a big house is arduous work and honours each person in the community.

Differentiation between rich and poor

With continuing transformations, the differentiation between rich and poor in Phuc Tam has considerably increased in the past few years. As with Lam Tien, it is easy to see that most of the wealthy households are Kinh. In the village as a whole, five Kinh households are rich. Their wealth is expressed in possessions like a brick house with ferro-concrete roof, a motor-bike, a TV set, and such modern means of production as a milling machine and a rice-husking machine. The estimated yearly income of these households is 15–20 million dong. The heads are men aged from 38 to 47. The number of household members varies from five to eight, and the working members from two to three. These households know how to profit from business, hence their success. They all have roadside shops for selling goods and services to the public.

Most poor households are Tay. Mr Hoang Van Tich, the village chief, and Mr Hoang Van Thanh, the party cell secretary, state that there are five poor families who run short of rice about one month per

92 PROFIT AND POVERTY IN RURAL VIETNAM

year. They live in shabby cottages, and their utensils and furniture are of little value. Two of the heads of those households are widows who lost their husbands at an early age. The smallest household has two members, the largest seven. There are several reasons for their poverty and each family has its particular circumstances. For instance, the family of Mr Ngo Dinh Tho (80) is poor because they have no son to do the heavy work.

One of the aims of the collectivist model was to eradicate economic stratification, while the market model builds on self-interest and entrepreneurial skills.

The role of Tay people in social life

During our stay in Phuc Tam, we realized that although the Tay are poorer than the Kinh, they play a greater role in social life. In fact, the Tay hold nearly all the leading positions in the commune. In Phuc Thinh the leading positions of chairman and party secretary are held by Tay. Among the heads of the commune's mass organizations only the head of the Women's Union is a Kinh. As regards the village chiefs, twelve out of thirteen are Tay. The Tay here appear self-confident and clever at finding solutions in social affairs. They have both authority and power in the commune.

What surprises us most in Phuc Tam is the Tay standard of education. From information gained in Phuc Tam, we learned that Tay children rarely leave the school even at the lower secondary level. The district statistics for boys and girls attending upper secondary school show that out of seven children, six are Tay. The fact that the Tay have a higher standard of education than the Kinh can also be seen in the number of persons holding degrees.

An interview with Mr Luu Duy Noi, a Tay farmer, shows how open this Tay household has been to innovations like forestry and education. Mr Noi (56) retired from forestry work in 1990.

> It was good when we still had a subsidized system, but the adoption of the contract system made things bad. That was the main reason why I retired, although my poor health was the official reason.

We asked what had made it bad, to which he replied,

> Because the worker had to work harder and he got less pay. The cultivated wood was destroyed by fire or by wood cutters. When workers were allotted forest and worked all day, they had to worry about protection while being completely exhausted.

His case also illustrates how investment in the children's education has prevented him from reclaiming more land. Mr Noi has six adult children and sizeable assets of land: 5,600 square metres of wet-rice

CUSTOM AND COMMERCE IN PHUC TAM VILLAGE   93

land, of which he himself has claimed 2,400 square metres, and 7,000 square metres of forest garden with bamboo, palm, and styrax. The land was cleared by his forefathers. With six children, one would expect that he has enough hands to cultivate and tend the land. Yet, only the fifth child, the first son, is a farmer and lives in Mr Noi's house with his wife and child. One of the four daughters is also a farmer and married to one as well, but all the others have been educated beyond the expectations of peasantry. Three daughters are teachers, two of them in secondary schools, and the youngest son is a student in a medical university. Consequently, when the land of his forefathers was allocated, Mr Noi did not have enough children to take it over. The household found itself short of labour. Its basic economy is subsistence, but with assets to generate cash for consumption. We discuss Tay culture.

> All my children are bilingual from school. At home, we use Tay to address our children and grandchildren.
>
> *Q: What do you want to keep alive of Tay culture?*
>
> A: It is difficult to say. Vietnamization takes place everywhere. But the Tay language is most important to preserve, although Vietnamese is the medium of education. Besides the language, oriental medicine is a Tay heritage. I do not use modern medicine; instead I use oriental medicine with strong alcohol. A traditional medicine doctor lives 4 kilometres from here. Moreover, weddings and funerals play a significant part in our local life.
>
> *Q: Do you pay contributions to those family celebrations?*
>
> A: Yes, contributions come from many families. Usually we only pay contributions to funerals. Local families support one another in investment and need. Mutual aid is our tradition. We do not see much ethnic dressing here. For my generation they were compulsory. My children can choose.

The culture of the Tay in Phuc Tam has been influenced by Kinh migrants as well as by the national Kinh majority culture. To a certain extent, the Tay have assimilated or become Vietnamized. They have a good knowledge of Kinh culture and they are fairly fluent in the Vietnamese language. By the same token, Tay culture has exerted a considerable influence on the Kinh, as can be seen in the house construction association, begun by the Tay and adopted by the Kinh migrants.

There are other customs that the Kinh have learned from the Tay. According to Tay custom, if a member of a household dies, the village families will offer a bundle of fuelwood, a chicken, some kilograms of glutinous rice, and a small sum of money to the bereaved family.

94 PROFIT AND POVERTY IN RURAL VIETNAM

The organization of the funeral was entrusted to a *cai co*, a person appointed by the people of the village. When the cooperative was set up, this traditional Tay practice fell into disuse and the role of the *cai co* passed to the leader of the production brigade.

This custom was practised by the Kinh when they came and settled to clear and farm new land. Mr Pham To Nga recounted that among the Kinh there was a certain Mr Phan Van Quang who did not practise this custom. In 1988, when Mr Quang's father died, most of the Tay in the village did not go to the funeral. Thus, the coffin had to be carried by the close relatives themselves. According to Kinh custom, family members and the close relatives do not carry the coffin. It has to be done by villagers who are not kith and kin.

When studying the changes occurring in the village, we were surprised to see that the Tay in Phuc Tam and those living throughout Chiem Hoa district have changed their dress very little compared to the residents of Minh Dan village. Dress constitutes an easily changing cultural item, especially near an urban area. However, up to now women in middle and old age wear their ethnic attire. Only young girls and men dress in Kinh style.

Why do the Tay in Phuc Tam village or even the wider Phuc Tinh commune place such emphasis on social and cultural life? First and foremost the Tay have a long history and Chiem Hoa district has been their domicile since time immemorial. Second, this place was one of the many revolutionary bases against the French under the leadership of the late President Ho Chi Minh. Many brave deeds, which were highly regarded by people throughout the country, were initiated here. Chiem Hoa is at present involved in a project worth many billions of dong for restoring and preserving places of historical significance. The Second Congress of the Workers' Party of Vietnam was held at Dan Hong commune in 1951.

Chiem Hoa is actually the home of several leaders of Vietnam, for instance Madame Ha Thi Khiet, Tuyen Quang provincial party committee secretary, and Mr Ha Quang Du, minister of youth, sports, and physical culture. Both are ethnic Tay from the district.

SEVEN

Substitution of a Failing Management Model

CHIEM HOA FOREST ENTERPRISE – ITS EVOLUTION AND DECLINE

Chiem Hoa forest enterprise was established in 1962. During its first decade it exploited the natural forest by logging timber. Since 1973, its main responsibility has been was to provide the Bai Bang Paper and Pulp Mill with raw material. The introduction of state forestry in the 1960s challenged the traditional thinking of local farmers. Until then they considered the forest as something given by nature, ownerless, and an endless resource which could be freely used. Now forestry became a commercial venture almost like an agricultural business. The trees needed to grow and be tended to become products.

When we visited Chiem Hoa forest enterprise in 1987 and 1989, director Bui Phuong Dien was the chairman of the trade union. The men who received us in 1994 wore well-tailored suits, shirts, and ties. We remembered them in sweaters and casual jackets. It was easier to distinguish between managers and workers in 1994. In introducing the Vietnamese participants at our meeting, director Dien this time mentioned their ethnicity.

Our notes of 1987 indicate that the enterprise far exceeded official production targets set by the state. The deputy director informed us then that the enterprise started to sell planks to the delta in 1985. It negotiated with the districts and in exchange received cash, foodstuffs, or other consumer goods for their workers. The enterprise made direct contacts with other enterprises. The state target and the unofficial target coexisted. This opened new gates. In 1986, the enterprise doubled the

Figure 24: Director Dien at Chiem Hoa forest enterprise, 1994 [EL].

official target in bamboo and traded 500 tons to obtain consumer goods and schoolbooks. In 1987, they were to sell planks, bamboo, and pulpwood to Bai Bang, Thai Binh, and Hai Hung. The deputy director was already worried: "We harvest 1,000 hectares and plant 500 hectares of new forest. We are harvesting too much and planting too little."

Obviously the enterprise was looking for ways to compensate its workers for the support not provided by the state. Eventually, logging came to a halt. Since 1992 the enterprise has had to restrict exploitation and renew the forest resource. Workers have not logged since 1992, only planted. Before the logging ban, the forest was exploited in a disorderly manner. According to the director Dien, the ban had initially helped the enterprise to control the disorder.

Since 1982, the government has implemented a policy of entrusting farmers with forest land for reforestation and management. By the

SUBSTITUTION OF A FAILING MANAGEMENT MODEL   97

end of 1992, the policy was widely implemented in the area surrounding Chiem Hoa forest enterprise. This is because the Tuyen Quang peoples committee had in 1990 requested all forest enterprises to review their land areas and to keep for themselves only those areas of forest land that they could manage commercially in an effective manner. The remaining areas would be returned to local management and were thus entrusted to farmers for commercial forestry.

In 1987 the enterprise had 32,000 hectares of forest; 22,000 were allotted to the villagers between 1990 and 1992. The shrinkage of land to 10,000 hectares facilitated control of slash-and-burn cultivation. Another advantage was that the rest of the land was allotted to local people who husbanded their own piece of forest.

The present natural area of Phuc Thinh commune is 2,140 hectares. Of that 1,141 hectares is forest land, including the forest land of Chiem Hoa forest enterprise. Some 554 hectares belong to Phuc Thinh commune. Of the commune's forest land, 359 hectares were entrusted to farmers' households, while 59 hectares of forest land were protected, and a total area of 139 hectares were bare. In sum, 80 hectares of the bare land have already been distributed to households, and steps have been taken to distribute the remaining 59 hectares as well.

The new social forestry programme gave an impetus to local farmers and encouraged them to become involved in commercial forestry. If the farmers plant and tend trees as raw material for paper, they will have stable, regular customers. They may also receive capital and technical support from the state and the forest enterprise. Our interviews in Phuc Tam revealed that the farmers wanted to take part in the commercial forestry. Six out of ten households declared that they wanted to engage in forestry, provided that the forest was not too far away. Only the heads of three households said that they were not interested. One of them was a fertilizer dealer, another a butcher, and the third already had a large forest garden.

During this period, management began to sign contracts with workers and villagers. There were two kinds of contracts.

* *The short-term contract* falls into two stages: growing and protecting. In the first stage, the worker must clear the land, dig holes, and sow the seed. Thereafter, the trees have to be tended four times a year and constantly protected. The three or four first years are the most important growing period. After that, the trees are strong enough and the main task becomes to protect them against destruction over the next ten to twelve years.

* *The long-term contract* embraces the whole rotation cycle. The rotation period, the business cycle, takes nine to fourteen years. Inspections are made quarterly during the growth period to ensure

98 PROFIT AND POVERTY IN RURAL VIETNAM

the quality required for full monthly payments. As regards protection, full pay is based on the contract and the size of the land. The trees are counted and the missing trees are investigated. The salary is then paid quarterly.

The present role of Chiem Hoa forest enterprise in developing a new awareness about forestry as a means to produce consumer goods is even more important than before.

The forest and forest land

According to the commune's authorities and the leader of Chiem Hoa forest enterprise, most of the forest and forest land has owners. This means that the enterprise is at the stage of completing the formalities for entrusting forest to farmers and forestry workers. The forest and forest land can be divided into the following categories:

1. *Forest areas that had been planted using government capital before 1993*, such as the forest land of Chiem Hoa forest enterprise. The whole area covered by this type of forest has been entrusted to the protection of workers and farmers. The households that received the forest had none of the rights contained in the 1993 Land Law. This forest land was still fully owned by the enterprise. However, they received certain payments from the enterprise. Seen from the perspective of ownership, the beneficiaries had no real rights to manage, tend, protect, and enjoy the fruits of the process. In the ten interviewed households, we did not meet anyone who had signed a contract for forest protection.

2. *Naturally exhausted forest land* was entrusted to farmers for management and protection. It is still unclear to what extent the five rights (see p. 11) applied to this type of land. In reality, some households understood that they simply had the right to manage and exploit the entrusted area. They did not have any aspirations to demand the five rights of land users. The important thing for farmers was that nobody could violate and exploit that area. They did not yet take account of the right of collateral, transfer, lending or inheriting.

3. *Forest gardens around farmers' houses* have been regarded as their own land since 1982. Some farmers complied with the formalities to obtain official certificates at the same time as the formalities for getting wet-rice land were discharged. According to the land register of production brigade leader of Phuc Tam village, thirty-five of the forty-four households (79.5 per cent) had their forest gardens approved by the local authorities. Twenty-seven out of thirty-three Tay households (82 per cent) and eight of the eleven

SUBSTITUTION OF A FAILING MANAGEMENT MODEL   99

Kinh households (73 per cent) had forest gardens. The official document also sanctioned the custom among the Tay of taking the natural land near their houses as their own garden land. The Kinh migrants were influenced by these customs. Mr Ha Phuc Nhu's household had the largest area (1.65 hectares) and the second largest was Mr Nguyen Van Thuan's, with 1.02 hectares. Of the ten households interviewed, there was only one that did not have any forest land. This is quite different from what we found regarding agricultural land. The entrusting of forest land to the majority of households was a sound expression of forest management. Possibly the concentration on pilot communes in Chiem Hoa district ensured the extremely important results. Our study shows that the households have a better sense of non-formal ownership of forest gardens than concerning exhausted forest land.

4. *Bare land and bare hills that can be reforested* are referred to as forest land. Some of the ten households wanted to have forest land for tending and conserving, provided that the land was reasonably near their houses. Thus they refused to accept forest land in Dong Dinh and Dong Lung. The forest land had to be used according to the instructions of Tuyen Quang provincial party committees, as noted above. Households with forest land have the five rights according to the 1993 Land Law, provided that the trees had closed their foliage.

If we classify the above four types of forest and forest land in terms of clarity of the five rights, the fourth category ranks highest. By contrast, the first category (i.e. cultivated forest land entrusted to households for protection) ranks last. In the medium- and long-term future, the last three categories of forest and forest land will come into incomplete household ownership according to the 1993 Land Law. In reality, the naturally exhausted forest land entrusted to households gave each household a certain area of forest without payment to the government. Even though few households were able to benefit, this situation was better than leaving the forest without an owner, as had happened in recent years.

There is no concrete evidence of the implementation of the five rights. However, there were conflicts between some households over the boundaries of the forest land. It is the growth of the market economy that makes land rise in value. Land is badly needed by the villagers here, not only for cultivation and husbandry, but also for business operations. In past years during the process of distributing land to farmers for long-term use, many disputes have arisen over the distributed land. This phenomenon did not exist in past decades.

100   PROFIT AND POVERTY IN RURAL VIETNAM

There have been six cases of land disputes among the people in Phuc Tam. One case arose because of religious beliefs. The Kinh are afraid of big trees growing near graves. They believe that if the roots of the trees penetrate deep into the grave, the members of the family may fall sick. The place of burial of Mr Nguyen Van Nhuan's mother belonged formerly to the area under the management of the co-operative. Later, this land was distributed to Mr Luu Duy Kinh, a Tay, for long-term use as forest land. When Mr Kinh planted trees near the grave, Mr Nhuan protested for fear of that the roots would penetrate the grave of his mother. He requested Mr Kinh to plant the trees 10 metres away from the grave.

The other five cases of dispute concerned individual interests in the ownership of forest gardens, ponds, or rice-fields. Among them was the dispute between two paternal cousins named Ngo Dinh Phu and Ngo Dinh Dac. Both men had received forest gardens as a legacy from their fathers, but owing to unclear borders between these gardens, a dispute between the cousins arose. The village authorities had to intervene and settle the issue. The case was solved in 1993.

Besides the conflicts between individuals, there were also disputes between individuals and the collective. That was the case of Mr Nguyen Van Nhuan, who had encroached upon the common land of the cooperative to set up a stall for selling goods. The village authorities ordered him to dismantle the stall and give back the illegally occupied land to the cooperative.

Among the disputes that have taken place, there were also two cases of dispute between the Tay and the Kinh themselves. These conflicts show that under the law of value, controversies can emerge between different ethnic groups as well as between close relatives.

In general, the conflicts related to forest land were more numerous than those related to rice land. Possibly the main reason for this is that the ownership of forest land was not previously approved and regulated by law. The law made the land more valuable and people came to understand the value of each square inch of land. And the value was so high that every household tried to raise disputes over land in their own interests.

The impact of self-management of land on the farmers' lives
One change in living conditions was that swidden cultivation will soon end. In Phuc Thinh commune there were only twenty households working the swidden land that they had reclaimed earlier. According to the local authorities, this cultivation method would end very soon. It is worth noting that the underlying cause for swidden cultivation was the pressure of food supplies in the mountainous region. In the

north of Vietnam land is scarce, while the yield was low before the revolution and in some severe years afterwards during the period of collective production. This forced people in mountain regions to produce food on slash-and-burn land for their survival. Although the size of the population has increased, while the number of rice-fields remains the same, in the early 1980s and especially from 1989 onwards the shortage of food among the farmers decreased. In fact, the rice yield rose from 1.5 tonnes per hectare in the period before 1989 to 4–4.5 tonnes in the 1990s. Consequently, improved living conditions have recently reduced the farmers' need to burn forest for cultivation.

Farmers have gradually taken over the management of agricultural production and have adopted a commercial orientation in their use of land. This process has been implemented step by step, and by observing traditions and achievements of the Vietnamese revolution. So far the implementation of the Land Law has not caused great disturbance in the countryside. Although there have been major achievements in a short period of time, one should be aware of the limitations on the long-term development of Vietnamese agriculture.

Accompanying the changing land relationships has been the policy of free prices and free business practices. They act as a general incentive for the development of agriculture. Farmers have good opportunities to adopt intensive farming. It can be argued that the whole Doi Moi process in Vietnam began with the renovation of agriculture.

In 1973 the revolutionary state installed the Chiem Hoa forest enterprise to manage forestry in the name of the Vietnamese people, and opened the land for migrants from the plains. About twenty years later agricultural land, forest and forest land is allotted to local and migrant farmers and forestry workers. We now turn our attention to the latter.

EIGHT

Modernization by the Market

MODERNIZATION BY COLLECTIVIZATION

The demographic composition of the brigade

When we visited Brigade 481 for the first time in 1987, we came to understand how the life in a brigade was organized. The workers had broken away from their families of origin and become integrated in production collectives. As state employees they received salaries, and had access to nursery and kindergarten, health care and pensions – things coveted by the farmers. They worked to reach targets set up by the state and the best of them were rewarded quarterly by moral incentives and bonuses. Their relationships were production-based in contrast to the lineage-based bonds of the old farmer families. Moreover, we got to know how the financial crisis of the state had affected the workers.

Brigade 481 consisted of ninety-two workers, of whom sixty-six were women. Although the great majority of the workers were married, only nineteen couples lived in the brigade, while many families were split. Thirty female workers had absentee husbands. For example, Mrs Va's husband had been in the army since 1968. He visited the brigade now and then. In five years, when he retires, he will return to live with his family.

Likewise, six other men had left their families in their native villages. They too would return home in the years to come. The brigade leader, Mr Quy, had been in forestry for twenty-four years. In 1975, he married a woman in the delta. She stayed there and took care of their eldest child and Mr Quy's mother. The youngest child lived in Brigade 481, the nursery looking after him. In a few years' time the family would reunite in Hai Hung.

There was a surplus of unmarried women (seventeen), but only one unmarried man.

The brigade population was young; only three people were over 40. As can be expected, there were lots of small children, nearly one hundred under 11 years of age. Indeed, the brigade population deviated markedly from the families in the nearby villages by its gender imbalance and the restricted age range, with few teenagers and a missing older generation.

More than two-thirds of the workers had their roots in the Red River delta. Mrs Mau was recruited from Thai Binh in 1973. She was one of the 140 young people who arrived at that time. Her husband was also from Thai Binh; they met at Chiem Hoa. After fourteen years Mrs Mau still considered Thai Binh to be her home.

By 1987, about half of the migrants belonged to the second generation. Most of them were children of forestry workers. The remaining workers were from local ethnic groups, mainly Tay.

The workers' educational level was relatively high. Ten workers had completed ten grades. Almost all of them were women from the delta. Men with ten years of education did not usually choose to work in the forest (Rubin 1987). Fifty-four workers have seven to nine grades of schooling, and the rest four to six grades.

Figure 25: A row of collective houses at Brigade 481, 1989 [EL].

104   PROFIT AND POVERTY IN RURAL VIETNAM

The brigade as a production unit

The brigade was a total institution, where workers lived and spent their leisure time. The rooms in the collective rows were small and dark. Here, as elsewhere, the walls inside did not reach to the roof. Every sound is audible throughout the house: weeping infants, daily chatter, quarrels. Few secrets could be kept and everyone took part in the life of the others.

Some temporary houses had recently been hit by a tornado. A family with six children woke up when the roof collapsed in the middle of the night. Nobody was hurt, but the heavy rainfall soaked them all.

Because the state was unable to provide the necessary means for their workers, the enterprise encouraged families to produce their own food by providing them garden plots and building materials for private houses. Twenty-three households had been able to build their own houses and to move out of the collective since 1983. Moreover, some second-generation workers stayed in their parents' houses in the nearby village. The employees of the brigade comprised indirect and direct workers, that is white-collar and blue-collar employees. The indirect workers in Brigade 481 were three members of the board and five women who worked in the nursery, kindergarten, and the primary school. In the transformation of society, the socialist model laid great emphasis on the collective care of children.

The direct workers were divided according to their tasks: three groups collected pulpwood, five planted trees, one group worked with lacquer, one fed buffaloes, another produced food, and the last one combined forest service and guarding. The groups usually had six to eight members.

Two-thirds of the workers in the harvesting groups were men, as were all the group leaders. Out of thirty-eight workers in the planting groups, only one was a man. Here all the group leaders were women. The group leaders earned extra: they received 1 per cent of the total value of the piece-rate system. It is worth mentioning that five of twelve group leaders belonged to local ethnic minorities. It was the brigade leader who picked the leaders.

The working groups had quarterly plans to fulfil. The brigade received the production targets and time schedule from the enterprise. At the end of the month the working groups went through what they had achieved since the previous meeting. First the brigade board and the group leaders would meet. Afterwards another meeting took place with all the workers.There were six party members in the brigade: three women and three men. Three were local ethnic people, and three were Kinh. The brigade leader was the secretary of the party cell.

MODERNIZATION BY THE MARKET

Other members were the vice leader, the secretary of the brigade trade union, and leaders of working groups. The power in the brigade rested in their hands. The party had a monthly meeting and discussed issues concerning production and living conditions. When the cell reached decisions, they would instruct the workers to implement them.

Before 1979, Brigade 481 mainly worked in forest maintenance. In 1979, they began to fell trees and they harvested 120–150 hectares each year until 1984. Then there were just 80–100 hectares of forest left.

Mass organizations like the trade union, the Youth League and Women's Union had branches in the brigade. They acted as intermediaries between the party and its members; that is, they mobilized their members behind the policies, and, principally, they brought the opinions of employees, youth, and women to the party. They all met monthly.

How did the brigade organization function in practice? The role of the state was crucial. Almost everything depended on the state. Workers were paid in cash and kind. The most basic ration was the supply of rice. Worries about the food supply were an underlying concern for all the brigades we visited in 1987, including Brigade 481. Critical periods in the past were not forgotten: delays, transport difficulties, cuts in the rice ration, the failure of the crop in the north, all of them created uneasiness that was both hidden and open.

In 1987, the workers received only 70 per cent of their rice rations. They obtained cassava or maize instead. Five kilograms of cassava was equivalent to 1 kilogram of rice; 1.2 kilograms of maize was equivalent to 1 kilogram of rice. If the enterprise was not able to provide cassava and maize, the workers would receive money instead. In the recent past, they had been compensated 25 dong per kilogram of rice. The state price for rice was 5.2 dong per kilogram. However, we were told that the free-market price was 110 dong per kilogram.

The rations included other items as well. However, it was the end of May, and Brigade 481 had not received any meat or kerosene since February or sugar since March, and soap had only been received for the first quarter of the year. Mr Long, a father of six children, was very upset about the unreliable deliveries of rice rations in 1987:

> Last time my family received just 60 per cent of its rations, only 18 kilograms. We don't know when we will get more rice but we fear that we have to wait about a fortnight. We only have 2 kilograms of rice left. However, we have bought paddy rice from local farmers. Those 80 kilograms correspond to 40 kilograms of rice that is ready for boiling. Forty kilograms of rice lasts ten days. At present we eat too little rice, just 800 grams per meal for the whole

family. In addition we eat sweet potatoes and cassava. The only reason to have a state is because the state supports the people. However, now people have to tolerate not having enough rice.

The insecurity about food came up in all the interviews. The brigade nurse, the nursery and the kindergarten teachers speaking for the children, the brigade leader and deputy leader, as well as the workers, brought up the topic. What did the workers do, when there was no rice left? According to the trade union representative, Mrs Va, they could always borrow from someone. For example, they could go to the store-keeper in the brigade. Unfortunately, at that time the brigade had no stored rice.

The remuneration system and the delayed wages
The average monthly salary in 1987 was 285 dong. In addition the workers received allowances and bonuses. They could also sign contracts and be paid according to how much they produced. The system of remuneration was complex and rather incomprehensible. The allowances were based on geographical location, seniority and inflation; the aim was to attract workers to the forestry. The bonus systems were of two kinds: one was partly based on the piece-rate system and partly

Figure 26: State employees had access to nursery and kindergarten [Susanne Rubin].

Figure 27: A planting group in action [EL].

on how disciplined the workers were. The second type followed the emulation model. The enterprise ranked brigades according to their production results, technical performance, and living conditions, into the best, average, and a third unlabelled category for those at the bottom. In 1986, Brigade 481 received 5,000 dong as a collective bonus for rather good results. They bought fish fry for the common fish pond with the money.

The best working groups were selected. In Brigade 481 three working groups were considered as socialist labour groups in 1986. Further, there were six "emulation fighters". Their salaries were multiplied by 1.5, making a sum of 1,400 dong. The "advancing workers" received a smaller sum of 650 dong. The emulation fighters and the advancing workers were chosen every quarter. The workers received the bonus partly in money and partly in consumer goods. The goods came from the delta and the foreign trade company of the province, in exchange for export items such as plank and bamboo. The previous year, the chosen workers received a blanket. It would be more correct to say that the blanket was sold to them for 2,800 dong. However, they paid only 1,400 for it. Since the price on the free market is 4,000 dong, many workers sold the blanket to get extra income.

Seasonal variations in forest work and thus monthly income made it even more difficult to estimate how much the workers earned. We tried to establish the extremes by asking about the highest and lowest salaries. A 31-year-old man involved in harvesting earned the most. The monthly variations in his salary ranged from 371 dong to 6,485

108   PROFIT AND POVERTY IN RURAL VIETNAM

plus a bonus of 1,500. We were told that he was strong and had a "sense of responsibility". He also happened to be the chairman of the Youth League in the brigade and was married to the deputy leader. There were about thirty other workers who earned more or less the same amount, twenty-two of them men and eight women.

The worker with the lowest salary was a woman with two children. She was weak though not ill. She worked in a planting group and her salary fluctuated between 276 and 950 dong per month. With two small bonuses she attained a yearly income of 7,151 dong. There were about ten workers who earned almost as little as she did; virtually all of them were women.

The average yearly cash income in Brigade 481 was close to 10,000 dong. Calculated on the price that the enterprise used to compensate for rice that the workers did not receive (25 dong per kilogram) it was equivalent to 400 kilograms of rice. Yet, if we used the free-market price, it was equal to only 90.9 kilograms of rice. However, the salaries were often delayed. According to the brigade leader, the most recent salary they had received – for March – was paid at the end of May.

The socialist model of modernization was eroding. The state could not keep to its plans and commitments. There were no means for investments, for salaries, consumables, not even for daily necessities. Changes were already taking place, although at that time we were not able to grasp their significance.

Forestry workers and local people

At the policy level, there was a new concern about relationships between forestry workers and local people. The management strove for integration of the brigades and the villages. "There used to be differences between the local people and the forestry workers. We are trying to organize so that they can work in cooperation", said the deputy director.

The forest enterprise intended to involve more farmers in forestry when they were not tending crops. The enterprise had to apply to the village council for land, residential land, and garden land, so that their workers could invest in the family-based economy. The forest enterprise and the village council also had common interest in the construction of schools for farmers' and workers' children.

Since 1987 Brigade 481 had had an elected member in the village council. Similarly there were representatives of the Chiem Hoa forestry workers on the councils of seven villages. We asked the representative from Brigade 481 about the topics she raised in the village council.

MODERNIZATION BY THE MARKET

We usually take up the conflicting interest of trees and land between between farmers and forestry workers. The farmers do not understand that the forest must survive. There are forest guards, but that is not sufficient.

Besides the issue of rice supply, concern about forest protection was an undercurrent in several of our discussions. There were three forest guards in the nearby cooperative. According to the brigade leader:

They will guard the forest from buffaloes. They will also see to it that the harvested wood is not stolen. In addition, there are state forest guards belonging to the forest department.

Already in 1987 an outline of the new Doi Moi policies was visible, even if the conditions continued to worsen for some time.

Shortage of work in 1989

When we visited Brigade 481 two years later we found there had been no change in the food supply, only monthly variations. In September and October 1988, the whole brigade was short of food; the rice had to be borrowed from the enterprise. A few families were to face hardship before the next harvest. In 1989, the workers had to procure their food themselves, except for rice. However, they received only 70–80 per cent of their rations.

Mr Long, the father of six, had recently retired and his rice rations had thus been reduced. Hitherto, all his six children had received rice rations, but when the family planning policies were suddenly more strictly applied, the two oldest children got no rice rations. Mr Long was depressed. In a few years, the teenagers would be out of school and would work for their own rations. But how to bridge the gap in the meantime, when you lived on the edge?

The first generation of Chiem Hoa workers were retiring in the late 1980s. About fifty workers retired each year. The workers were encouraged to leave since there were not enough jobs for all of them. Now when the private sector was expanding, the number of state employees would be limited. About 50 per cent of the workers of delta origin in Brigade 481 returned to their native villages, compared to 30 per cent for the whole enterprise. This explained why many families continued to live in the collective rows although they could have had a simple private house with a 300–500 square metre plot of land.

In Brigade 481 fifty-seven people continued to be employed in forestry. However, there was not work for all of them. The supply of hard wood would be scarce until the new plantations matured for harvest in 1994. To be candid, the enterprise did not receive enough money for all the plantations they had planned in 1989.

110   PROFIT AND POVERTY IN RURAL VIETNAM

In order to cope with a surplus of twenty-one workers, the brigade had picked out a team of thirteen to raise pigs. The team consisted of "mothers with many children" or "weak workers". Being weak meant, for example, rheumatic illness and backache. All members of the team were women. Furthermore, twenty workers (thirteen men and seven women) participated in the most recent harvest in other brigades. The brigade also applied work-sharing. At the time, eight women shared jobs.

Compared with other Chiem Hoa brigades, conditions in 481 were harder. Other brigades had more ancillary occupations. Brigade 481 is not well placed to develop the family economy. It was difficult to find residential land for private houses, gardens, and fishponds. At this point in our briefing the brigade leader and the deputy director of the enterprise entered into a lively debate in Vietnamese. When it ended, we were told that it took time to remedy forest destruction. The forest was badly damaged: 5,000 square metres had been declared to be "missing". The relationship between the forestry workers and the local farmers had been tense for a long time.

The plantations had to be protected. The livestock are generally allowed to graze freely. There can be up to forty buffaloes untethered. In negotiations with local people about special grazing areas, some land was allotted as a common grazing area. But the families were scattered, and needed more grazing land. The guards tried to keep the buffaloes away from plantations and the farmers had to pay fines. In addition, much wood-cutting took place along the roadside. The wood was sold as firewood on the open market. The three forest guards in Brigade 481 did not make much difference.

There was not much timber to be harvested before 1994. The area of harvested forest land was bigger than the newly planted areas. Meanwhile, employees had to diversify by growing tea, digging fishponds, and planting commercial trees. The leaders had to create faith in the future without making promises that they could not keep. The workers' faith in the future had to contend with a 5–6 year interruption in harvesting. They hoped that after this period there would be jobs for them, or at least for their children. The second generation had been promised the right to work. However, for families who already lived on the verge of misery, 5–6 years was a very long time.

Interview with Mr Thanh, the brigade nurse
From May 1987 until April 1989 twenty-seven children were born, Mr Thanh informed us. Many women had passed the peak of fertility, 70 per cent of women of reproductive age used IUDs, and three women had been sterilized. Five women had had abortions in 1988

MODERNIZATION BY THE MARKET 111

and only one to date in 1989. The control of fertility is more efficient in the forest brigade than in Phuc Tam village.

When the new brigade leader mentioned the three unmarried mothers in the brigade, Mr Thanh responded. Actually, he said, there were only two single mothers, since he did not think that a 23-year-old girl qualified as an unmarried mother. In his view, an unmarried woman should be over 30 to be socially recognized as a single mother. Therefore, the young woman who was jilted by her lover when she was pregnant was not an "unmarried mother" in the same sense as the others.

The enterprise leader took part in this discussion. He accused married women of being selfish, for monopolizing their husbands even though there were unmarried women with no fathers for their children, the born and unborn. Vietnamese women very much opposed the return of concubinage. Therefore, they supported the prescription that a married man who fathered a child by another woman should remain anonymous. An increase in single motherhood has been reported, and it was locally estimated to be 8 per cent among female forestry workers.

Mr Thanh argued that even when the father's name is concealed from the public, he could still support his child surreptitiously:

You see, the father and the child are of the same blood. Rumours and gossip circulate in the brigade about the identity of the father. But the man is free to take on the obligations for the child or to evade them, since his identity is safeguarded. The unmarried mother and the father usually agree to save his marriage and reputation. Eventually, the child will learn who its "underground father" is.

As we listened to these men, we recalled the fate of Ms Sau. Her love story must have evoked many arguments. The views of the leader and the nurse echoed those controversies. Sau was one of the single mothers. She was cheerful and lively and had an impressive capacity to garden and do household chores with her single arm, often assisted by her 8-year-old son, Toi. Having lost her arm in a work accident, she was in 1989 a forest guard.

Sau was not sure of her age. Her mother had died in childbirth and other people had looked after her. Nobody cared about her age. In her late teens, Sau was recruited by Chiem Hoa. She was only about 20 when a heavy bamboo trunk fell and crushed her arm.

A few years later, she fell in love with a fellow forestry worker, the father of Toi. He wanted to marry Sau. However, since he already had a wife and three children in the delta, he had to request a divorce. To this end all three of them went to his native village. They were subjected to every pressure to save the first marriage. The man was unable to put his love for Sau above his moral duties as a stepson and husband. Sau and Toi returned to the brigade alone.

Figure 28: Sau was cheerful and lively and had an impressive capacity to do household chores and gardening with her single arm [EL].

Sau was the only unmarried mother I had met who openly revealed the identity of her child's father. Her capacity to improve their living conditions was limited. I found myself counting my fingers. How many years would it take before Toi could support his mother? Again, we faced a vulnerable household that had to survive a gap before its burdens diminished or its resources grew. The whole of Brigade 481 struggled to survive while the plantations reached maturity. Exhausted parents exerted themselves until their children could relieve them.

BRIGADE 481: MODERNIZATION BY THE MARKET

Eventually, logging came to a halt. Since 1992 the enterprise has had to restrict exploitation and renew the forest resource. Workers have not logged since 1992, only planted. Before the logging ban, the forest was exploited in a disorderly manner. According to director Dien, the ban had initially helped the enterprise to control the disorder.

The ban has made workers' living conditions extremely precarious. They depend on temporary payments for survival as they need cash for staples such as rice, kerosene, etc. The enterprise had to find agricultural land for the employees in the valley and on the slopes. In 1993, the enterprise lent between 2,000 and 5,000 square metres of wasteland from the remaining 10,000 hectares to each household. The land is only lent to cover the present critical conditions. The workers can keep it until they leave or retire. Once the logging ban is lifted, the

MODERNIZATION BY THE MARKET   113

remaining workers will mainly live on their salaries. Retired workers can also work as contractors.

It is an irony of the fate that just when the market expanded, the logging ban stopped most of the forest activities. Thanks to the foresight of the forest enterprise in promoting family economy and the new opportunities of petty trading, the workers were able to make both ends meet, while the forest grew and the enterprise adjusted to a new order.

The shrinking number of employees at Chiem Hoa forest enterprise highlights the changes of the 1990s. It also exposes the constant labour surplus in the past (see Table 5).

Table 5: Employee numbers at Chiem Hoa forest enterprise, 1970–94

Year	No. of employees	Women (%)	No. of brigades
1970	1500	60	21
1987	1323	64	19
1989	1109	–	16
1994	325	55	14

How have these changes affected workers in Brigade 481? When we visited them in 1987, the workers had to cope with uncertain food supplies; by 1989 they were also short of work. How many of them had now left the brigade, and how many remained? The statistics for Brigade 481 are given in Table 6.

Table 6: Employee statistics for Brigade 481, 1987–94

Year	Employees	Women	Men	Children
1987	103	65	38	102
1989	78	54	24	107
1994	27	17	12	60

Obviously, we would not be seeing many of the previous workers.

Brigade 481 in 1994

The location of Brigade 481 along the main district road and near the district town of Chiem Hoa has both advantages and disadvantages.

114   PROFIT AND POVERTY IN RURAL VIETNAM

Communications are good and create good trading opportunities. However, the protection of the forest is difficult in a densely populated area.

At the brigade, some houses have disappeared and the roof of the central stone house is damaged. Dogs have invaded the yard and they run around barking, fighting, and mating. Some look scabby, some look well kept and friendly. Chickens and hens peck for grains in the grass. Now and then a cat appears. They all assemble to sneak pieces of pork and chicken bones off the floor when we eat.

Mr Ha Quang Trung, the new brigade leader, cannot tell us much about the people. Many more workers have retired between 1987 and 1993. The reasons they gave are set down in Table 7. Of seventy workers, eleven have returned to their native homes in the delta. In addition fourteen workers have moved to another brigade. Nine women have married local Tay farmers.

Table 7: Reasons for retirement in Brigade 481, 1987–93

Reason	Total	Male	Female
Full retirement	7	6	1
Poor health	32	9	23
Regulation 176	31	8	23
Total	**70**	**23**	**47**

In the past brigade leaders could easily inform us of the household statistics. Now, it is more difficult to define the brigade population. Since 1993, the collective houses have been abolished or sold to the workers. Workers have moved into private houses and live scattered along the road. They are busy generating supplementary incomes. Many retired workers still live in their houses within the brigade's settlement. However, Mr Trung did know that Mr Long and his six children eventually succeeded in returning to the delta. The family even had a house built in advance. The economic autonomy of the households had increased and the brigade's control had loosened. This fluid transitional situation made the statistics even less accurate than they used to be. We were told that there were in total twenty-six households, plus a single mother.

What has happened since 1987?
We ask the new brigade leader to tell us what has happened in the 1990s.

MODERNIZATION BY THE MARKET   115

In 1992, the forest enterprises in the district changed to a new system of production, in which local farmers also take part in forestry. In May 1992, the enterprise was instructed to close the forest gate and stop logging. Since then no logging has occurred. The ban means a shortage of work and a surplus of labour: 1994 is the worst year yet. Since the beginning of the year there has been no work, not a single task. Workers have to switch to other sources of income to make ends meet.

And Mr Trung himself, what does he do?

> For my part, I have a salary of 120,000 dong per month. We own a rice-husking machine. My wife retired in 1989, now she and our children use the machine and husk 500 kilograms of paddy per day. It yields 25,000 dong minus gasoline, etc. The net earning per day is 10,000–12,000 dong. However, the problem is that we all are forestry workers.

We also ask Sau, the forest guard, about what has happened since our last visit. Sau herself retired in December 1993 after twenty years in the forestry. She retired because of poor health and received a lifetime pension, because she was injured at work. Her monthly pension is 190,000 dong.

Although society in general has made great progress in these years, living conditions in the brigade have not improved because of the logging ban. Since 1989, there has been almost no work. People are sitting idle, it is almost like unemployment, and the enterprise has not got enough land to allot to the forestry workers. Many workers have returned to their native land and some female workers have married local men.

Two or three workers have become farmers. When there is no wet-rice land available, most of them turn to vending, brick making, and petty trade. There is a great demand for firewood. Brick making requires much firewood, and the farmers steal so much firewood that no forestry worker wants to sign a contract to protect the forest. Of the forestry occupations, protection is the easiest. However, it is not suitable for women, because it is risky and dangerous. Sau comments:

> In my time as forest guard, I established very good relations with the villagers. They supported me.

> Previously the brigade had a board comprising the brigade leader and representatives of the trade union, Women's Union, the Youth League, and the party. Now there is no board any more. This only means that some posts are no longer there. We have still connections to the Women's Union in the commune. Functions are amalgamated. The brigade leader is at the same time also a party man and

116   PROFIT AND POVERTY IN RURAL VIETNAM

statistician. This is because the enterprise cannot afford to pay all those functionaries. From the workers' point of view there is no change.

Q: Which years have been the worst?

A: I suffered most from 1989 to 1992. Since my retirement, I have felt more relaxed. My economic conditions are almost the same as in 1987. You should know that there is great disappointment, criticism, and anger among the workers.

In 1992 Sau bought one of the houses at the brigade centre. The residential area is 450 square metres including a garden with bananas and sweet potatoes. She had to borrow 500,000 dong to buy it, and she has not been able to repay it yet. What is even worse, her health is deteriorating:

> You know, the accident when my arm was severed and my skull was injured, whenever the weather changes I suffer from headaches. This year I have been very sick. I have a kidney disease. My urine has blood in it. I do not know how to treat it. The wounded arm is very painful at present. In the accident in 1985, the nerves were severed. The pain is terrible; it feels like electric shocks all the time. It is getting worse and worse.

> As a woman with only one arm, I feel desperate. Life is difficult for people with two arms, and I have only one.

Strategies of retirement

Owing to the prevailing economic strategies, in only one case were both husband and wife still forestry workers among the thirteen interviewed households, whereas the other spouse either had retired or had another occupation (teacher, map drawer, daily labourer, construction worker, police). Similarly, among the six interviewed retired workers, there was only one forestry worker couple. The remaining forestry workers were married to a farmer, nurse, kindergarten teacher, or a soldier, and one worker was a single mother.

Mrs Mau retired due to "bad health". This was just a pretext for leaving the brigade, she said: her health is excellent. Her husband is still employed but he has had no work since 1992. They built a beautiful stone house that year. They are enterprising and have several sources of extra income. The family will stay close to the Brigade 481. Thai Binh in the delta is no longer home.

Mr Thanh, the nurse, and his wife retired in 1994, also due to bad health. They live in a simple private house at the back of the brigade. Their pensions amount to 500,000 dong per month. They have pigs and Mr Thanh also trades along the roadside.

MODERNIZATION BY THE MARKET 117

Mrs Va's husband eventually returned after twenty-five years in the army. They are both Tay. In 1990, they were able to build a stone house on the roadside.

Mrs Mau (the previous deputy leader of the brigade) and Mrs Va (the previous chairman of the trade union) were once powerful people, members of the party and the brigade board. Since 1993, the mass organizations have not exercised power within the brigade. The previous leaders seem to enjoy the fruits of Doi Moi. They also exemplify the generational transition taking place.

Compared to the past, there are few children. The nursery is closed and one of the nurses, Mrs Na (30) has become a forestry worker:

> In 1989, when you visited us, we still lived in the collective house. At that time I was a nursery teacher. In 1990, when the enterprise reduced its workers, many indirect workers became direct workers: this also happened to me. We had no choice. It was hard to become a forestry worker. I miss my former job very much. My husband encouraged me. He promised to do the hard work for me.

At present Mrs Na is pregnant. Her husband, a construction worker, hopes this second child will be a boy.

The fate of motherless (and fatherless) children

It is a coincidence that our stay in Brigade 481 took place when the father of Sau's son paid his first visit since he returned to the delta. Sau confided:

> The father was happy to see his son, but the son was not happy to see his father. He has been away too long. Toi remains cool. Frankly, I do not feel happy at all. The father came here empty-handed since his wife controls the money. He has three adult children in the delta.

The brigade leader had earlier described how the man had come with a bag with two pieces of bread as a gift in one hand, and a raincoat and an extra pair of clothes in the other. Obviously, Sau was deeply frustrated with his "empty hands", given her debts, her pains and her great need for support. It is hard when those who owe you something have nothing to give.

One day, Sau invited us to dinner to commemorate the anniversary of their daughter's death. We did not even know about the daughter. The girl was only six when she was fatally bitten by a dog. At dinner we met Toi's father. Mr Luong is a sturdy man in his fifties. His face is lined and there is a gap in his front teeth. He had prepared the meal.

Toi played a waiting game. Why did his father abandon them? His feelings are mixed. The situation is stressful for Sau. She suffers pain, looks tense and tired, and talks loudly. We all play the role of happy family. Mr Luong confides that he lost his mother when he was born.

118 PROFIT AND POVERTY IN RURAL VIETNAM

Sau and he found each other through their shared fate of losing their mother at birth. Luong's father gave him up for adoption; that was long ago. He has recently married off his eldest daughter. He ends his story by saying: "My family situation is complicated."

Yes, we all know. The brigade leader, Mr Trung, and a neighbouring single mother join us for a drink after the meal. It is remarked that Sau and Mr Trung come from the same district in Thai Binh province. It is thanks to Mr Trung that Sau has been able to buy her house from the brigade for only 500,000 dong. People who have their roots in the same native soil support one another.

Mr Trung is the father of three sons. His wife greatly wanted to have a daughter. When the third child also proved to be a boy, she despaired. Her wish for a daughter was so intense that she dressed the little boy as a girl and let his hair grow. He was treated as a girl until a teacher refused to accept this pretence any more, and told the parents that the boy would not be welcome at school until his hair was cut.

We drank rice wine by the light of a large kerosene lamp, borrowed for the occasion, while sitting on low wooden stools with our knees drawn up.

THE CAPACITY TO SWITCH

Being a forestry worker when the gate to the forest is closed has not deprived workers of their means of livelihood. The policy of providing subsistence land and investment credits has created new opportunities. "Generally speaking, we can say that the difficulties we face today are less than the problems we faced in 1987 and before", says the enterprise director.

By local criteria, people are wealthy when they have enough food, a brick-and-tile house, a motorbike, TV set, radio-cassette, five to seven heads of cattle and four to five pigs. Average people have some of those possessions. Nowadays even the poor have enough food. They eat three meals per day. They live in temporary houses of wood and bamboo with earthen floors and thatched roofs. Their children go to school. However, they lack investment capital. They have no fishponds, no cattle, no TV, no radio-cassettes, etc. The poorest among the poor are the single mothers who still live in collective houses. They eat food of poor quality and have only two meals per day. There are twenty such single mothers within the whole enterprise. The trade union subsidizes them.

Who are the wealthy?

It is difficult for a foreigner to estimate the subsistence value of livestock and cultivation. We have therefore ranked the nineteen households

Figure 29: The key to economic success is diversification. Burning bricks is a common source of extra income [EL].

interviewed according to their 1994 cash income as reported by the workers. It remains to establish what makes some people wealthy and others poor.

Two pairs of productive hands

The key to economic success is diversification, the ingenuity in finding and combining different sources of income. The second major asset is labour. We speak first and foremost of family labour. If we define households who earn under 3 million dong per year as poor, and those who make 15–20 million dong as rich, we end up by having five of each kind among the nineteen households.

Basically, they are all forestry worker households. What then accounts for the difference in income? At present they all live under the logging ban and have to find other means of survival. In the words of Mr Nho:

> Our main occupation, forestry, has become a supplementary occupation, and vice versa. Some people face problems and some were able to adopt in time and obtain other sources of income.

Mr Nho is the head of a wealthy household, in fact the wealthiest. He and his wife earn more than 20 million dong per year. However, he calculates an income of only 10 million, since he reinvests half his earnings in production. Both Nho and his wife joined the forestry in the 1970s. At first they lived in a collective house but in 1986 they

120   PROFIT AND POVERTY IN RURAL VIETNAM

were able to move out and build a small private house. They both belong to the local Tay people. They are a strong team; at 36 years of age, they do not suffer from any aches yet.

The couple has several sources of income: they raise pigs and sell a tonne of pork per year for 7 million dong. They earn 500,000 dong per month by distilling alcohol, and 6 million dong by growing lemon grass. As a newly appointed brigade leader for a neighbouring brigade, Mr Nho has a wage of 100,000 dong per month.

Nho has signed a contract with the enterprise to protect the forest near his house. After the harvest he will plant new trees according to the enterprise's plan. He will not enjoy full economic autonomy, as the forest is still owned by the enterprise.

Being local Tay people, the couple belong to a kinship network:

> Whenever I make a big investment we receive support. Of course, I also support my parents with cash and some other materials. The obligation to support is mutual. Our custom is mutual responsibility.

In 1991, the Nho family built a large brick-and-tile house not far from the main road. They did not need any support from the enterprise.

> It rests basically on self-reliance. We had no loans. We used our own money. In my opinion, this house is still a temporary one. I want to build a house with a flat roof and steps to the second floor. So far we have no electricity.

In summary their advantages are: two pairs of productive hands; two forestry workers, both healthy and able; a stable marital relationship; two healthy sons, 10 and 12 years old; a solid family network of mutual support locally well anchored; favourable location with access to customers; ambitious and well informed about options available.

In all the wealthy families, we found stable working couples, though not necessarily two forestry workers. A worker might be married to a kindergarten or primary school teacher or a retired soldier, all of whom add their wages or pensions to the household economy. They all contribute almost enough to cover their daily needs.

Mr Sep and his wife, a teacher, are an example. He retired from forestry in 1991 when the enterprise changed to the new system:

> I engaged in various kinds of work. I purchased rice and waited until the price rose. I worked as a butcher and sold pork meat. I engaged in petty trade.

The economic strategies seem to be the same as those applied in Phuc Tam village. Today, Mr Sep's household has a fishpond for the sale of fish, and a newly planted garden of fruit: orange, apricot, plum, and papaya. Being a teacher, Mrs Yen, earns 300,000 dong per month. Mr Sep's pension adds 190,000 dong. In this diversified economy the

MODERNIZATION BY THE MARKET

profit varies year by year. Mr Sep is reluctant to establish any firm annual income.

Their conspicuous brick-and-tile house was built in 1993. It includes a separate kitchen, toilet, well, and pigsty. The roof is flat. "The cost of it was 38 million dong. I took no loan. I still I have 5 million dong left." Having several sources of income, they do not risk becoming destitute if they should fail in one activity.

The enterprising Mrs Minh

The economic diversification among households that earn 10 million dong or more a year, includes burning of bricks, contracts for *trai*s with cash trees, and investing in rice mills.

Mrs Minh shows marked enterprise. She is married to a war veteran who was on the battlefield from 1968 to 1975. He received a head wound that affected him mentally. He had to retire from his previous work as a map drawer. Mrs Minh has an 800 square metre garden near her house within the brigade site.

> We already had a private house near the road in 1989. We had to move to this house after my husband engaged in gold digging and lost a lot of money.

Mrs Minh cultivates 200 square metres of wet-rice land. She has cleared a wilderness for tea. She has a breeding pig and fatted pigs for sale and chickens. In addition she gets money from brick making and vendoring, and she has part of a large collective fishpond. She took a

Figure 30: Some husbands had engaged in gold digging in the Lo River – a dangerous and risky activity [RL].

122   PROFIT AND POVERTY IN RURAL VIETNAM

2 million dong loan for digging the pond and for fish stock, which she has already repaid. The interest rate was 2.5 per cent.

Mrs Minh's younger brother, a snake seller, is visiting her: "There are all kinds of snakes here, poisonous as well as non-poisonous." He shows a mark where a snake bit him on his left hand. There is a large scar. "It happened a year ago when I put my hand in a basket believing it to be empty. It was not." His flesh rotted and he had to be treated by a doctor. He also treated himself with leaves and herbal medicine.

> I go to restaurants in Hanoi and I even go to China to kill and prepare snakes for tourists. In early 1990s, this was a lucrative business, yielding me 10 million dong per year. The accident in a Chinese restaurant meant a great loss. In 1994, since lunar new year [three months] I have earned 3 million. Yesterday, my younger brother lost five kilograms of snakes worth 300,000. He had not closed the sack properly. They are somewhere around here.

Yes, at lunchtime we saw a crowd of boys taunt a snake with long sticks. They ended by killing it.

Mrs Minh has the idea of diversifying the pond animals and exporting fresh water turtles to China. She is now considering keeping snakes for sale. Two young local men accompany Mrs Minh's brother. They help to catch snakes and sell them to a snake dealer. They also get snakes from other boys. The profit is satisfactory. Obviously Mrs Minh has grasped the potential of this market.

Mrs Minh has earned nothing from forest work since the logging ban. However, she fares well. She has imagination and initiative. She expands, innovates, and diversifies. She invests all her energy in the future of her two teenage sons. Mrs Minh is an exception to the rule of two pairs of productive hands.

What makes people poor?

We ask some forestry workers why certain people are poor. Some blame the victims: "They eat up everything instead of saving money. They miscalculate." Others point to social conditions that inhibit a family's capacity to be involved in production: small children, bad health, being a single mother. Still others mention unpaid debts, lack of land, and poor-quality houses.

Mrs Mui and Mr Vinh: sacrificing everything

We visit a few poor households and draw our own conclusions. Mrs Mui and her husband, Mr Vinh, are the poorest of the poor. She is a Tay woman employed as a forestry worker. He is a daily labourer, a Kinh, an outsider from Thanh Hoa province. Mrs Mui has no work in the forest because of the logging ban. Since 1994, the enterprise has

MODERNIZATION BY THE MARKET

not even been able to make the small emergency payment of 30,000 dong per month. Mui and Vinh raise pigs. Vinh collects firewood, Mui sells it on the market. They grow cassava and lacquer trees in their garden. The cassava is both for themselves and the pigs. Their incomes are irregular: "We live from hand to mouth. We have no storage, no reserves."

The clay walls in the house are cracked. The room is bare with earthen floors, an old hammock, and a bed.

> The house was built by my husband. We took the wood from the forest. We could not have helpers because we could not afford to serve them meals. We are short of food ourselves.

We asked if her family supported them in any way?

> We have no family support. My parents are very old and they have six children. Five of my husband's brothers live here in the neighbourhood. They are all poor. The fishpond nearby belongs to my husband's brother. Sometimes we ask for fish. However, we have become reluctant to ask because we seldom have anything to give in return.

The core problem is their 4-year-old disabled daughter, Tam. She was born without a rectum.

> We do not understand the reason for it. No one on either side has suffered from an illness like that. We practise normal sexual intercourse and we do not use any drugs.

When Tam was five weeks old she was brought to the Swedish Children's Hospital in Hanoi. The doctor told them that the daughter needed to undergo four sets of treatment, and Mui and Vinh made the next appointment. Including medicine and treatment, plus accommodation and food in Hanoi for the parents, each visit costs about 2 million dong. Where do they get the money? On one occasion they sold their house so that Tam could be taken to Hanoi. Another time they borrowed 2 million from a bank. And Tam got her treatment. But they have not been able to pay back the loan, and they simply have no means to take Tam to the hospital for the fourth and last time. As it is, Tam cannot control her bowels. So, she can neither go to the nursery nor play with other children. Mui and Vinh worry about their daughter. They are themselves short of food:

> There are no improvements in my life; it is the opposite, from bad to worse. Some years ago there were gold diggers on the Lo River and my husband took part and earned money. It is very dangerous because of the landslides. Many people were killed.

An outsider, jobless, landless, with five grades of school, what else can men like Vinh do? The couple have sacrificed everything to save

Figure 31: The parents have sacrificed everything, sold what they had and put themselves in debt to save their daughter [RL].

their daughter, sold what they had, put themselves in debt. Literally, the child is like a millstone around the parents' necks. Should they abandon her and let her die rather than all three being doomed? They are still under 30 and could have another, healthy child.

The pale mother looks like a holy virgin with the sleeping child on her lap. Are there any agencies that care? We decided to use Tam as a test case to see if it was possible to find any agency that could intervene on her behalf. First we talked to Mr Trung, the leader of Brigade 481. He explained that the brigade had no means whatsoever to intercede. We took up the case at our final meeting with director Dien, Mrs Phan from Women's Union, and other forest enterprise officials.

Because of the logging ban, the enterprise faces severe economic difficulties. In addition, its previous responsibilities for the health of the workers and their children have ceased. Since May 1994, workers are included in a new health insurance system. The insurance embraces only the employees, not their children. From now on, children are the sole responsibility of their parents. Furthermore, we were informed, the trade union has provided Mrs Mui with support. However, they follow state regulations for welfare. The regulations assert that assistance can only be given twice a year, each time to a maximum of 40 kilograms of rice. This amounts a total to about 80,000 dong.

What other options are there? The Red Cross and the Committee for the Protection and Care of Children are the right organizations, but

MODERNIZATION BY THE MARKET 125

no level – local, district, province, or central – could pay the full support. They give only 50,000– 100,000 dong. In a very special case, the maximum support could be 200,000 dong.

Our enquiries confirmed that there is no support available from Vietnamese sources. Therefore, we visited the Swedish Save the Children office in Hanoi and requested them to provide the 400 dollars needed to cure Tam in Hanoi and help her parents to restore their finances. Save the Children's representative promised to find a means to cure Tam. Six months later, Tam and her parents had been to the Children's Hospital.

Many poor families are hit by disability and illness. Why should the child of just Mui and Vinh receive help? We felt a latent resistance among some Vietnamese. Weren't there other more deserving parents? Bonuses and special benefits should go to people who deserved them. Why should these particular people be favoured? All this smelt of injustice, or at least of arbitrariness. We worried that such sentiments would affect Mui.

Mr Truong and Mrs San: unable to see new options

Until recently, Mr Truong and Mrs San were both forestry workers. Truong retired in 1993; he was then 35. His pension is 150,000 dong per month. Their daughter is 10 and their son 9.

Truong and San do extra work to protect the forest and they have also signed a tree-nursery contract. The problem is that the forest does not offer them work and does not pay for the work they are doing. They see forestry as their main occupation. They have the skills needed and do not plan to do any other kind of work. They simply do not know how to find new incomes.

Truong and San regard themselves as poor, because they have to eat potatoes and cassava. Their temporary house is very simple. The garden is 600 square metres. Usually they breed and sell two pigs annually and the money obtained they spend on food. At present "there is nothing to invest in". They receive no support from their families. Instead Truong has to assist his siblings who are even worse off. He gives them 10,000 dong or paddy now and then.

So why are they poor? They started poor in poor families, and cannot count on any support for investment or in need. They do not eat well. He has suffered from a stomach illness for five years, and her health is poor. They have no surplus energy nor flexibility to switch to other sources of income.

Another worker in similar conditions expressed these sentiments:

The old system was better. The state took care of everything. There was work and there was food. Now the state does not care

126   PROFIT AND POVERTY IN RURAL VIETNAM

at all. There is no subsidiary system and the workers with a lot of money get more, while workers with little money get less.

Some workers are imprisoned in the past, unable to see any new options.

A widening gap in the next generation

Nowhere is the parents' involvement in their children's education stronger than in Chiem Hoa. The forestry workers in Brigade 481, especially those who are successful, lay great stress on the education of their children. Education has replaced the land as a source of future security. Mr Hien and Mrs Huan have three sons who are in grades 7 to 12. They go to the local school in the morning and in the afternoon they have foreign language training (in a private school). They learn English.

> As forestry workers, we do not own land. Thus we hope for the highest possible educational achievement for their future. The boys are above average level at the school standard. We, my wife and I, only have seven grades. We intend to educate our children as much as they wish.

Mrs Minh comments on her son, Duc, who is in the Grade 6:

> We pay 36,000 dong per year in school fees. Together with various contributions, we pay 200,000 dong per year. My oldest son, who is now in the army, was not good at school. Duc, my second son, does very well and I will try by any means to get him to university.

Hoa (8) is in grade 2. Her mother says:

> We pay 4,000 dong per month for extra education in two subjects: Vietnamese literature and mathematics. The best pupils are selected for extra education. We also pay 40,000 per year for the construction of the school. Also, we contribute to school funds like "protecting young talent", teachers' festivals, charity funds and insurance. Since Hoa started grade 2, we have paid 50,000 dong in total plus gifts to her teacher.

It should not be a surprise that, with one exception, there are no children from households earning less than 10 million dong per year among the parents quoted above.

Workers with low incomes cannot afford extra lessons after ordinary school hours. For about half the workers in Brigade 481 the contributions and fees demand considerable sacrifices. The poorest have nothing to forego.

Toi, the son of Sau, the single mother with a single arm, has to repeat grade 8 before he can begin the next grade.

> I would like him to continue, but our circumstances are very bad. The brigade leader wants Toi to continue through grade 12 and then

MODERNIZATION BY THE MARKET 127

go to a vocational school. Toi failed last year due to our miserable family conditions. Every day he has to go to the market and sell firewood. We need money to pay our debts for the house and a breeder pig.

It falls to the boy to compensate for the lack of a father and the left arm of his mother.

Children of the poor often labour hard for the subsistence of the family. In Chiem Hoa, the demand for firewood is high. Mr Toan has a permanently ill wife and a retarded son. He has recently bought a buffalo to transport firewood from the forest plantations. Toan lets his daughters, Thu and Tan, sell the wood on the open market. They transport one bundle at a time on a bicycle. The sisters also collect and chop wood. They are in grades 5 and 8 and are good students. The school fees for grade 5 are 40,000 dong per year and for grade 8 over 80,000.

Education has become more competitive and costly, and the parents' ability to support their children is now more crucial than before. There is a growing contradiction between the family support of particular children and the universal ethos of the school.

THE SOCIAL IMPACT OF THE MARKET

When the rice yield fell and the agricultural cooperatives failed to reach their production targets, the collective attempt at modernization had to be dismantled. People were short of food and the state was bankrupt. As we have seen, the cooperatives as well as the state enterprises adopted their own unofficial strategies for survival. Most of these strategies were later recognized and adopted by the party. The economy was liberalized, the land redistributed, the brigades and cooperatives more or less dissolved, and households were recognized as primary units of production.

With the advent of Doi Moi, families have to contend with the market. Because its geographical location on a main communication route, Phuc Tam and Brigade 481 are more advanced in terms of goods and cash than Lam Tien village and Minh Dan brigade. A market economy of goods and money has penetrated deeply and affected nearly everyone in the locality. If commercialization of land is the precondition for a shift from a subsistence economy to goods production, Phuc Tam's location along the road has made the shift easier.

The inhabitants of Phuc Tam village are more interested in owning land than those in Lam Tien. Furthermore, our interviews with household members revealed that they want to own land for their children and grandchildren. The conditions for goods production and agricultural

128 PROFIT AND POVERTY IN RURAL VIETNAM

surplus are favourable, and thus ripe for a quick shift from subsistence to the production of cash-crops.

We have described how the transition to a market model opened up a rapid process of economic diversification and commodification that has brought wealth to many households and improved the living conditions of the vast majority of households in Phuc Tam and Brigade 481. From next to nothing the households of successful farmers and forestry workers have attained a cash income equivalent to about US$2,000 per year. This comes on top of a high level of self-sufficiency in food. By and large, people no longer suffer from a shortage of food.

In Chiem Hoa, the roles of the Tay and the Kinh are partially reversed as compared to Lam Tien. Indeed, the Kinh have a higher material standard, whereas the Tay play a far greater role in social life.

While the living conditions improve, the gap between poor and wealthy is widening. Why do some people remain poor? They are poor because they lack the social assets that make others wealthy. Theirs is an inherited poverty. Their parents and grandparents were poor. They had too many mouths to feed. They were motherless. Their fathers left. They were abandoned, old and childless, migrants and outsiders, ill, disabled, disordered. They were guinea pigs for enforced ideologies and unsustainable political economies.

People can be an asset, but they can also become a burden. When health care was privatized and people had to pay for education, then the poor, the sick, and those who did not have supportive family networks, were the losers in Brigade 481, Phuc Tam village and elsewhere.

Whereas both the old rural family and the socialist production units were based on collective obligations, the Western idea about the market rests on an image of "an economic man" who has to be liberated from networks of obligations, of other people as burdens, who limit his self-interest, independence, and individual freedom.

An opposite strategy builds on collective self-interest, and in Vietnam it tends to be family interest (and class interest). The threat of poverty lends urgency to mutual obligations. We are told by Vietnamese sociologists that people share annual celebrations of ancestors and recognize a common genealogy; they revive rites, they pay contributions to large, kin-based funds. They want to protect their families and be able to meet the challenges and risks inherent in the market model of modernization. It is debatable whether we are witnessing a momentary revival, or if features of the traditional family will persist.

However, the changes are easily exaggerated. Mutual support in rural families has persisted all the time. Support between generations

Figure 32: A planting group at rest. Their prospects working solely in state forestry look dismal [EL].

Figure 33: Mr Hien and Mrs Huan became forestry workers in 1972. Since 1993 Mr Hien has diversified into producing bricks for sale [RL].

is extensive and part of the moral order in the villages. Besides, the forestry workers who lived with their workmates far from their delta communities were mainly recruited from poor families with many

130   PROFIT AND POVERTY IN RURAL VIETNAM

children (Liljeström *et al.* 1988). Generally, family bonds are assumed to be weaker among the poor, mutual support more limited, and there is less to be transferred between the generations. Nevertheless, the migrant Kinh keep in touch and send their parents gifts. They visit each other, they send their children to stay with the grandparents, and many return to the delta when they retire.

While people in northwestern Europe assumed and built up the economic independence of the nuclear family for centuries before industrialization, in Asian societies like Vietnam, mutual dependence and generational support were the rule. While in our European world, marriages were postponed until the couple could make ends meet, the farmers in north Vietnam saw to it that their children married young but were able to survive by living together with the husband's parents (or in some circumstances, with the wife's parents). Thanks to extensive support from the older generation, they were able to establish their own households early.

Indeed, rural under-employment, improved communications, commodification, and urbanization, are forces of change. Yet, the plants that evolve from different historic roots are not necessarily the same.

CASE THREE

"Neither Bat nor Rat"

NINE

Advancement and Deprivation in Khuoi Nieng Village

BACKGROUND

By now the reader is familiar with typical features of Doi Moi: farmers' households gradually taking over production links; workers leaving the collective rows and building their own houses; enterprise managers reducing their workforce and signing contracts with both farmers and workers; land being redistributed; and first and foremost, fewer people being hungry and underfed. The workers at Vinh Hao forest enterprise applied the same strategies of retirement as workers at Tan Thanh and Chiem Hoa, and while the family economies expanded, the gap between rich and poor grew wider. Here we shall concentrate on the special impact Doi Moi has had on Khuoi Nieng village and Brigade 5 of Vinh Hao forest enterprise.

In contemplating the spirit of commerce in Khuoi Nieng village we could not help thinking that the residents suffered from market mania. The flood gates are opened and all contained forces burst forth. Enterprising households here make more money than anywhere else we have been. So far we have reckoned incomes of wealthy households in tens of millions of dong: in Khuoi Nieng they earn hundreds of millions. Big money means hired labour.

The contrast between the rich part of the village and the poor part behind the streams is striking. Yet, when a 100-million-dong man blames the poor for being poor, he seems to be avoiding the real issues.

134   PROFIT AND POVERTY IN RURAL VIETNAM

The workers in Brigade 5 displayed similar improvements to those in other brigades we had already visited. However, where the commodity economy was bustling in Khuoi Nieng village, the workers in Brigade 5 seemed to lag behind.

We were also confronted by some unintended effects of Doi Moi. The current absence of any forums where workers can complain and be heard had created discontent. We listened to complaints about arbitrary treatment. Did some people line their pockets at the expense of others? Did some cadres withhold information or did they simply lack social skills? Did fear and uncertainty prepare the soil for suspicion? We were aware of the danger of being partisans and getting involved in issues without having the full picture nor time to stay.

We found the Vietnamese metaphor "Neither bat nor rat" a telling statement for the current situation where socialist ideals are challenged by the hard reality of market forces.

KHUOI NIENG VILLAGE

Ethnic composition

Khuoi Nieng village and Brigade 5, Vinh Hao forest enterprise, are located in Vinh Hao commune, Bac Quang district, in southern part of Ha Giang province, not far from the main highway between Hanoi and Ha Giang township. The population of the commune, just over 4,000, consists of eight ethnic groups including Dao, Kinh, Tay, Nung, Co Lao, H'Mong, La Chi, and Hoa.

The most numerous are the Dao with over 2,000 people, while the smallest group, the Hoa, has only four persons. In the whole commune there are 729 households dispersed over ten villages. The economy is mainly based upon agriculture with tea and oranges as the main commodities. Because the commune lies near the highway and the intercommunal road not to mention the many households near the Vinh Tuy town, its commercial and business activities are expanding strongly.

Turning left from the highway, one enters the intercommunal road passing through Khuoi Nieng village and quite close to Brigade 5. The distance to the commune people's committee is 9 kilometres and another 20 kilometres separate this village centre from the district town.

The households in Khuoi Nieng village are scattered. There are ninety-one households, with 467 persons divided between four ethnic groups: Dao, Tay, Nung, and Kinh. The Dao have sixty-eight households, the Kinh seventeen, the Tay four and the Nung two.

The village is divided into two main areas, properly called Area I and Area II. Actually, people still call them Brigade 1 and Brigade 2, since the agricultural cooperative still exists nominally. Area I was

Figure 34: Dao farmers at the village tea house [EL].

the original Khuoi Nieng village, comprising seventy households today. The distance to Area II is about 10 kilometres in the direction of the big forests. It is also called "the deep forest area". In 1985, the Dao residents migrated here from Vi Xuyen district in Ha Giang due to the insecure situation on the border with China. This was a totally voluntary migration without any prior arrangement. Vinh Hao commune had to accept the migrants from the border area, and grant them permission to reside permanently in Khuoi Nieng village. This is why the inhabitants of the two areas have no close contacts or even cultural affinity. Life in the two areas is very different.

The village name means "Nieng stream" in Tay. Why does an area dominated by Dao have a Tay name? According to Mr Ly Van Liu (69), Khuoi Nieng was set up in 1948. Before that there was only dense wild forest where the neighbouring Tay came to collect bamboo shoots, mushrooms, or to hunt. The first people to settle here were the so-called long-dressed Dao. Some seventeen households with thirty-nine people came from Tien Kieu village about 10 kilometres away. The main reason for the migration was exhaustion of their cultivable land. The newcomers settled at the Nieng stream; the fifty-eight Dao households in modern Khuoi Nieng are mostly descendants of the seven original families.

The Kinh families settled here in 1987. They were workers from Vinh Hao forest enterprise or people from Vinh Tuy town. The Tay arrived here from Dong Yen commune nearby about ten years ago.

136   PROFIT AND POVERTY IN RURAL VIETNAM

The Nung, who are mainly former forestry workers from Vinh Hao forest enterprise, settled here about eight years ago.

Khuoi Nieng village is in a valley surrounded by low hills. Its inhabitants live scattered along the Nieng stream, and along other streams like the Co, Nga Hai, Na Me, and Na Phay. All these streams are tributaries of the Lo River which flows parallel to the highway. This means that there is a communication waterway between Khuoi Nieng village and the Red River delta.

The riverine networks make the topography of Khuoi Nieng rather complex. According to Mr Dang Van Hinh, village head, the stream bursts its banks in the rainy season and people have to travel by raft or small boat. Normally the distance is not great, only 1 kilometre at most. This is an advantage for local commodity production.

Impact of the contract system

Khuong Nieng is one of the nine agricultural cooperatives set up in the early 1960s in Vinh Hao commune. At that time all main means of production were collectivized, including the wet-rice-fields. Rice land previously owned by individual households now fell under the ownership of the cooperative.

As elsewhere in northern Vietnam, collective land ownership did not allow for effective use of the rice-fields. Consequently, the farmers' lives in Khuoi Nieng became extremely difficult. The family of Mr Dang Van Hinh, now rather well-off, suffered from a food shortage two or three months per year during the period of collectivization.

In 1981, Khuoi Nieng cooperative started to contract some production links to households. By the end of 1980s, it contracted out all rice-farming land to the households. The land was allotted according to the number of household members of working age. For those below the working age, three persons were equal to one working person. The same applied to two persons above working age.

This method of land allocation provoked many complaints among the agricultural households, especially when Resolution 10 was issued in 1988. Most cooperative members held that those below or above working age need as much food as people of working age. Land allocation on this basis was seen as unfair. Since 1991, the allocation of wet-rice land has been based upon the total number of household members. According to Mrs Ly Thi Nhuan and some others, after the reallocation of land was made on this basis, there were no complaints in Khuoi Nieng.

Mr Ba Van Duong, the present chief manager of Khuoi Nieng cooperative, notes that each household member was allotted an area of land corresponding to eleven bundles of rice seedlings, tantamount to 242 square metres. (A bundle is a measurement unit in Khuoi Nieng.

Each bundle of rice seedlings equals 22 square metres of land.) However, according to data collected in May 1995, five households out of nineteen interviewed had no rice land at all.

Table 8: Land area of households interviewed in Khuoi Nieng

Head of household	Ethnic group	Total farm area (m^2)	Members in household	Farm area (m^2/person)
Dang Van Hinh	Dao	3,000	4	750
Ly Vasn Liu	Dao	2,700	6	450
Ban Van Dai	Dao	1,800	5	360
Ly Van Thai	Dao	1,400	4	350
Pham Van Nhon	Kinh	1,600	5	320
Ban Van Hop	Dao	1,000	4	250
Hoang Van Kien	Dao	1,150	5	230
Ban van Duong	Dao	1,080	6	180
Hoang Van Quyen	Dao	720	4	180
Ban Van Minh	Dao	850	5	170
Truong Van Vinh	Dao	720	5	144
Ban Van Loi	Dao	500	5	100
Dang Van Thang	Dao	260	3	87
Bui Van Hoa	Dao	0	5	0
Ban Van Thiep	Dao	0	4	0
Chu Vam Huynh	Tay	0	4	0
Le Van Dien	Kinh	0	4	0
Ly Xuan Hieu	Dao	0	4	0
Ly van Tai	Kinh	(no data)	4	(no data)
Average		**883**	**4,5**	**195**

138 PROFIT AND POVERTY IN RURAL VIETNAM

According to Table 8, the average land area per household is not even. What struck us was that all these five landless households had not complained to the cooperative or the local administration. They accepted this situation and even appeared satisfied with it. The main reasons are:

- The husband and wife in the household with no farmland (as shown in Table 8) were newly married in 1989, and the cooperative had largely completed the allocation of wet-rice land by the end of 1988.
- The average farmland per capita in Khuoi Nieng is very low. Therefore in 1990 and later in 1992, when the cooperative reallocated land, the average per capita area was even lower owing to the increase in the population. By April 1994, the average area of farmland per capita was only 159 square metres. Therefore some households, such as Mr Hieus's and Mr Huynh's, refused to take their allotted land.
- Of the five households with no farmland, four had large gardens. For instance, the average garden per capita for Mr Hieus's household is 3,000 square metres. All five households grow orange trees in their gardens. This might be the main reason why there were no complaints about the unequal land area per household.

Land disputes in Khuoi Nieng

We assumed that land disputes had occurred in Khuoi Nieng during the land allocation process under Resolution 10 on contractual quotas. With the promulgation of the 1993 Land Law, former land allocations to households were legalized. However, the reality in Khuoi Nieng was unexpected: there have been almost no land conflicts in the village in recent years, except in two cases. These were claims for ancestral land from before the establishment of the agricultural cooperative.

The first case concerns Mr Ban Van Danh, manager of Khuoi Nieng cooperative for ten years. Mr Danh's household contributed three *mau* of farm land (one *mau* is equal to 3,600 square metres) to the cooperative. When the allocation took place, he claimed his old farmland. However, he was given only two *sao* (one *sao* is equal to 360 square metres) of his former land. He was allowed to select one *sao* land in the fertile upstream area and one *sao* downstream in the poorest land.

The second case concerns Mr Truong Van Nguyen. When he joined the Khuoi Nieng cooperative, his household contributed one *mau* of land. In late 1988, when the cooperative allocated land according to Resolution 10, Mr Nguyen reclaimed his former land. The cooperative allotted his household 0.5 *sao* upstream and 0.2 *sao* in another place. Although Mr Nguyen is still dissatisfied, he has to accept the

ADVANCEMENT AND DEPRIVATION IN KHUOI NIENG 139

allocation because it is agreed to by the majority of the cooperative's members.

Cassava, a subsistence crop; orange, a commodity

It is unusual for valley people to use cassava as a subsistence crop. One must first understand the natural conditions of Khuoi Nieng and how these conditions affect planting practices.

Khuoi Nieng valley is narrow and divided by the numerous streams into small plots of land. Almost all wet-rice lands here are terraced fields. According to the village officials, Area I has only 2.7 hectares of rice-field, of which 0.66 hectares give two crops per year. This land is not enough for the subsistence of seventy households. More land could be turned into wet-rice lands. The reason for not doing so lies in the old way of cultivating land in this area. The Dao traditionally cultivate burnt lands. It was only after 1960, when the cooperative was set up, that the land was used for rice cultivation. On the other hand, the rice-fields here are affected by alum and the yields are low. Almost all households use only dung because they believe that nitrogenous fertilizer will harm the land. The highly esteemed rice variety "I" from China usually yields 120 kilograms per *sao*.

When allocations of agricultural and forestry land started, slash-and-burn cultivation became less frequent as there was little land left for this purpose. It was used by families who cleared land for the forest Brigade 5 for 200,000 dong per hectare and the privilege of planting upland rice on burnt land, or by poor families who planted upland rice on the nearly exhausted patches of burnt land.

Maize, normally ranked second in the mountains of northern Vietnam, is not common in Khuoi Nieng. It is mostly planted on the alluvial land along stream banks, and yields 700 to 800 kilograms per hectare. The agricultural extension service in Bac Quang district has introduced a new variety of maize called Biocid for experimental growing. According to experts, this variety could yield up to 1,100 kilograms per hectare.

Fortunately, Khuoi Nieng can boast a highly prized crop, namely cassava. The soil and the climate are suitable for growing this plant and there is no need for manure. After one year of planting, a bunch of cassava can weigh 3–4 kilograms. It can be planted anywhere: near the hedges, in the garden, along the streams, or on burnt land. The variety planted in Khuoi Nieng is local and is usually called white cassava or banana cassava.

Cassava is supposedly a subsistence food but only a number of poor families have to eat it. Some people use only the fresh buds as vegetables. Families here sell cassava and other crops to get rice. Many families derive large incomes from cassava. This is the case of

140   PROFIT AND POVERTY IN RURAL VIETNAM

Mr Dang Van Hinh's family which in 1994 had an output of 35 tonnes. Other families average about 3–4 tonnes per year. People also use cassava for fodder and for distilling alcohol. The waste from distilling is fed to the pigs. In 1994, Mr Hinh's family raised as many as forty pigs. However, at the time of our field trip to Khuoi Nieng, a swine plague had killed many pigs. Several families told us that normally they could sell 300–400 kilograms of pork per year (live weight). In some cases, as in Mr Ban Van Buong's, they sell as much as 600 kilograms. Cassava is also used for fish breeding, its stems and leaves being good for fish.

Mr Dang Van Hinh told us that at the general assembly of the co-operative in 1994, the people in Khuoi Nieng concluded that on past experience, planting cassava helps to strengthen the family economy. A number of families also found cassava good to grow with other plants, for instance styrax, cinnamon, and tea. Their experiences show that the land had fewer weeds and cassava shaded the other crops in their first years. Cassava is used as a short-term crop to meet immediate needs while the long-term crop is orange trees. The return from oranges covers expenses and even gives a good income.

According to Mr Ly Van Liu, the venerable old man of the village, several households have been growing orange trees since 1965, using plants from Vinh Tuy. However, it was not until recently that oranges have achieved commodity value. Previously people grew oranges for the pleasure of eating them, and only occasionally sold them to get money for salt, kerosene, or other necessities. It is only under the impact of the market economy that the economic value of orange trees is being realized.

Now, the price of oranges is rising and they are purchased directly from the orange trees owners. Since Doi Moi, the people in Khuoi Nieng have expanded their orchards. In Area I, orange trees are now grown by every family. Even such a poor family as Mr Ban Van Hoa's grows at least eighty trees, while Mr Ban Van Tiep and his family grow as many as 140 trees. There are families who grow up to 600 trees. The household with the highest output in 1994 was that of Mr Cam Huynh, a Tay. He picked over 6 tonnes of oranges. In comparison, several families have calculated that a palm tree can yield twelve leaves annually at 300 dong per leaf, while each orange tree yields 30 kilograms of fruit worth 100,000 dong.

The local climate is suitable for growing orange trees, but their growth depends on where they are planted. Normally the trees need manuring only after several years. Weeding is essential and time-consuming, thus families need to hire labour. Weeding should be done four times a year and it is costly. To weed one *sao* of orange trees would cost 80,000 dong per year.

ADVANCEMENT AND DEPRIVATION IN KHUOI NIENG 141

People recounted how busy the village was during the orange harvest. Traders came by bicycle, motorbike, car, and even on foot to buy the oranges. Some orange crops were sold even before the harvest. These crops belonged to poor households that could not wait until the selling season.

An important issue has emerged concerning how to preserve the newly harvested oranges and reap the most favourable price. In Khuoi Nieng there are two ways to preserve them: one is to store them in bamboo frames in a hole in the ground. The hole is covered with bamboo. In this way, oranges can be preserved for up to three months. The other way is to put lime on the orange stalks, wrap the fruit in an arrowroot leaf, and keep them indoors in a cool place. In this way oranges can be kept one or two months.

Emergence of *trais*

In Khuoi Nieng the *trai* have emerged over the past two years. We first heard about them at Lam Tien village. Here five families have set them up, including Mr Hinh, the village head, and Mr Duong, the chairman of the cooperative.

The emergence of *trai* is linked to the development of the market economy in Khuoi Nieng and is closely associated with the distribution of agricultural and forest land. I asked Mr Pham Van Nhon why he had set up a *trai*. He said that he intended to develop his family economy on the basis of agriculture. From this he would prosper and create jobs for his children. Mr Hinh and Mr Duong saw this as a proper way to enrich themselves.

The *trais* are at some distance from the homes, the nearest being 500 metres away. The average area is 5–6 hectares and four out of five *trais* are practising cultivation and breeding. They cultivate short-term crops to finance long-term ones. They first make full use of their low-lying wet-rice fields but also carry out slash-and-burn cultivation of upland rice or cassava. They also raise pigs and poultry. Mr Hinh, for instance, breeds half of his pigs at his *trai*. The pigs are used both for immediate family needs and to generate investments for the long-term cultivation.

The long-term investments are in orange growing, tea and general afforestation. These plants and trees have strategic importance and are expected to provide high incomes. After three years, the oranges are expected to yield their first harvest. Tea was introduced by the district's agricultural extension services a year ago. Recently, cinnamon has appeared in this area and many families grow it in their forest gardens and their farms/estates. Mr Hinh planted cinnamon in early 1995 and succeeded in producing 10,000 saplings. Many local households have registered their intention of buying saplings.

142   PROFIT AND POVERTY IN RURAL VIETNAM

Since 1993, some households have started growing Tam Hoa plums, apricots, and lychees. Mangletia and styrax have also been grown on farms and forest gardens. The trees can be used as timber after ten years.

People are also engaged in fish breeding on the *trais*. They use the natural terrain when damming streams or excavating marshy land. The species are mainly flowery dory, black carp and Indian mud carp. Pigsties are located at the edge of the ponds so that dung and waste can sustain the fish.

Mr Nhon noted that he had invested about 50 million dong in his *trai*, including payment of hired labourers to dig the pond and break fresh ground, and to buy breeder plants and breeding animals. He derived these funds from different sources such as animal husbandry, rice husking, and cassava and orange sales. A number of households have borrowed 2–3 million dong from the bank. This is not enough to meet the farmers' needs.

Of the five households, two (Mr Duong's and Mr Hinh's) have hired labourers to work the *trai*. These labourers live on the site as guards and workers. Mr Duong hires an old Dao man and his wife. They tend the goats and pigs to earn additional income for themselves. Mr Hinh's family hired an old Dao woman aged over 50 who has no family. She does the guarding and weeds the orange and tea crops, digs holes for orange saplings, etc. Other families use their own members as labourers. These can be adult sons or other relatives, such as Mr Son's younger brother from Bac Thai province.

Management of garden land

Farmers' households in Khuoi Nieng now regard garden land as an indispensable part of their livelihood. Indeed, garden land is more important than farmland for households in Khuoi Nieng. This is completely different from the customary views of farmers in northern Vietnam; normally, rice land is paramount.

In Khuoi Nieng (as shown in Table 8), five of nineteen interviewed households had no rice farmlands. On the other hand, all the interviewed villagers had orange gardens. We have already mentioned the role of the garden economy in general and the orange garden in particular. To a large extent, most households will rely on incomes from their orange gardens in the near future. For almost all households, orange gardens will guarantee sufficient food, even if they are not concentrating on food production.

At present, many of the nineteen households face economic difficulties. Take, for example, the households of Mr Hon, Mr Thiep and Mr Diem. Their lives still hover between occasional sufficiency and

ADVANCEMENT AND DEPRIVATION IN KHUOI NIENG

Table 9: Garden land ownership in Khuoi Nieng

Head of household	Current orange plantations		Future orange plantation	
	No. of trees	Area m^2	No. of trees	Area m^2
Phan Van Nhon	600	15,000	no data	no data
Ban Van Loi	300	7,500	40	600
Ly Van Hieu	240	6,200	0	0
Hoang Van Kien	235	5,800	200	5,000
Ban Van Duong	170	4,250	no data	no data
Bui Van Thiep	140	3,700	20	500
Bui Thanh Minh	130	3,250	100	2,500
Dang Van Thong	130	3,250	70	1,750
Hoang Van Quyen	120	3,000	380	9,500
Ban Van Hop	100	2,500	0	0
Ban Van Dai	100	2,500	100	2,500
Cam Van Huynh	100	2,500	500	12,500
Dang Van Hinh	100	2,500	no data	no data
Ly Van Thai	100	2,500	100	2,500
Truong Van Vinh	100	2,500	100	2,500
Ly Van Liu	90	2,250	100	2,500
Bui Van Hon	80	2,000	10	250
Hoang Van Tai	70	1,750	no data	no data
Le Van Dien	50	1,250	50	1,250

Note: For future orange plantation, 0 = no further production plans.

144   PROFIT AND POVERTY IN RURAL VIETNAM

occasional shortage. However, we predict that in the coming two or three years their standard of living will rise considerably thanks to the orange trees that are flourishing in their gardens, promising bumper harvests in the future.

The policy of allocating forest and forest land, and legalizing garden land of various types for each household, is enabling the farmers' family economy to adapt to the market economy, and is turning farmers from subsistence producers into commodity producers. The renovation of land relationships has opened the way for other changes in the rural economy, including new ideas about the land needed by each household. Table 9 (see previous page) illustrates the new ways of thinking in Khuoi Nieng village.

In comparison with the farmland allocated to each household, we can see that garden land farms the largest part of the productive land in each households. In future, Khuoi Nieng farming households can live by and enrich themselves by tapping the potential of the garden to grow orange trees.

It is clear that conditions for the garden and forest economies are favourable in Khuoi Nieng, while wet-rice land is an additional source of income. The renovation of land relationships is changing production and business in this region from mainly subsistence production under centralized planning to commodity production in a market economy.

To support long-term forest growing, farmers' households in Khuoi Nieng rely on the income generated from their orange gardens. As we have seen, these in turn require the income from short-term crops. In this way farmers in Khuoi Nieng have devised appropriate ways to cope with long-term forest growing. This is a steady form of development with little need of outside support.

In fact, remarkable changes have taken place. After several decades of separation from the forest, highland farmers who used to live by forest farming are now bound economically to the forest farming again. This is just a beginning. It is a positive sign; it reinstates the traditional link between the ethnic groups and the forest and mountains, and restores the balance between man and nature in the northern mountain region of Vietnam.

Bustling market

The market economy has become very active along the intercommunal road. Shops and inns have emerged, bustling with life. The first shop ever opened along this road belongs to Mr Nguyen Son. Others have followed, for example, selling eels, frogs and turtles and providing services like tailoring clothes, repairing motorbikes, taking and developing photographs and selling jewellery.

Figure 35: Although there are many new jobs and goods in Khuoi Nieng, cutting bamboo for use as ropes is still a necessity [EL].

Along this road, another eight shops sell sweets, cakes, beer, alcohol, glutamate, fish sauce, salt, peanuts, instant noodles, etc. The shopkeepers usually buy their goods from Hanoi, a day-long trip by motorbike. There are also services like rice husking and milling, and battery charging. Three motorbikes, two from the village and one from the forestry Brigade 5, offer taxi services. There is also a cassava-purchasing agent who buys from growers and sells to traders from the plains. Other agents trade in turtles, snakes, eels, and frogs.

Among the families engaged in trade, six are Kinh families and two Tay. They all live at the roadside. The habits of the Dao families have also changed. Earlier they were reluctant to live near the road; they feared the lack of cultivable land and grazing. Also, they did not want to live away from the hills and the forest. Many Dao families now actively seek to reside near the roadside. Such is the case of Mr Ban Van Duong's family, who sold their big stilt-house for 5 million dong to build a temporary house near the road. His sole reason for doing this was business. In 1994, he earned enough to build a three-storey house with a tiled roof and separate kitchen.

Mr Duong has opened a tailor's shop. He bought a sewing machine and invited a veteran tailor to teach his wife the trade. In two months, he paid 200,000 dong to the teacher and his wife qualified as a tailor. She bought another sewing machine and hired a woman whom she in turn taught to be a tailor. They make clothes for customers in the village and in Brigade 5. A shirt costs 8,000 dong and a pair of trousers 10,000.

146   PROFIT AND POVERTY IN RURAL VIETNAM

Mr Duong is himself trading oranges and cassava. He acts as an agent to merchants from the plains who come to the village to buy oranges for sale in the urban centres. When we arrived in Khuoi Nieng he was busy buying cassava. Since 1994, Mr Duong has bought thirty lorry-loads of cassava.

Mr Hinh has his house about one kilometre from road. He has energetically sought business deals. He joined Mr Hoang Van Vu, from Vinh Phu province, in breeding fish. Mr Vu came to Khuoi Nieng village in 1992 to buy timber and firewood. He ferried the latter by draft to the plains. When he met Mr Hinh a second time they discussed joint undertakings. Since then, they have engaged in different business activities together, including breeding fish and growing cucumbers. They learned cucumber-growing techniques from Mr Vu's wife, whose village is famous for its cucumbers. Later on, the partners intend to expand their commercial cucumber production. Mr Hinh has started growing cinnamon saplings, too. For all these activities, he borrows and buys land and hires daily labourers.

Some years ago, gold fever hit the village. Many people hoped to change their lives. Now the fever has abated, but three families still in the business are those of Mr Son, Mr Hinh and Mr Tinh, mentioned above. Mr Hinh and his partner have dug for gold not only in the Lo River, but also in the Gam River in Chiem Hoa district. The total returns have reached 100 million dong (about US$10,000).

Mr Son and his wife exemplify the new opportunities opened up by the market economy. Over the last six years, Mr Son has had eleven different occupations: farming, leasing buffaloes to the Vinh Hao forest enterprise, motorbike repairs, showing videos to forestry workers at Brigade 5, breeding turtles and frogs, trading these animals as well as eels and snakes, digging gold, tailoring, breeding poultry, managing a photo shop, and trading oranges. His wife has just opened a cosmetics shop.

Not all Mr Son's businesses have been successful. Sometimes he has failed and his family has lost a great deal of money. Now the big profits come from orange-growing. In the immediate future Mr Son is planning a cassava-processing scheme. According to his calculations, a processing workshop would cost him 46 million dong in machines and equipment, not counting the costs of purchasing raw materials and hiring twenty labourers. We took our leave from him and his wife in an atmosphere of promise and enthusiasm.

Coexistence of hired labour and mutual aid

The market economy in Khuoi Nieng has created a demand for hired labour. The most common work is digging holes for orange trees, weeding and transporting oranges, breaking new ground for cultivation,

ADVANCEMENT AND DEPRIVATION IN KHUOI NIENG 147

and setting up new gardens. Some households hire labourers for slash-and-burn cultivation. Labour is also hired to look after the *trais*. The main reason for hiring labour is because a single household simply has too many jobs to do. This is especially true for households that combine agriculture with trading and business.

Hired labour has been common in Khuoi Nieng for only about three years. It is closely linked to the emergence of oranges as a commodity. Who are the employers and who are the hired labourers? The employers are well-off and medium-income people. They hire labour all the year around. In Khuoi Nieng, there are six such households. We do not have exact figures of their incomes, but the families of Messrs Dang Van Hinh, Ban Van Duong, and Nguyen Truong Son have incomes in the range of hundreds of millions of dong. Medium-income households also need hired labour, especially at harvest time.

Hired labour comes from those of medium income and below. Labourers either work for well-off families or for people of their own level. Labourers can be of the same lineage as their employers or be workers from Brigade 5 of the forest enterprise.

The price of hired labour is fairly uniform in the village. Excluding piece-work, the price is 10,000 dong per day. If the labourer has lunch at the employer's house, he receives 7,000 dong. The price for hiring someone to look after a farm is calculated differently. For instance, Mr Hinh has hired an old woman to live at his *trai*. He pays her 60,000 dong per month excluding food and lodging. Though hired labour is common in Khuoi Nieng, no one makes a living from that income alone. Even the two poorest families in the village, those of Mr Tiep and Mr Hoa, only work five or six days a month for other people. People with enough resources may sell their labour for money too.

Earlier, work exchange and mutual aid were common among the ethnic groups of the mountain region of northern Vietnam, because they were essential for economic self-sufficiency. In Khuoi Nieng today, they are superseded by hired labour. Work exchanges only take place among the same kin. Poor families who simply cannot afford labourers exchange work for slash-and-burn cultivation, sowing and weeding.

Despite the rise of commodity economy and hired labour, the community spirit in Khuoi Nieng survives. This is expressed in mutual aid for weddings, funerals, house-building, and at times of sickness and misfortune. The village community has a rule for funerals: each household that comes to pay respect to the bereaved family helps by bringing 2 kilograms of rice, one bottle of alcohol, a bundle of joss-sticks and votive papers. People also share in digging the grave, carrying the coffin and preparing meals.

148 PROFIT AND POVERTY IN RURAL VIETNAM

Families with sick members enjoy the concern of the whole community. Relatives and villagers usually give money and rice or do the field work on their behalf. To facilitate mutual aid and assistance, the lineage or village usually undertakes to raise the money to aid the affected family. During our stay in Khuoi Nieng village, Mr Ban Van The (40) fell seriously ill. His relatives from the village and from other localities brought him rice, chicken, bananas, and eggs. The village administration summoned inhabitants from Area I to raise money to help Mr The with medical treatment in Hanoi.

Trading and business as well as hired labour do not diminish the tradition of mutual aid and assistance in the community.

Changes in traditional culture

Khuoi Nieng village is an area where conditions favour exchange relations and easy communication arising from the market economy. This also affects traditional culture, especially Dao culture. In other areas of northern Vietnam, Dao (especially the women) normally preserve their ethnic dresses, their architecture, language, and other customs. In Khuoi Nieng, the Tay and Kinh ethnic groups strongly influence the Dao.

This is most clearly seen in housing. Formerly, the Dao were mostly nomads, and their houses were simple and portable. Once they settled under the fixed cultivation and settlement programme, they started to build houses on stilts in Tay style. Now the Dao build houses like the Kinh, that is one-storey houses on the ground. According to Mr Hinh, the village head, young newly weds no longer want to live in stilt-houses. One-storey houses are no more costly than traditional houses and houses on stilts require much more land.

The Dao have also changed the way they dress. Only older people over 50 dress traditionally. However, on special occasions people still wear their ethnic attire. They also keep one or two sets of traditional dress for wearing at the end of their lives. According to Dao belief, dead persons should wear traditional clothes so that they could be recognized and welcomed by their ancestors.

AREA II: THE BACKYARD OF THE DEVELOPMENT

Area II of Khuoi Nieng is almost half a day away from the main village because much of the distance, at least 5 kilometres, can only be covered by foot. The path follows a winding stream on its way to Lo River. In fact, we had to cross Ngoi Chi stream no less than sixty-eight times! The people of Area II live in a small, narrow valley surrounded by dense forest.

Most of the Dao living here, twenty-one households, migrated from Vi Xuyen district. They live in traditional stilt-houses made of bamboo

ADVANCEMENT AND DEPRIVATION IN KHUOI NIENG 149

and other materials. Under the floor, there is a shelter for livestock: buffaloes, pigs, and poultry. The main source of cultivation is slash-and-burn cultivation. A normal upland rice yield is 150 *cum* per hectare. This, however, is insufficient; people have to mix their rice with cassava, maize, and vegetables. Cassava is best suited to the soil here and is regarded as the main food plant. However, unlike Area I where cassava is mostly sold or used as fodder, in Area II cassava is frequently part of the daily diet.

The households in this valley have no experience of orange-growing. According to Mr Hinh the soil is suitable for orange trees. So far only two families have grown oranges and they harvested sweet crops.

The guiding principle in Area II is self-sufficiency in food. Oil and salt are provided according to the norms of Project 327 (a government afforestation programme with special support to local people in the mountain areas). Therefore, people have only to buy other necessities such as clothes and domestic utensils. However, to buy these necessities, they have to travel a whole day to the market on the far side of the highway or to Vinh Tuy town.

Generally Area II is short of everything and up to one-third of the families constantly lack food; thus they have to eat cassava instead of rice. We visited the 53-year-old Mr Dang Van Sang and his wife, the poorest family in this area. The wife has given birth to six children of whom three died in infancy. One daughter, aged 18, is deaf. Mr Sang has had pain in his stomach for two years and cannot do heavy work.

Figure 36: Father and son in Area II [EL].

150   PROFIT AND POVERTY IN RURAL VIETNAM

His dwelling is a shabby hut and nothing in his home is worth more than 10,000 dong (equivalent to US$1). The family members do not even have sleeping mats. Since the family moved here, their house has had to be rebuilt four times. In 1994, it fell down because of a rainstorm. The neighbours assisted in building a temporary shelter. The family eats cassava and tries to survive by begging.

Poverty begets disease. Area II is notorious for its malaria. The four children of the Ban Van Yen family are all affected. People here have no mosquito nets and use only smoke to keep mosquitoes away. Between 1985 and 1995 five children died from unknown diseases. To cure illnesses people turn to herbs in the first instance, and to Western medicine in the second. People also pray: two priests are in charge of the prayers.

A thorny problem in Area II is education. The nearest classroom is 6 kilometres away at Brigade 6 of the Vinh Hao forest enterprise. In 1994, using voluntary contributions, a young teacher started a class for fourteen children between 6 and 12 years old. After two months, the class no longer operated.

On return to Area I, we asked Mr Hinh how poverty had affected the mentality of the people of Area II. According to him, the crux of the matter lies in the population's mode of living and thinking. They adhere to the old ways and do not know how to change. We asked Mr Hinh why the officials and youth did not guide them. He laughed in agreement and said that they plan to do this in the near future.

What is the real cause of poverty in Area II? Did Mr Hinh give a satisfactory reply? This question stayed with me all the way back to Hanoi and, sad to say, remained unanswered.

TEN

Reconciliation of Hardships in the Past

VINH HAO FOREST ENTERPRISE AND FOREST LAND RELATIONSHIP

The history and development of Vinh Hao forest enterprise is similar to that of other state-owned companies in northern Vietnam. The enterprise was set up in March 1960 as part of the "new economic zones" policy whereby Kinh people were expected to improve the less developed uplands. Also, the overpopulated Red River delta where the Kinh came from was to be alleviated of the burden of feeding itself.

The forest itself was a national asset used to support the impoverished state treasury. During the 1970s and 1980s the forest in the northern provinces was also used by the military as a source of income.

Initially, quite a few people were moved into an area of 31,000 hectares of state forest land. The 700 or so Kinh workers who settled in collective houses of the Vinh Hao forestry brigades were young and unmarried, and over half were women. Other migrants from the delta were settling down as farmers in the newly established cooperatives. The difference between the incoming farmers and workers was that the former came with entire families and sometimes even with entire villages. The workers were individuals, although they were recruited in groups. They did not necessarily come from the same village but often came from the same district.

According to village elders in Vinh Hao commune, the forest was dense and the local population, comprising different ethnic groups like Tay and Dao, lived by dry- and wet-rice cultivation in scattered hamlets in the valleys and on the hills.

151

152 PROFIT AND POVERTY IN RURAL VIETNAM

The initial task of Vinh Hao forest enterprise was to harvest and supply bamboo to the delta provinces under the central plan. The forest of more than 31,000 hectares was spread over eleven communes in Bac Quang district, although over time it became evident that the forest enterprise could not manage such large areas, nor provide work and food for so many people. By logging wood, mostly bamboo, local farmers found ways to use forest area for agricultural purposes. Deforested areas were successively handed over to neighbouring agricultural cooperatives.

It was not until 1976, when Vinh Hao enterprise was declared to be part of the Bai Bang Paper and Pulp Mill, that reforestation started in earnest. The main task of the enterprise changed to planting trees for pulpwood. The forested area had dropped to 11,000 hectares and was scattered in parcels. There was a growing concern about the protection of the planted forest. More than 20,000 hectares of forest and forest land were returned to local administration.

Mr Nguyen Thai Oanh, director of Vinh Hao forest enterprise, still has to settle border disputes with local people. According to him, with an area of 11,000 hectares the enterprise only existed on a map. In fact, in many places local forest gardens were included in the enterprise land. In 1990, following Directive 5 of the people's committee of Ha Tuyen province, the enterprise again reviewed the forest and forest land areas under its management. It kept only those areas that the enterprise could manage and do business on. Thus, in 1990, the management area of the enterprise was reduced to about 6,000 hectares; the rest was returned to the local communes. This land was later allocated to households wherever possible. Actually, many areas of wasteland and bare hills cannot be allotted to households as they accept only forest land close to their residence for ease of forest cultivation and protection.

Along with the reduction of the enterprise forest area, the communes undertook to allot forest and forest land to farmers' households. In Vinh Hao commune, forest garden lands have been legalized. Whoever had a little forest garden was allocated additional forest land.

Of the nineteen village households interviewed, the two with the smallest forest and forest land areas have an average of 0.5 hectares each. The one with the largest area has 8 hectares. The average is 3.02 hectares. Only four of the nineteen have their ancestors' forest land. This possession is now legal. Does this show that the Dao ethnic group has turned less natural forest land into forest gardens compared to the Tay in Lam Tien village? The process of reviewing the forest and forest land areas of Vinh Hao forest enterprise enabled the ethnic groups of this mountain region to live by forest farming legally. Does this lessen

RECONCILIATION OF HARDSHIPS IN THE PAST   153

the pressure from farmers to reallocate wet-rice? Does this reduce disputes over wet-rice land?

There have been many disputes over newly distributed forest, forest land and former forest gardens in the area of Vinh Hao forest enterprise and Khuoi Nieng village. According to Mr Phan Van Thoan, who is in charge of forest protection at the enterprise, there have been nearly 200 disputes over forest land, forest gardens and agricultural land along the highway between Hanoi and Ha Giang province, under the control of Vinh Hao forest enterprise.

Most disputes arose over land that was not legally owned by anybody. This land was worth little in the past. However, in the market economy, if it is forest land lying along the highway, its value has increased rapidly. Moreover, after the promulgation of the Land Law, the Vietnamese government legalized the land management and land-use rights of each household.

In Khoui Nieng not many land disputes have occurred. Only two of the nineteen interviewed households had been involved in disputes over forest land. Mr Ban Vai Dai in Khuoi Nieng had a dispute with Mr Si in Vinh Tuy commune. The local authorities settled the conflict by allocating the disputed land to Mr Dai's household, because it was his ancestor's forest garden land that had been allotted by Vinh Tuy commune to another household. Another land dispute, between Mr Dang Thanh and Dinh Long commune, has not yet been resolved.

If a plot of land under the commune's management was allocated by the forest enterprise in error, the enterprise will hand it over to the commune. If a plot of land is mistakenly allocated by the commune to a household, that household must enter a joint venture with the enterprise to plant forest. The enterprise will then grant a certificate to that household. This manner of settling disputes is generally favourable to the local people. The most important thing is to ensure that disputes do not have a negative impact on afforestation in the region.

Relations between Vinh Hao forest enterprise and the communes of Vinh Hao and Dong Nien changed drastically in 1993 when Project 327 came into being. The aim of the project is to reforest land by long-term distribution to the farmers. An underlying objective is to curtail shifting cultivation by encouraging farmers to become settled. As part of the Project 327, the forest enterprise has leased land to the farmers on ten-year contracts. The contracts are provisional. The reason for not making them permanent is, according to the director of the enterprise, land-use conflicts between the enterprise and the commune. For the same reason, there were only provisional contracts in the whole of Ha Giang province at that point (April 1995), and there were still no clear regulations for allocating forest land.

154 PROFIT AND POVERTY IN RURAL VIETNAM

The officials of Khuoi Nieng village confirm the lack of certainty:

> The enterprise does not cooperate with the commune and our village. For instance, they just announce that the forest at Brigade 6 belongs to them. But we do not agree. Actually, it is the leader of that brigade who has declared several hundred hectares of forest to be his. Because the biggest problem for local farmers here is the lack of agricultural land, we want more forest to manage.

Another aspect of forest land allocation is that the forest land destruction has stopped. A former brigade leader comments:

> Earlier, during the subsidy system, we had great difficulty in protecting the forest. The farmers just entered and logged the trees for their own consumption. They even organized sales to the Bai Bang Paper Mill. They did this to get food. They were hungry as shifting cultivation did not yield enough. The direct protection of the forest is now more effective.

Relations between Brigade 5 and Khuoi Nieng village

The socioeconomic conditions of forestry workers and farmers have been both similar and different depending on the prevailing policy and particular regional features and predicaments. The watershed between before and after for both groups is the allocation of agricultural and forest land to households. This is, however, an ongoing process; the first steps away from total collectivization began in 1981, and the last will probably lead to complete private ownership of land. Moreover, agricultural and forest land have been allocated under different terms. Yet, both farmers and forestry workers are now more answerable for production on the land.

In Vinh Hao the forestry workers were employees until 1990, and were taken care of by the brigade. The brigade was a closed economic and social unit. Local villages were inhabited by various ethnic groups, among them also Kinh farmers who had migrated from the delta. The farmers' work was managed by principles similar to those of the forestry brigades. The major change began in the early 1980s when farmers gained greater control of food production. They also had kinship ties in the area. As we have seen, these ties are significant in securing investments and a respectable family reputation as well as help in crises.

Most of the forestry workers interviewed said that they did not have a close relationship with nearby farmers. That has not changed over time. Nevertheless, we found some cases of contact and support. The school at Brigade 5 has received farmers' children since 1988. One forestry worker reported that they had lent money to some farmers in Quyet Tien hamlet. They were poor and needed money to feed their small children.

RECONCILIATION OF HARDSHIPS IN THE PAST   155

Another example of contact between workers and farmers was revealed during a visit to a worker's house. There were ten bicycles parked outside the house. They belonged to farmers who grow rice on enterprise land. It was not clear if this activity was regulated on paper somewhere and if someone was making money out of it. As we understood it, the aim was pure food production for subsistence. "What to do when people have nothing to eat?" It shows the pragmatic and spontaneous solidarity among people who are in the same exposed situation.

The plantations of styrax and mangletia trees in Vinh Hao are quite extensive. They constitute a dormant fortune. After four years, when it is time for harvesting, the forestry workers and farmers who now manage forest land areas will certainly prosper. Consequently both workers and farmers clamour for forest land for plantations. Except for the continuing differentiation between the haves and have-nots, the social and economic situation of workers and farmers will converge. They have a common interest in land for housing, gardening, livestock and cultivating rice, cash-crops and trees. The ability to bargain for land is therefore crucial. With healthy labourers in the household and access to hired labour outside, the future of households in Vinh Hao should be promising unless Doi Moi has some unforeseen consequences.

FORMER BRIGADE WORKERS RECOUNT

With logging and increased plantations, the number of brigades of Vinh Hao forest enterprise increased. Brigade 5 was established in 1974. At that time it consisted of a permanent housing area and a mobile team. Most of the workers we met were recruited between 1975 and 1985. Many of them, including the women, had formed parts of a mobile logging team.

A woman, now 41 years old and retired because of ill health, came to Brigade 5 in 1974:

> During the years from 1976 to 1984 we had to move around with the logging unit to different places. We moved very often. We were logging bamboo, styrax and mangletia.

A former brigade leader remembers those years:

> The workers were young and had no families. They came from the delta and they planned to stay for a short time only.

> Women wanted to return to have a chance to meet a husband. Six or seven workers applied for transfer. Only one was approved, because the worker was admitted to another occupation. When they wanted to work closer to their native places, there were no forestry enterprises in the delta, so they could not be employed as forestry

156   PROFIT AND POVERTY IN RURAL VIETNAM

workers. Changing occupations was not possible either as no other employers would accept them. Besides, there was a shortage of labour in the forest.

Six out of the nine men we met in Brigade 5 had been in military service between 1978 and 1985. Although the disastrous war against the US ended in 1975, Vietnam continued to face a difficult situation because of its political and military commitments in Cambodia and Laos. The "lesson" administered by China in early 1979 in the form of an attack on the northern border meant that military mobilization continued in Vietnam.

Two of the six workers who were mobilized to defend the border with China feel still affected by the hardships they went through:

> The year 1978 was the most difficult in my life. I left my home for the first time. I was only 19. We had two kinds of work, planting trees and guarding the border. We lived on shelters and slept on the floor. There was not always enough food. Those years damaged my health. I suffered from malaria when I returned to the forest enterprise. In 1987, 1988 and 1989 I was severely ill. Once I stayed in hospital for six months. They injected me against malaria. Since then I suffer much less when I have malaria. Last time was in 1992.

The other worker was also struck by malaria while in the army:

> By the end of 1985 I had malaria again. Since then I have suffered from malaria once a year. The medicine I take does not help much. I feel weaker and weaker every year.

As before, when men were at the front, the women replaced them.

Women replace men

In forestry, women were already the majority among the workers. Their predominance grew further when the male workers were mobilized. Some women in Brigade 5 bore witness to those years:

> We were in the mobile logging units and we had to move once or twice every year. Even those living in the more permanent brigades were often shifted between them. Most of us were women, because the men were in the army. We worked hard and had very little to eat, only wheat seeds and cassava. Many of us fell ill. Today we still suffer from malaria, back pain, aching joints and other diseases that sap our strength.

Another effect of military mobilization was that many workers married late, at about 30. Some women were never able to marry. Whereas the women's right to become mothers was recognized, all single mothers we met had their own particular reasons for having a child or two.

RECONCILIATION OF HARDSHIPS IN THE PAST   157

Even for married couples it was not easy to establish family life. Often, a worker noted, husband and wife had to work in different brigades and even different enterprises. Thus, many married mothers had to assume all the everyday responsibilities for children and household. A retired worker describes the situation in those first years:

> Many workers were young women and they made up 70 per cent of the total labour force. Some older ones were able to move to other brigades to get married. Some married locally and left the forestry. Some remained unmarried.

"Everybody's father is nobody's father"

In Vinh Hao forest enterprise as elsewhere in northern Vietnam, the state took care of employment, work distribution, salaries in cash and kind, housing, and the schooling and health services. In principle private business was not allowed.

The system also had a practical *raison d'être*. During the war and the prolonged near-war, the rationing system was a way to make both ends meet with a growing population and limited food production. State employees were guaranteed a regular supply of all vital consumer goods and could buy them at a subsidized price. The distribution was fair in the sense that manual workers such as those in forestry, got a higher ration of rice (up to 21 kilograms per month), while white-collar workers received less (only 13 kilograms). Again, problems arose when the forest enterprises were not able to pay salaries on time and just gave workers a reduced rice ration, a ration that was far too small to survive on.

Brigade leaders had to rush to the farmers to buy rice for their workers as the state was unable to deliver enough. And open markets were few and had a limited variety of goods. One former brigade leader remarked:

> At the time the workers were totally dependent and the cadres had to solve many problems like children's illnesses, maternity leave and lack of food. And when the rations were delayed the brigade leader had to go directly to the farmers and buy rice as the market did not have enough for sale. If he did not, the workers would refuse to work.

Forestry work was very much directed from the top down. The enterprises received their orders from the state in form of yearly plans. As the former leader in Brigade 5 expressed it:

> The state gave a budget to the enterprise, which directed production at each brigade through the brigade leader. The brigade itself was staffed with officials who gave orders to the workers. If they could not fulfil the plans set by the enterprise, we had to

158 PROFIT AND POVERTY IN RURAL VIETNAM

borrow workers from other brigades. The machinery of control was heavy; nevertheless, the production was not efficient. The workers had no responsibility and they were totally dependent. So they handed over everything to their superiors.

We asked whether there were any strikes or signs of protest.

No, there was never any strike, but the workers went slow. Or they pretended to be ill. At that time the brigade leader had to go to the workers' houses and persuade them to go to work. They might go to the site but not do any work. Another big problem was that nobody felt directly responsible for the protection of forest. The property belonged to nobody, so no one cared. Or as a Vietnamese saying has it: "Everybody's father is nobody's father."

We brigade leaders had regular meetings with the enterprise leadership where we reported about the prevailing conditions in the brigades. Standing between those two forces was difficult. If I tried to satisfy one side, the workers became angry or the enterprise leaders were dissatisfied. I had sleeping difficulties because of the cross-pressure and all the worries. I felt relieved when I eventually retired after twenty-three consecutive years. Today, I feel relaxed and stronger. I sleep better.

The housing in Brigade 5 was much the same as that in Minh Dan and Brigade 481. However, here the kitchen was collective and sometimes the workers had their meals communally although the families used to eat in their rooms. There was no place for gardening and only a few kept chickens or even a pig. As in many other places, the kindergarten, school and health clinic all were simple and in need of equipment. A worker who came to Brigade 5 in 1978, still recalled:

Life was hard in the first years. I lived in a collective house for nearly ten years. First we were six men to a room, later four. My wife and I lived in a collective house until 1986.

A female worker who had worked in Vinh Hao since 1976 noted:

The first ten years I lived in a collective house, sharing a room with three other women. We had our meals in the collective dining room.

THE END OF THE SUBSIDIZED SYSTEM

Towards the middle of the 1980s, it became obvious to the leadership of Vinh Hao forest enterprise and the authorities in Vietnam generally, that subsidized prices and salaries that were administratively set were not an impetus for development. Besides, the state could not afford to continue the subventions to its employees.

The forestry workers had already started to draw their own conclusions about the unbearable shortages of food and other necessities.

Figure 37: Collective house in Brigade 5 in 1987 [EL].
Figure 38: The same house in 1995 – cut into pieces to serve as private houses [RL].

Couples moved out of the collective houses to build small bamboo houses nearby. Having a house and a garden meant additional income and hence rice.

The forest enterprise had to examine its mode of management which resulted in different forms of contracted work. As explained by Mr Oanh

160   PROFIT AND POVERTY IN RURAL VIETNAM

(the enterprise director) and Mr Hien (leader of Brigade 5), the contracts divided responsibilities between the enterprise and the contractors. The enterprise invests 70 per cent of the total value of the end product, i.e. by projecting and planning and by supplying seedlings and fertilizers. The contractors invest the rest through their labour, i.e. they clear the land, plant, tend, and protect. When the trees are logged, the enterprise gets back 70 per cent of the total wood production of each unit, and the contractors keep the rest to use as they like. There are no results from the contracts yet, as logging will only start in four years.

Most of the contracts were signed in 1992. Farmers signed provisional contracts of ten years' duration. Workers have yearly contracts whereby different stages of work are regulated.

Another measure to cut down the costs of the enterprise has been the reduction of workers. During 1988–90, half the 600 employees stopped working. In 1995, there were 200 left. The reasons given are the same as in other enterprises: retirement because of age, number of working years and bad health. It is also common for one family member, either husband or wife, to ask for retirement to be able to garden and farm. Many retired workers in Vinh Hao returned to the delta. Only two workers stayed out of the sixty-five who retired in 1993.

In this respect, Brigade 5 is an exception: over the past five years thirty workers have retired, but only five have returned to the delta. We enquire of the workers in Brigade 5 why they stay. They explain that they have no land or houses to return to. Their relatives are so poor that they cannot accommodate them. Here in the forest they have a piece of land and a house to live in. Most workers say that their lives are better than those of their farmer parents and siblings.

Another good reason for staying in Brigade 5 is the Swedish aid given between 1987 and 1992 to construct private houses, a school, a kindergarten and a power station. This was to support Vietnamese plans to transform the brigades into forest villages with more diversified activities and a reasonable infrastructure.

The Vietnamese state, through the enterprise and with Swedish aid, made a direct subvention of 50 per cent of the cost of a normal one-storey stone-house with three rooms. The house is worth about 6 million dong. The family had to pay half of this sum. Some small houses worth 1–2 million dong were built especially for single mothers. We met three of these women and they had all paid 670,000 dong.

In 1989, a sub-brigade called 5B was set up some 3 kilometres into the forest. The idea was to be nearer the worksite. Initially there were twenty-five workers living in collective houses. Three years later, they started to build private houses near Brigade 5 because of the better facilities like electricity and school. Today, there are only four people left at Brigade 5 B: two workers, a teacher, and a male nurse.

RECONCILIATION OF HARDSHIPS IN THE PAST 161

Another example of renovation in the Vinh Hao forest enterprise is the forest protection measures taken by Brigade 5 in Khuoi Nieng village area. In 1994, this forestry brigade started to employ "hired thugs" or rangers to protect the forest. Since then, the destruction of Brigade 5 forest has basically stopped. The payment of large sums to these hired hands falls outside the normal mode of management for a state enterprise.

A "hired thug" is paid 1 million dong per month, while Mr Hien, leader of Brigade 5 only got 320,000 dong between January and April 1995; that is 80,000 dong per month. The use of hired labour was a break with management practices; the ends were more important than the means. The "hired thugs" were very effective. Their employment reflects new attitudes among the leaders of the state enterprises in the region.

Constraints on forest development

It is obvious that there are some administrative constraints on forest development in this region. These constraints can be overcome by improved administrative procedures without much financial support.

The first obstacle contains all the regulations of the operating agencies in the administration regarding the age of the forest which can be harvested. Despite the shift to a market economy, the regulations still bear the hallmarks of imposed centralized planning.

Another constraint is the application procedure for permits to log forest. Mr Oanh said that the workers of the enterprise and the farmers' households working with the enterprise to cultivate forest work very hard "from dawn to dusk". Ironically, when their forest is ready for logging, they have to try very hard to obtain permits to do so. The procedures are:

- inventory of the forest to see whether it has reached the harvesting age
- outline of harvesting design
- submission of design for approval by Vinh Phu Service Union
- grant of logging permits by the Ministry of Forestry
- report to the local provincial people's committee
- report to the local provincial forest protection department
- report to district forest protection station
- application for permit to sell wood for paper pulp to be signed by the chairman of the local provincial people's committee
- transport permits from the provincial forest protection department
- once harvested and transported, tax payment should be made to the local district's tax authorities

162   PROFIT AND POVERTY IN RURAL VIETNAM

There are too many procedures! And of course there are fees at each stage of the procedures. Such fees are not part of the state budget, but only contribute to inflate the price of paper pulp. They also create added burdens for the hard-working forest growers.

The third constraint is the logging ban issued by the Tuyen Quang provincial people's committee. We do not want to discuss the objectives of this order. We only want to raise some factual assessments of its effectiveness.

The decision to "close the forest gate" occurs when the need for pulpwood of the Bai Bang Paper Mill does not decrease. In a market economy, demand should determine the volume of logging for paper production. While in Tuyen Quang province forest enterprises have not been allowed to harvest pulpwood, in the lower basin area of the Red River the Bai Bang Paper Mill openly purchases paper pulp without regard to its origin, if the price is right.

In such a situation, only those who strictly obey the ban suffer. These are mainly the state forest enterprises. Lumber from these enterprises is still cut, not by growers and owners, but illegally by other people. The illegal wood can easily be marketed at Bai Bang Paper Mill. Moreover, the price of wood has increased since the decision to close the forest gate. That stimulates the illegal cutting of wood grown by the forest enterprises!

Some management activities and administrative decisions have been inconsistent. Some of them reflect the process of renovation and the shift to a market economy, while others still bear the marks of centralized planning. These uneven changes are obstructing the forestry development in the northern mountain regions of Vietnam. How then did the forestry workers participate in those transformations?

How to make a living in a forest village
Today Brigade 5 looks very much like a village. All collective houses have been removed or divided into private ones by demolishing sections of the long stone houses. The brigade is situated on a small dirt road 3 kilometres from the north–south highway. On the way to Brigade 5, one passes Khuoi Nieng village.

The forest village has seventy-five inhabitants today, of whom fifty still work in forestry. About half of them are women. As late as 1990 there were more than 100 workers. Among residents, there are retired workers, teachers, carpenters, and others. Twelve couples are forestry workers and in twenty-three households only one of the spouses is a forestry worker. Retired workers, single or not, are no longer included in the statistics.

We wanted to know more about employment conditions in Brigade 5. What methods are used to become wealthy? The workers' opinions are compiled below:

RECONCILIATION OF HARDSHIPS IN THE PAST   163

- *To obtain much forest land and let other people like farmers work on it.* Actually five workers' families have hired labour in 1994. Among them are the brigade leader and the head of the trade union.
- *To invest in cash-crops on forest trais.* In Brigade 5, the cash-crop is oranges. Three families here, including the brigade leader, have such *trais.* According to the enterprise leadership, it is only rich families who can afford this. It is entirely a family business and the investment capital is usually borrowed from the bank.
- *To raise animals, in the first instance pigs.* Out of the fifteen interviewed families, twelve raised pigs. The resulting income is used for staples like rice.
- *To own or have access to a fishpond.* About half the families are regularly able to add fish to their menu.
- *To enjoy good health.* Most interviewed workers had health problems: malaria, aching backs and joints, headaches. Women suffered from infections related to IUDs. Some workers were seriously disabled. A chronically ill worker seriously affected the household's living conditions.
- *To have access to at least two labourers.* According to the former brigade leader, everything now depends on the labour that people command. Labour is needed for the contract with the forest enterprise and the family economy. In fact in Brigade 5, only families with adult children, and workers with siblings living permanently in the brigade, are able to mobilize enough labour.

The most common activity for expanding the family economy is cultivating orange trees, usually on a piece of land near the housing area. Families also raise pigs and have fishponds. Many families cultivate rice in their tree plantations. The harvest varies from 100–400 kilograms of paddy per year.

In comparing the salary from forestry with earnings from the family economy, rich and average families have income from these two sources in a proportion of 50/50. Poor households have almost no additional income to their forestry wages and without exception they comprise single mothers or other single women and newly established families. How do they cope? A total salary of 1 or 2 million dong per year covers only the cost of rice for one or two people and nothing more. Some of the poor hire their labour out to other families. Both men and women work on orange *trais* and rice-fields and in other seasonal jobs. Others borrow money and rice from workmates or dealers out on the highway.

So what does it mean to be rich in Brigade 5? Yearly income should be 10 million dong or more. A family should have all the advantages mentioned in the earlier cases. Some four or five families have these. The

164   PROFIT AND POVERTY IN RURAL VIETNAM

lowest income is 1–2 million dong. We met five such families. Thirty-five households are average which means any income in between.

Who personally are the richest and the poorest in Brigade 5? Everyone knows the poorest to be Ms Loi, the single mother of two children, and Mrs Nguyen who has lived alone with her son for five years. The youngest of Ms Loi's children is 1 year old. Although Loi is utterly poor, there is nothing miserable in her way of being. She is lovely, spontaneous, glad and caring. Still, her son's asthma worries her. The three live in a solid stone house built with SIDA aid. In order to get food, Loi has to go deep into the forest to cut fuelwood and collect bamboo shoots for sale. She also does extra work as a day labourer for local farmers.

Mrs Nguyen's husband was eventually admitted as a worker in the brigade at the end of last year. She is expecting their second child in a fortnight. Nguyen's mother had just arrived from Vinh Phu to assist her daughter. This support is typical: it is an expression of close relationship in the maternal line although a daughter is considered to be "lost" or "flown" when she joins her husband's family at marriage (Hy Van Luong 1992; Pham Van Bich 1997).

The couple paid 300,000 dong for their house in 1993. They were able to borrow from the enterprise after the special assistance programme ended in 1992. They have repaid the loan, but they are now forced to borrow both cash and rice, since the drought destroyed their last rice harvest. They live on the margin, but their long-term prospects appear good. They have planted thirty orange trees in their small garden. In three more years there will be fruit. The husband is strong and healthy and besides forestry work, he is a day labourer at a farmer's orange *trai*.

At present, according to the brigade statistics, there are four single mothers among the active workers. Two of them cohabit with men outside the brigade. One of the men is a carpenter from the delta who turns up now and then. He has made beautifully carved furniture for the mother of his child in Brigade 5.

The brigade nurse, Ms Dung, has two sons with a former worker of the enterprise. The boys are 8 and 5 years old. Dung is a Kinh from Thai Binh province; her beloved is a local Tay. His family refused to accept her and found their son another wife. The father of Dung's sons lives ten kilometres away. He does not support them as he now has his own family to provide for, Dung explains.

Loi receives no support from the fathers of her children. She and nurse Dung are only able to serve their children two meals per day; breakfast and dinner, and possibly a very light lunch. They eat rice mixed with cassava all the time. However, the single mothers in the brigade try to assist one another although they are all poor. They avoid approaching the better-off families.

RECONCILIATION OF HARDSHIPS IN THE PAST   165

One of the richest people is Mr Don (38) who has been the trade union leader for three years. He refers to himself as a common worker. In 1976, he came to the brigade. He married ten years later, after six years in military service. Both he and his wife come from the same district in Hai Hung province, but from different villages. His wife retired because of bad health, and she now works entirely in the family economy. There are only two labourers in the family, since the children are still small. Nevertheless, Mr Don and his wife are among the five families that manage the most forest land (4 hectares). Last year they hired labour. Their total income was 25 million dong. Most of the income comes from the forest and the rest from the family economy, including a small kiosk which they run in the brigade. Their brick house was part of the housing project.

Worsening social conditions

Mr Phan (54) was the leader of Brigade 5 from 1986 to 1991. While comparing current conditions with those in the past, he reports that the social insurance is weaker today. Not much attention is paid to the workers when they are ill. The previous system with rations and sick allowances reflected societal priorities that have been swept aside in favour of other considerations.

Mr Phung Van Loi, a worker and a father of three children, was infected by meningitis. He spent two months at hospital in Hanoi. No one from the enterprise realized how serious the disease was. They gave him an advance payment of 100,000 dong, and he received 70 per cent of his salary for the months he was ill. However, he spent nearly 1 million for the treatment, yet still left the hospital too early because he could not afford to stay longer. He is still very weak, and suffers from headaches and backache after the illness. Sometimes he finds it hard to turn his head. Due to the illness he had to borrow 5 million from his parents and sisters. The money was spent on the treatment. Now the debts and the pain remain.

Another worker broke his leg and was sent to Tuyen Quang provincial hospital. According to this worker, the insurance system does not work satisfactorily and so people try to cure themselves. As the medicine he received at the hospital did not work, he went to the market for traditional drugs.

We were told about several cases of recurrent malaria in Brigade 5; some of these were children. Even managers at top level confirm that the present insurance system does not seem to work:

> It does not cover all expenses when someone falls ill. And the clinics and hospitals favour only those patients who can pay. The consequence for ordinary people is a worsening of conditions.

166   PROFIT AND POVERTY IN RURAL VIETNAM

The state of things in Brigade 5 was distressful in other ways too. There had been three cases of theft. One morning, when Mrs Than and her husband had gone to the forest and the children were in school, their house was broken into and what they had of value was stolen: the radio, clothes and about 1 million dong of savings, money to be spent for the coming New Year celebrations (*Tet*). Mrs Than and her husband went to the brigade leader for help. Mrs Thanh had to do the talking as her husband's hearing is impaired. The brigade leader was busy with other things. They turned to the village police, who did not come to the brigade. They wrote to the enterprise manager and applied for an allowance, since they had no money for celebration of *Tet*, and it was near the end of the year. They never received an answer. All the thefts in the brigade remained unsolved. The workers felt neglected, and left in a state of suspicion.

To all this one has to add the controversies within the brigade school. The school has five grades and four teachers. The teacher of grade 4 had recently been fired. The pupils' parents were upset and wanted the popular teacher back. According to them she had been treated unfairly.

Nearly 50 per cent (fifty of one-hundred-four) of the pupils are from local minorities, Dao and Tay. The teacher of grade 3 commented:

> Dao children are sometimes difficult. They are not very good pupils. If a teacher blames them, their parents come to school and quarrel with the teacher. Some pupils stop coming to the school. They cannot read and write.

We asked her what was the drop-out rate?

> I do not pay much attention to those who stop. I do not remember numbers. One Dao pupil in my class recently stopped coming.

The school worked in two shifts due to the "lack of classrooms". Yet, out of the four classrooms only two were in use. The brigade nurse and her children lived in one classroom, and another one stood empty. We frequently felt puzzled by what we saw and heard.

Generally, because social policies and mass movements have weakened, women felt more vulnerable about the whims of individual cadres in the brigade, and farmers and dealers on the main road. Some women meant that they were not treated with respect and did not receive land and work in proportion to their abilities. They were ignored when they asked for support to repair their houses, dig wells, etc. The women referred to the old brigade board which had several leaders. They also missed the party, trade union, and Women's Union. In these forums they had been given a voice and their problems could be addressed. Now decisions were being taken without their knowing the grounds for them. People felt that they did not have the same rights as before.

ELEVEN

Current Ambiguities

WORKERS' VOICES ON DOI MOI

We wanted to know how Doi Moi had changed the workers' economic and social conditions. One of the former brigade leaders (1982–86) noted:

> Previously the workers handed everything over to the state. They were paid without regard to the work they had done. Now the workers are responsible for the end product and get paid accordingly. A disadvantage with the old system was that the forest was not protected since nobody took responsibility and there was no control. A particular feature in this brigade is the Swedish aid for housing and infrastructure. Thanks to this support, the workers can concentrate on creating gardens and fishponds, thus giving a good start to the family economy.

The other brigade leader shared his opinion:

> Now the workers can decide when they work and how they use their time. And they can take care of their food themselves. They are more free and self-confident. There is no strict discipline any more.

Were there any disadvantages to the new system?

> Yes, socially it is a weaker system. The party and the mass organizations like the trade union, the Women's Union and the Youth League have no influence any longer.

Other workers would agree about the disadvantages, yet they were less sure about the benefits of the new system. A female worker who married late noted:

> Before I lived in a collective house. Life was easier without family. Now it is difficult to manage the food situation. We lack food

168   PROFIT AND POVERTY IN RURAL VIETNAM

three months of the year, so we have to eat cassava, maize, and potatoes.

A single mother, who once worked in the Women's Union in the delta, said:

Life is much better than before. But it depends mainly on the family economy. Earlier, we waited for brigade cadres to act. Now we decide on work ourselves. It is freer and it is better. However, there are fewer activities within the trade union and the Women's Union. Earlier, everything was collective, now everybody has to manage his or her own affairs, so people are less interested in mass movements.

Another voice was heard, also a woman:

The workers have no representatives nowadays, not in the trade union, nor the Women's Union.

Other changes deal with forestry work as such. Earlier, there was enough work, both logging and planting, and it was equally distributed. Now that work is directly related to salary level, there is an interest among workers to have land for forestry work. According to many workers, they have too little land and thus limited income from forestry work. During the four first months of 1995, few if any salaries had been paid. Accepting that forestry work is seasonal, the yearly total salary is still only half or less of the total income.

According to all the workers we talked to, the biggest problem in the brigade is the shortage of work. As salaries are work-related, the workers' demands for more work are understandable. The perceived shortage of work runs counter to the views of the enterprise, which plans to recruit more workers to cope with an alleged excess of work. There seems to be a lack of communication in respect to the availability of land and access to work.

To sum up the changes, the characteristics of the present situation are:

* better family economy because of private houses and gardens
* higher quality of forestry work, including protection, due to decentralization of responsibilities
* sense of greater freedom in life
* less social security including high costs for health services and education
* living conditions increasingly dependent on strength and health, number of labourers, networks of kin and friends, and individual ability
* organizations like the Communist Party, the trade union, the Women's Union and the Youth League adopt a lower profile.

Figure 39: Dao woman in Area 11, Khuoi Nieng village [EL].

Discontent in Brigade 5

As soon as we started interviewing forestry workers about their lives before and after Doi Moi, we noticed that something was troubling them. Gradually, we learned that the prevailing frustration and tension were directed at one cadre. Was he the victim of collective criticism because he happened to be the nearest leader? Did years of deprivation and present insecurity demand a scapegoat? Did the disappearance of old representative bodies for workers mean that complaints festered? We cannot tell. Yet, we chose to record the voices of both male and female workers, ordinary workers as well as those in a higher position in the brigade. Below are given some of the criticisms voiced:

> There are bad ways of behaving here. People do not help one another. (Interviewee no. 1)

170 PROFIT AND POVERTY IN RURAL VIETNAM

> I feel very critical of the leadership. They change the conditions too frequently. It is difficult for us to follow the changes and know our rights. (Interviewee no. 2)

> The leadership here is rigid and unqualified. The cadre says there is no more forest land to allocate, yet he has taken 8 hectares for himself. He is the biggest landowner in the brigade. (Interviewee no. 3)

> The leadership here is not professional. In fact, everybody wants to leave this brigade and go back to the delta, even though we have quite a good material life here. The economic and social conditions are potentially good. It is the organization and the management that is bad. The cadre has too much power. He is not capable. (Interviewee no. 4)

These examples of indifference and arrogance were summarized by a worker: "He does not care if the worker lives or dies."

In confronting the director of the enterprise with some of these complaints, we got the impression that he was taken by surprise and was not aware of the situation. According to him, the enterprise never refused any worker more forest land:

> There is an excess of land. Anybody who wants land can have it. In Brigade 5 there is so much work to do that we plan to recruit more workers. We plan to secure work for people already in the brigade.

> *Q: What about the way salaries are calculated and the irregularity of payments?*

> A: These are the rules of the state and everybody knows it. The kind of work that should be done in planting is fixed, how often trees should be tended, etc.

> *Q: Who checks the work performance?*

> A: The cadre. The assessment is made once a month and the salary is based on that. The salaries up to March 1995 are paid.

> *Q: Who pays the salaries and takes the money to the workers?*

> A: The cadre.

> *Q: What about the workers who have only two meals a day and eat cassava for most of the year?*

> A: We have no information that there are families with such problems.

Obviously, in the new system, there is only one person who acts as a link between the brigade and the enterprise. What happens if that person fails to provide accurate information? Then the enterprise is ignorant about the problems at brigade level, and the workers are left out or misinformed.

CURRENT AMBIGUITIES

It is not our role as researchers to judge the situation in Brigade 5, but it is clear that in the new system workers are much more dependent than before on the professional ability of key persons in the enterprise and the brigade. The workers have no common avenues to express their needs and demands. In fact, they now depend on the benevolence of one person.

THE ENTERPRISE'S AND VSPU'S VIEW OF DOI MOI

We wanted to ascertain from the director the enterprise's view on the effects of Doi Moi.

Q: What main impact has Doi Moi had on the enterprise?

A: Previously we asked the state for money, and it was provided. Now we have to borrow money.

Q: So you are now an economic unit that has to survive alone?

A: Yes, but the problem is that we have no investment capital. We have asked to borrow money from the Vinh Phu Service Union (VPSU) [formed in 1986 to supply Bai Bang Paper and Pulp Mill with raw fibre] at 0.24 per cent interest per month but we have not been granted it. We do not understand why. We cannot afford to borrow on the market where the interest is 2.5 per cent. So we have to undertake unscheduled activities like setting aside 30 hectares of forest for a match factory in Hanoi and contracting out forest to farmers.

Q: What are your responsibilities towards the workers?

A: We have to create jobs for the workers and pay salaries. We have to take care of the social welfare system and follow the general rules of production.

Q: What is your main problem?

A: Frankly, we have too many bosses! Different enterprise activities are controlled by different authorities. Take logging, for example. It is controlled by the district through the Forest Protection Station [*Kiem Lam*]. When it comes to borrowing capital, we have to turn to the VPSU. The total operations of the enterprise are under the district and the province. Production plans should be reported to the VPSU through the district and the province. Finally movements like the party, the trade union and the Women's Union are at the district level. We would prefer our board of directors to be left alone by the other levels. We want to run the business ourselves!

Later, in trying to understand the implications of the ongoing change, we asked Mr Ham, the deputy director of the VPSU, for his point of view.

172   PROFIT AND POVERTY IN RURAL VIETNAM

Q: How have the changes affected your Union?

A: We still are responsible for six enterprises, our task is still the same: to plan, manage, and finance production and take care of the workforce and its living conditions. The enterprises report to us. And their two main tasks are also still the same: to plant forest and to harvest trees. We also borrow money on the behalf of the enterprises to invest in plantations. We still manage the final products. The infrastructure is also our obligation as well as the management of the labour.

What is new for the enterprises is that they can decide for themselves how they want to use their profits. They can generate business freely. And they do not pay tax to us as before. But they must sell only to us and certainly not to the free market. The reason is that the VPSU's main duty is still to supply the Bai Bang Paper and Pulp Mill with raw material. The selling price is now following the market, and today's price is 350,000 dong per tonne at Bai Bang.

The problem for us is that the market in paper raw materials is totally chaotic. There are many private operators now. They have no land or forest, but they are allowed to buy and sell raw material. This leads to frequent theft of our products. There are companies that combine wood sales with tourism! We have requested to the state that only those who have access to the forest land should be allowed to sell raw material.

Q: What about the logging ban in Tuyen Quang province?

A: It is still in effect. The workers survive thanks to the family economy. The problem is with VPSU and our enterprises in that province. We have borrowed money for the plantations, but we cannot repay because there is no income from the logging.

Q: We have encountered a lack of confidence between the workers and leadership in Brigade 5. Do you have any comments?

A: We are striving to reduce the administrative costs. Consequently, we often have only one or two people in the brigade leadership. However, workers have the right to protest and report to the director of the enterprise. The leader is wrong, if he thinks he can decide by himself on the number of hectares and the calculation of salaries. This is fixed by regulation.

TO BE MASTER OF ONESELF – YET SOMETHING IS LOST

During our talks with the forestry workers and other residents of Brigade 5, one expression was frequent: "We are now our own masters [*lam chu*]." This is, of course, an important and universally welcome change. For obvious reasons, the abolition of the total state involve-

Figure 40: Mrs Luong, a forestry worker in Brigade 5B. She considers her health to be normal, which means aches in the back, joints and head [EL].

ment benefits workers and others who are not dependent on subsidies and who have both the knowledge and the capacity to adapt to a self-management system. In this system the family plays an increasingly important role as the base for social, economic and cultural security.

In Vietnam, this is a step back to the period before nationalization and collectivization. Collective ownership was an attempt to abolish dependence of private wealth and establish an egalitarian society based on citizenship and solidarity. Even if this was never achieved as planned, it raised expectations among people like the forestry workers, that their contribution of labour and ideas was important to society as a whole. They had certain rights within the hierarchy of an authoritarian system.

Nowadays, the workers themselves must plan for an acceptable living. Most workers, both men and women, welcome the changes. What we have seen, at least in Brigade 5, is a situation where one

174   PROFIT AND POVERTY IN RURAL VIETNAM

system is abolished but a new one has not been created. The workers are now in a vacuum where, on the one hand they are free to develop their own economy, but on the other, they have lost their rights as employees and citizens to exert their influence through the party, the trade union and the Women's Union.

They do not have a platform any longer. Instead they compete with others who seemingly set their own priorities and use the new opportunities in their own self-interest. It is probably not coincidental that the most stringent criticism came from the women: generally, they are the people who have lost the most. As only hard labour now counts, and as they are particularly concerned with health and education, they look back to the previous system and see its advantages. It is telling that they do not talk solely in economic terms. Above all, they miss the atmosphere of mutual help and solidarity. Now you should be a master – but on your own.

It looks like the farmers in Khuoi Nieng are benefiting from the market while the workers languish in a situation which is neither bat nor rat. Doi Moi seems to have created a beast that is difficult to define.

– SCENES FROM HOANG SU PHI SUNDAY MARKET –

CASE FOUR

"All Have to Eat Rice"

TWELVE

Poverty and Environmental Degradation

BACKGROUND

In order to reach Hoang Su Phi district from the Hanoi–Ha Giang highway, travellers must negotiate two lofty passes at an altitude of more than 1,000 metres with clouds below them. Then the road twists and turns round hairpin bends for dozens of kilometres. The potholed road itself is proof of the extremely difficult transport conditions. Of the twenty-seven communes in the district, only seven are accessible by car.

Our first impressions of the parched rice-fields were underscored as we approached Hoang Su Phi district at the end of the dry season. Unlike the plains of north Vietnam and some of mountainous localities we had recently passed through, where spring rains made the trees blossom, here the vegetation withered from lack of rain. In 1991 the average annual precipitation of Ha Giang province was 3,088 mm while Hoang Su Phi district recorded only 1,746 mm.

Po Lung mountain village and Hoang Su Phi forest enterprise are typical of northern mountain locations. They are remote and inaccessible – relatively speaking. Indeed, in the northern periphery they are close to the district centre of Hoang Su Phi. Further, they are marked by low biological productivity, a degraded environment, disease and health problems, and they lack a development paradigm tailored to these special conditions (Rambo 1996).

Mr Phuong Quay Phin, chairman of the district people's committee, refers to a survey made in 1994, according to which:

- 30 per cent of the population has enough to eat and adequate clothing.

Figure 41: After unloading the horses, the men take them to the stream that runs at the bottom of a ravine [RL].

- 30 per cent face extreme poverty. They do not have enough food and clothes. They may be short of food for three to five months a year.
- 40 per cent are average. They are short of food for briefer periods, four to six weeks, but can cope.

Hoang Su Phi district is home to ten ethnic groups, the largest being the Nung (17,510), Dao (16,399), H'Mong (6,114) and Tay (5,284). The total population is 51,000. Here, the national majority is a minority. Half of the work force at Hoang Su Phi forest enterprise consists of local ethnic groups. The people in the neighbouring village, Po Lung, are mainly Nung.

We had not previously visited Hoang Su Phi forest enterprise. It deviated from the other three enterprises by having the prevention of an ecological catastrophe as its main objective. Accordingly, this case is about environmental degradation and poverty, about disease,

Figure 42: Nung woman selling alcohol at the market [RL].

illiteracy, and population growth. All this might sound gloomy. It surely contrasts with the lively and colourful market of Hoang Su Phi.

HOANG SU PHI SUNDAY MARKET

The market of Hoang Su Phi is as old as the district itself, but Sunday as market day is an innovation from the 1970s. It meets the needs of public employees who only have Sunday off. All the district centres in the mountains in the North have adopted Sunday markets. The Hoang Su Phi market has been a focal point for traffic across the border. Tradesmen from China bring goods with them and buy local products. Dealers from Hoang Su Phi go to China.

By Saturday evening people from remote areas begin to converge. By Sunday morning, further groups of people arrive by foot, often accompanied by small horses carrying their goods. After unloading the horses, the men take them to the stream that runs at the bottom of a

180 PROFIT AND POVERTY IN RURAL VIETNAM

ravine. Especially popular is the thermal spring rising from the volcanic mountains. Three small bridges connect each side of the river.

The market scene reflects the cultural diversity of the region. Women wear their ethnic attire: the Nung in black and indigo, sometimes with blue headscarves and blue waist-belts. Many women are adorned in silver jewellery: necklaces, bracelets, silver buttons on their bosoms, and engraved silver plates at the back of their headgear. They stroll in small groups and seem to display themselves on a marriage market, demonstrating their beauty and their assets. Ethnic endogamy is the rule, although not without exception.

Many peasant women are dressed in a shade of blue that bears testimony to time and many washes. The Nung women sell bundles of firewood. They also bring vegetables, grain, and cassava. They sell traditional medicines and alcohol distilled from cassava. Wine is not made from rice here. While the women rest on their heels with their bottles and plastic cans, they take the occasional gulp of alcohol themselves and offer cups to thirsty children. The women also serve meals to hungry customers.

The black and bluish colours of the Nung dominate the market and form a backdrop to the bright dresses of the H'Mong. H'Mong Hoa women wear rich garments in brilliant colours: red, green, blue, yellow, purple, white and black. Their short skirts stand out, as do their wide-brimmed hats with pearls and coins hanging from them. The garments emphasize the short and sturdy build of the women. The women sit and embroider all the time, observing what goes on around them. Yarn in clear and strong hues is the H'Mong Hoa women's niche in the market. Customers gather around them. There is a demand for yarn and for homespun black cloth. The H'Mong also sell perfumed mushrooms, a local delicacy.

The women are in the foreground of the market, while the men form the background. This is not only a visual impression; it also highlights the market as a female arena. The Vietnamese peasants look to the local market for the margins that sustain life. What goes on in the village or city markets determines to a large extent how well the average family lives. It is here that most farm surplus is sold and it is here that the most significant prices are negotiated: how much for some onions, for a pair of slippers, a piece of cloth, a bicycle chain or a package of cigarettes.

At this most important crossroad of the Vietnamese economy, Vietnamese women act as the arbiters quasi-exclusively. Nearly all market stalls are run by women. In the towns, there are few Vietnamese-run shops that are not openly or discreetly controlled by women. But not only do women form the overwhelming majority of all active merchants in the country, they also constitute the mass of customers. I would not hesitate to assert that more than half (probably a great deal more than half) of all commercial transactions at the point of sale involve no men on the other side (O'Harrow 1995). No doubt, the young women who look on learn from their mothers that women ought to keep some money in their own pockets.

The men are more discreetly dressed. Only a few Dao men wear large black turbans which give them a priestly look. However, the men are not completely absent from business. They play their part by selling horses, goats, dogs, hoes and other tools, as well as the big home-made baskets that are carried on people's backs. A few village craftsmen sell silver jewellery from their pockets. Snakes as a delicacy and as a cure for failing potency are also male preserves.

Young mothers carry their infants on their backs. The small children wear lovely headgear, often decorated with silver coins. Here and there one sees mothers suckling babies. In the midst of their misery and hardships, the women create colours and maintain patterns and designs. One can only be impressed, as the mothers carry their babies in bags on their backs. Embroideries, colourful designs, pearls and silver coins, pieces of folk art, poetry in textiles, tell of the parents' hopes for their children. Those things are not for sale.

The different ethnic groups appear to have preserved their cultural distinctiveness. They strike one as being remote from the modern

Figure 43: Small children wear lovely headgear, often decorated with silver coins [RL].

182 PROFIT AND POVERTY IN RURAL VIETNAM

world. However, when a "cultural group" from the province visits the market, entertainment and information are mixed – that is, the loudspeaker blends popular music with the promotion of family planning. Eventually, the group invites people up on stage to sing and perform. A bold and self-confident H'Mong Hoa girl accepts the challenge and comes on stage. Her voice is powerful and expressive. She is rewarded with applause and 4,000 dong. She does not hide her satisfaction.

Then two young Nung women take their turn by singing ethnic songs; or are they modern hits? How could I know? I am surprised by their self-assured style, their stage presence, and their control of the microphone as they perform before a large audience. Do they achieve this by watching "cultural groups" at the market? Do they listen to popular songs over the village loudspeakers? Do they have access to films, radio-cassettes and TV? People walk long distances to places where they can watch TV. The capacity of the modern mass-media to penetrate even remote regions and innovate cultures in the midst of ethnic distinction is amazing.

PO LUNG MOUNTAIN VILLAGE

Po Lung mountain village is part of Vinh Quang commune. The area is known for having low annual precipitation. The rainfall was not enough to water the fields, let alone the forests, which were severely damaged. From the district centre, we could see only bare hills and mountain slopes with leafless trees in all directions. Climbing higher we saw a desolate scene: apart from some expanses of green forest near the Hoang Su Phi forest enterprise and different households, there remained only scattered terraced fields like scraps on a worn-out skirt. The soil is sandy. Is this a consequence of both low rainfall and ravaged forest?

The intense desire for rain was well illustrated on our arrival, when the chairman of the district people's committee, while briefing us, shouted: "It rains!" Thunder and lightning were heard and seen in the distance, but the rain that fell was not enough to relieve the parched land. Without rain the land becomes dry and hard and no plough can work it. Last year the crop failed; the rain came too late.

Po Lung is situated at an altitude of 800 metres. To reach the village, we had to climb 3 kilometres in a north-easterly direction. Actually, there are three tracks leading to Po Lung. The first time I was guided by the village chairman. We climbed for about 11 kilometres. The two remaining roads are less steep. Even so, it took at least two hours to go to and from the village.

The twenty-nine households are scattered along the high mountain slope. They stretch over about 2 kilometres. The village has 159 in-

POVERTY AND ENVIRONMENTAL DEGRADATION   183

habitants: eighty-one men and seventy-eight women. Earlier, during the Sino-Vietnamese war in 1979, eight families were evacuated to a number of lowland districts in Ha Giang and Tuyen Quang provinces. When Vietnam and China normalized relations, the state agreed to repatriate the families if they so wished. Between 1990 and 1992, four households have returned to Po Lung.

On the way to the village, as one passes the terraced fields and patches of burnt land, one sees forest gardens. Mostly, the gardens lie near the source of water. The houses are far apart. The Nung people usually live in houses on stilts. They keep domestic animals, buffaloes, horses, goats, pigs, and poultry below the living area.

Most of the fields look barren; nobody would believe that only decades earlier they were luxuriant with vegetation. The terraced fields have existed only since the beginning of the cooperative movement in the early 1960s. Prior to that, villagers used to burn and clear patches of forest and hilltop land to grow secondary crops. The population was still small. They led a semi-nomadic life and lived on crops grown on hilly land.

Mr Lu Sao Chi, who is a village elder, related that about sixty years ago the village had only five Nung households and seven Han households. The village was founded by the Han. Later on, Nung households from Po Lo commune (and even from China) came to settle.

Prior to 1982, Po Lung was part of the Dong Diu cooperative in Po Lo commune. During the Sino-Vietnamese war, the people of the district centre at Vinh Quang commune moved elsewhere in great numbers. Consequently, in 1982, Po Lung village was incorporated into Vinh Quang commune. The change was merely administrative.

Language barrier

Po Lung mountain village was the only one where we frequently needed someone to translate from an ethnic language into Kinh, the national language. Only four of thirteen household heads or their wives could speak Kinh. No more than about ten people in the whole village spoke Vietnamese, among them four women. However, their language skills are still poor, restricted to daily talk. They could not discuss political, social or economic matters. Mr Hoang Ngoc Chuong, chairman of the village administration, confessed that he often uses Nung to communicate state policies to the officials of Po Lung.

We asked Mr Sanh, the deputy chief of the village, whether he listened to the radio broadcasts of the Voice of Vietnam? He answered that he rarely did so. He admitted that he did not understand the broadcasts very well, and scarcely read newspapers or periodicals. In the whole village, only Mr Vang San Dinh could read newspapers and listen to the radio with real understanding.

184   PROFIT AND POVERTY IN RURAL VIETNAM

Mr Dinh (40) is a Han. He returned to the village in 1990 after being evacuated during the border war. Formerly he had been in the army and in many battles. He became acquainted with many Kinh. Moreover, he is now acting head of communal self-defence for Vinh Quang commune. Consequently, he has had more opportunity to speak the national language than anyone else.

Most villagers could speak only a few words of Vietnamese, like greeting, and asking about the age and native village of a visitor, and about the prices on the local market. Mr Sanh told me that he often turned on the radio to listen to the news, but his wife objected: it was too noisy, and made her deaf.

Although the village is not far from the district centre, the roads are impassable. However, the economy is based on self-sufficiency. The villagers have no need to go anywhere to exchange goods, and the dealers are not attracted to Po Lung. During my one-week visit, I met only two Nung people from Po Lo commune who brought young bamboo shoots to the village to barter for cassava, and a Nung who visited some acquaintances in the village. Several villagers went to the Hoang Su Phi market on Sundays to buy some basic necessities.

Social activities have also exerted a strong impact on communications. All positions in the village are held by men, except the head of the Women's Union. Nevertheless, this branch of the union has only a minor role to play. Even population control and family planning is under the direction of the village chief and deputy chief.

The poor understanding of the national language is also due to poor education. Two grade 5 pupils, aged 16 and 17, are currently the best educated people in the village. In the 1970s, the village also had two graduates from a medical secondary school. They now work in Ha Giang provincial town.

THE NUNG WAY OF LIFE

The Nung people in Po Lung have preserved much of their old culture. This culture has influenced the renovation process by both stimulating and restricting it. Here I deal only with some typical cultural features of the Nung.

Not even knowing the name of one's wife

Tinh visited the family of Mr Tai Chan Chao, one of the households who returned to the native village in 1990. Mr Chao (31) is married and has two children. Tinh asked the household head to tell him the names of his family members. When asked about his wife's name, he told Tinh that it was Tai Gia Chao. However, as an ethnologist Tinh knew that according to Nung custom a married woman is called by

POVERTY AND ENVIRONMENTAL DEGRADATION   185

the family name of her husband with the middle name of Gia. This name is also used for registration and in writing. For instance, from the names of family members in the register of domicile, one cannot ascertain the name and family name of the household head's wife. Hence, Tinh asked Mr Chao for his wife's names before she married him. But he shook his head saying that he really did not know.

Tinh was surprised, but there was no evidence that he was behaving abnormally. Afterwards, Tinh asked Mr Chao about the details of his marriage. He related that he and his wife were evacuated during the Sino-Vietnamese war. In the new settlement in Bac Quang district, they both worked in the same agricultural cooperative. They got married following the agreement by both families. He asked her about her name after the wedding, but she refused to tell it to him. He could not explain why.

Indeed, Mr Chao did not really care about knowing his wife's names. Tinh thought that he was a unique case. The next day he met Mr Tai Chan Minh (33). By chance his mother was present. Happily she remembered the maiden name of her daughter-in-law, Lu Thi May (38) for two reasons. First, according to Nung custom, the mother is responsible for asking the hand of the girl on behalf of her son (after due deliberation with her husband). Second, and more important, Lu Thi May is the daughter of her younger brother. Tai Chan Minh and Lu Thi May were cousins, a prevalent form of marriage among the Nung.

Nung marriage

When Tinh asked some village officials about the marriage, Mr Tai Seo Phin made it plain that men in Po Lung frequently married women from other villages without knowing their maiden names. Until now Nung marriages in Po Lung have been carefully arranged by the parents. When asking for a girl's hand for her son, a mother sought only to see the girl's face, her state of health, behaviour and age, but she did not ask her name. After marriage, the girl would take the name of her husband.

As long as the couple are childless, they address each other by using "I" and "You". They never call each other by their real names. After a child is born they call each other by the child's name, for instance "mother of A" or "father of B".

Prior to 1993, the average marriage age of Nung boys was 15 to 16. The marriageable age of girls was from one to five years older (even up to ten years) than the boys. In this way, when the daughter-in-law went to live with her husband's family, she would be a skilled worker and could cope with household chores. After 1993 early marriages waned dramatically, especially as population control and family planning became widespread. The administration and mass organizations have

186   PROFIT AND POVERTY IN RURAL VIETNAM

exhorted people to abide by the law of marriage and the family. There are clear stipulations about compliance with the defined marriageable age: 20 years for men and 18 for women.

In a Nung marriage all expenses are borne by the bridegroom's family. The expenses are rather high for a farmer. Prior to 1990, it was customary for the groom's family to bring the bride's family 120 kilograms of pork, 200 kilograms of rice, 100 bottles of alcohol, and 1 million dong in cash. Under the French colonial regime, the bridegroom's family had to give the bride silver bracelets, necklaces, and earrings. However, in 1950 the district and provincial administrations stipulated that for weddings, the bride's family could demand only 40 kilograms of pork, 30 kilograms of rice, 30 bottles of alcohol, and 300,000 dong. The cash contributions had to be used by the bride to purchase a quilted blanket, a woollen blanket, two sleeping mats, two trunks for dresses and jewellery, and also some cloth for the bridegroom's parents. And if the bride could raise more money by growing cassava or rearing poultry and pigs, she would buy towels for the bridegroom's uncles.

Until the present day the Nung still practise the custom that the wife stays at her parents' home after the wedding until she is about to give birth. At that point she goes to her husband's home to deliverher baby. During the intervening time, before she gives birth, she would pay occasional visits to her husband's family to help with farming work such as sowing, transplanting, reaping, and doing odd jobs. Similarly, the husband would do any job required by his wife's family. However, he is not permitted to sleep with his wife at her house.

This is one reason why Nung couples are usually slow to bear children, which usually begins two to three years after the wedding. For instance, I met Mr Den San San and Mr Tai Chan Cha; each have families with three married daughters who still live with their parents. One of Mr San's daughters has been married for four years. All Mr Cha's daughters, although married to men in other villages, continue to live in their parents' home. After having a child, a couple can make a separate home. It is the duty of the parents and siblings to help them in building a home and to provide them with such necessities as tools, seeds, cultivable land, household utensils, etc.

I interviewed a young married couple. Their three-room house on stilts was completed in January 1995. It is quite simple in design and construction and was built with funds accumulated by the husband's parents over many years. They received 2 cubic metres of timber, more than 150 bamboo trees of different varieties, 500 bundles of thatch in addition to rice, meat, and alcohol from those who helped in building the house. After the married couple began to live in their own home, the husband's parents gave them an area of land large enough to sow

Figure 44: All daughters, even when married, live in their parents' home until they are about to give birth [RL].

2 kilograms of rice seed, a terraced field big enough for 2.5 kilograms of maize seed, and a terraced field with over 1,000 cassava plants.

After making a home for themselves, how does the married couple live? In this mountain region where agricultural self-sufficiency is the norm, it is very difficult to define the role of husband or wife as either principal or secondary earner. Their contribution to farming is equal. The difference lies only in the number of production links allotted either to the man or to the woman. Owing to the fact that the wife is older than her husband, more experienced in farm work and more knowledgeable about production, the wife's role is much greater in the first years of living in their own home. During the course of married life, besides working on an equal footing with her husband, she continues to take care of household affairs, and decides on major daily works. In these scattered settlements and harsh conditions, how could a man survive and live with his family if he were to oppress his wife, his sole support?

Land relationships in Po Lung

Like many other areas in the northern provinces, Po Lung village has few field plots. In this region of immense rolling mountains and forests, the average per capita land is not small, but land that can feed people is scarce.

On our way from the district town to Po Lung village along a track for people and domestic animals, numerous bare hills and mountains

188 PROFIT AND POVERTY IN RURAL VIETNAM

extended before us. On their bare flanks, patches of land have been transformed into terraces. These are marvellous achievements by the peasants, who have toiled laboriously to expand the land available for food crops. Yet, the whole area of terraced fields in Po Lung has no gravity system for irrigation. The harvests depend 100 per cent on the weather. That is probably the main reason why the households are so inescapably poor. Only one of them has enough rice for the whole year, and the rest have to mix cassava or maize the year round. According to Mr Ren San Dung, nine households are short of food from the lunar new year to the sixth month of the year.

In this region, some essentials such as kerosene lamps, iodized salt, paper and exercise books are free and subsidized by the state. We often met groups of villagers going to the district centre to receive such items.

Mr Ren San Sang, chairman of the Farmers' Union, said that the people of Po Lung have never had enough food. Still, the years when they suffered the worst hunger was from the 1960s to the early 1980s, the period of collectivization. However, since about 1985 hunger has been alleviated, thanks to the contracting out of some work links to households.

In early 1990, Vinh Quang commune gave guidance to villages about the allocation of land to households. The main principle was to divide land according to the average number of inhabitants. According to Mr Hoang Ngoc Duong, the 60-year-old chairman of Vinh Quang commune people's committee, in Po Lung the amount of land was for 1.8 kilograms of seeds, equivalent to 360 square metres. However, since people believed that this allocation was only for contracting purposes, the distribution was not perceived to be fair. Thus, in 1994 after the new Land Law was enacted, the commune advised the villages about how to readjust the distribution between households. The basis for readjustment was as follows:

- There would be no change on land that a household had contracted for since 1990 and was still utilizing.
- Households that had too much land had to give back part of it. These households could choose the land they wanted to keep, but it could not be scattered or consist of only good land.
- The households with too little land were to receive more.

This mode of readjustment was welcomed by the villagers. We met none who expressed dissatisfaction with the manner of readjustment by the local authorities.

During the interviews we learned the reasons for this. These were twofold: first it was an attempt at fairness; second, the educational level of the inhabitants of Po Lung is still very low. Their concept of

POVERTY AND ENVIRONMENTAL DEGRADATION 189

rights is very basic and they feel no envy. It seemed that they did not know or care if the land they received was more or less than the average received by others. Thus, fairness only pertained to the manner of allocation. Actually, there is a big difference between households in average land per capita, as can be seen from Table 10.

Table 10: Area of household fields in Po Lung, 1995

Household head's name	Total area (by kg seeds)	No. of household members	Per-capita area (by kg seeds)	Per-capita area (m^2)
Ren San Dung	22	11	2.2	400
Tai Chan Cha	15	6	2.5	500
Lu Gia Thi	4	2	2.2	400
Thai Chan Chao	4.5	4	1.1	220
Tai Shao Phin	12	6	2.0	400
Vang Sao Cheng	5	5	1.0	200
Vang San Hui	9	6	1.5	300
Than Van Leng	7	8	0.9	180
Lu Seo Sao	9	8	1.1	220
Lu Seo Xi (B)	9	6	1.5	300
Then Sao Phin	5	6	0.8	160
Sai Seo Ngan	12	9	1.3	260
Lu Seo Ngan	10	6	1.7	340
Vang San Phan	9	6	1.5	300
Van San Cui	6.5	4	1.6	320
Lu Sao Xi (B)	12	8	1.5	300
Tai Sao Dau	10	8	1.3	260
Sai Sao Liu	9	4	2.3	460
Total	**170**	**113**	**1.5**	**300**

Source: Notes from fieldwork, 1995.

190   PROFIT AND POVERTY IN RURAL VIETNAM

Compared to Lam Tien and Phuc Tam the differences in land areas between households are largest here. Perhaps the fair manner of allocation and the low educational level have simplified the land relationships, since there were only negligible disagreements, except in two cases of conflict over water for irrigation.

Before collectivization, this water source belonged to Mr Sai Sao Vin. Then the water source was collectivized, too. During the period of contracting work and entrusting land to farmers, Mr Lu Seo Sao was given a plot of land near the water source. After the intervention of the local authority, Mr Sao had the right to use that water as in the period of collectivization. Another conflict of water source was also solved. Of course, when one of the households was permitted to use that water source, the other one could not feel pleased.

Some households in Po Lung had to move to other regions during the Sino-Vietnamese war. During their absence, their forest and field land were exploited by other households. When they returned, these households voluntarily returned the land without any intervention by the authorities. For example Mr Luu Khay Pha, a Han, was one of the evacuated householders. When he came back, he got back the whole area of forest and field land that he had held before.

Six of the eighteen households interviewed had much less land than the average. Three of those six were classified as the poorest in the village. Is the small area of arable land one of the causes of their poverty and shortage of food? If so, is it not necessary to readjust the allocation of land? In our view the answer is no. The differences in land areas are big, from twofold to fivefold. Still, the household that has the biggest fields has only 500 square metres per capita. It would be impossible to reduce the number of poor households by a reallocation of land. Any attempt to do so would only disturb socioeconomic stability.

In Po Lung we also studied the process whereby the landowners' rights were expressed in the farmers' daily lives. In this remote and high region, where the impact of industrialization is negligible, we saw no households that employed any of the five rights. It shows that socioeconomic circumstances have a marked impact on the implementation of the 1993 Land Law.

The struggle for survival

Rice mixed with other cereals is a common dietary item for all families in the village, including the six regarded as well-to-do. We often lunched with Mr Sanh's family. Mr Sanh was then deputy chief of the village. It was probable that these meals had additional dishes in honour of the guests. We noticed that the family had two rice pots: one was for visitors with rice only; the other contained rice mixed with cereals. We asked for rice mixed with sliced cassava so as to share it with the family.

POVERTY AND ENVIRONMENTAL DEGRADATION   191

The inclement weather in Po Lung had affected the growth of wet-rice. The average rice holding per capita is about 400 square metres, and monoculture is practised on this small area. The village does not have any irrigation system to allow for double cropping. The season for wet-rice growing is from early June to mid-July. If the cultivation is delayed there is no hope of a good harvest. Because fields are exhausted, households use fertilizers. With enough manure and much effort, the rice yield is about 1.4 tonnes per hectare. The harvest is precarious because of the weather. For instance, in spite of such investment in manure and labour in 1994, Mr Chi obtained only 80 kilograms of paddy because the plants were damaged by high winds.

The upland rice grown on terraced fields and burnt lands no longer has an adequate yield because the land is exhausted. Now that the policy is to entrust land and forest to households for management and cultivation, the farmers can no longer exploit the hilly areas as they would wish to. Thus, rice is mainly derived from wet-rice-fields. However, the present productivity of wet-rice-fields in favourable weather conditions is only 56 kilograms of paddy per capita.

Cassava is the second crop of major importance for many mountain regions; Po Lung is no exception. The only difference is that in other mountain regions cassava is mainly used for fodder or for commodity exchange, whereas in Po Lung it serves as the staple for the people. The reason for this is that they earn little from rice and other sources. People here say that the rice harvest is bad and cassava planting gives a poor yield.

Several well-off families with enough manpower, such as Mr Sanh's family, planted over 8,000 cassava plants in 1994. By contrast, along the village paths there are many patches of stunted cassava, weakened by the barrenness of the soil. Only after two years does the cassava yield starchy roots of little weight. The villagers cannot afford to manure the patches, because fertilizers must be used for rice.

Among the food plants in Po Lung, maize is the only cereal plant that is well suited to the weather and soil and that grows easily here. Maize produces two crops, in April and August. To obtain a yield of 4 tonnes per hectare per crop, the farmer must devote much time and energy to caring for the maize plants. The high-yielding maize plants require much manure, and households here cannot afford additional areas for maize. On the other hand, in years with low rainfall, such as 1995, forest maize was not grown much, because the soil was too hard to hoe.

Many varieties of plants have been grown, but with poor results. The Po Lung villagers practise only extensive farming, thereby getting low economic value because cultivation is for the sole purpose of self-sufficiency.

192   PROFIT AND POVERTY IN RURAL VIETNAM

All households plant bananas. Bananas come in three kinds: Tay banana, banana with kernel, and buffalo banana with the fruits as thick as a biceps and requiring nine months to ripen. Many households grow lychees. These are rather big lychees. For instance, those grown by Mr Sanh have a trunk as large as about 30 centimetres in diameter. When we arrived in Po Lung, the lychees were ripening and several trees gave a good yield. The black cuckoos, only seen in the season when lychees ripen, were crying forlornly. Mr Den San San told us the myth of the cry of this bird and we learned that lychees have long been associated with the Nung people. Although lychees yield well in Po Lung, they have been used chiefly for consumption, and few are sold at Hoang Su Phi market. Other fruits like grapefruit, jack fruit, and mango are mainly used for domestic consumption.

Each village household possesses its own kitchen garden which is carefully fenced against poultry. In this garden people usually grow mustard greens, cabbage, pumpkin, and radish for daily meals. Sometimes they sell some garden vegetables, but the income from this is insignificant.

Less developed animal husbandry

Once food supply is insufficient to meet human needs, the limitations of animal husbandry are readily apparent, especially as regards domestic animals feeding on cereals, like pigs and poultry.

The pigs reared in Po Lung are a local breed. Mr Sanh, deputy chairman of the animal husbandry section, explained that families in the village do not rear cross-bred pigs because they had heard that they had to be bathed every day and fed fishpaste.

Only middle-income and well-to-do families can afford to rear pigs. Mr Sin Seo Phung could not rear more pigs than the one of about 10 kilograms that he already had, because his family did not have enough to feed them. Households usually rear one, at most two pigs at a time.

Poultry rearing is mainly for family consumption during worship days and the lunar New Year. Two Nung groups have different traditions as to animal offerings to the ancestors. One group uses chicken and pigs, while the other uses ducks. This affects the choice of animal for rearing.

Those animals that do not require special fodder, such as buffalo, horse, and goat, are not bred in great numbers because of the shortage of grazing land. The whole village has fifty-seven buffaloes, used as draught animals to break the dry hard land. Some well-off families breed buffaloes for sale. Mr Tai Seo Dau breeds up to eight buffaloes a year for business. In 1994, the village still had two households without breeding buffaloes. These households are entitled to borrow funds from Project 327 for buying draught animals. Each household can borrow 1 million dong.

Horses are bred and used to transport goods between Po Lung and the district centre as well as other localities. Goats are bred chiefly for sale at the market. In spite of that, Po Lung village has only thirty goats. The most active breeder has no more than five goats. Again, the main reason is the shortage of grazing land.

This area of land has become all the more thirsty for rain over the past years, particularly in the dry season. Households must take care that their cattle do not damage the land of others in violation of the customs and regulations. People dare not let their cattle roam free and they tether their horses and buffaloes. Even grazing goats are tied to a tree or pole in order to keep them within a definite area. The majority of households still breed their domestic animals under the floors of their stilt-houses.

Few supplementary occupations

Besides agriculture, the Nung in Po Lung still practise some traditional supplementary occupations. First and foremost they make horse bridles from buffalo skin. One piece of buffalo skin cost 60,000 dong in early 1995 and could be used for sixteen bridles. Each bridle can be sold for 10,000 dong. Fifteen families in the village are involved

Figure 45: Mr Si makes horse bridles during the annual hunger-months in order to feed his large family [RL].

194   PROFIT AND POVERTY IN RURAL VIETNAM

in this occupation. People usually use their free time after farm work for this activity. In 1994, the households who made the most bridles, such as the family of Mr Lu Sao Chi, sold fifty sets and made a profit of 300,000 dong.

Blacksmiths are also traditional in the Nung community of Po Lung; currently, five families are blacksmiths. They forge knives and mattocks, chains and parts of horse harnesses. They also repair old knives and mattocks.

House building is an occupation that existed formerly but disappeared some time ago. In earlier times, the Nung in Po Lung lived in mud-walled houses. Mr Lu Sao Chi related that forty years ago only one household could afford to build a house on stilts. They learned the technique from Nung in other localities. Thereafter, simple houses on stilts have continued to be built everywhere in the village and, from the 1970s, people began to construct large and beautiful stilt-houses. They had to hire workers from other localities, and from the village for remuneration in cash and kind. In the early 1980s, the carpentry work for the frame and fittings cost about 50,000 dong. The house-owner would do the remaining work using the labour of his family, relatives, and neighbours. By the mid-1980s, more and more people learned how to make the wooden frame and fit it together. Professional carpenters could no longer monopolize the construction of houses. Today, people mostly help one another without requesting any payment for the carpentry.

Consequently, no commercial activities exist in Po Lung, though the distance between the village and the market is only 3 kilometres. In order to supplement their incomes, a number of poor people must hire out their labour in the village by doing odd jobs such as digging ponds, fencing gardens, or laying stones along the canal. However, the odd jobs are scarce, providing little supplementary income to the poor to tide them over their difficulties. When I asked Mr Dung, the village chief, whether anyone was working as a hired labourer on the district site, he shook his head.

Rich and poor

What makes the difference between rich and poor in a population where almost all households have to eat rice mixed with other cereals? The average per capita paddy output of the inhabitants here is 56 kilograms per year, whereas the per capita need for paddy must be around 300 kilograms per year. This paddy yield is not sufficient for the people, even when mixed with other cereals. They must supplement their ordinary incomes by selling farm products or handicrafts in order to buy more food.

POVERTY AND ENVIRONMENTAL DEGRADATION   195

Mr Lu Sao Chi, for example, solves the food problem in the following way. In 1994, owing to crop failure, Mr Chi obtained only 80 kilograms of paddy and over 500 kilograms of maize, not to mention 7,000 cassava plants. In order to ensure enough cereals for his seven-member household, he had to sell a dog for 120,000 dong, a goat for 140,000 dong, and 400 kilograms of manioc for 120,000 dong. In addition, he sold bridles for 300,000 dong. With this amount of money, he purchased over 400 kilograms of paddy. The family also had to sell a number of other things like chickens, eggs, cabbage, and bananas to cover other daily expenses.

However, like others in Po Lung, Mr Chi not only dealt with the food problem, but also with the need for status, which constituted one of the criteria showing if he was rich or poor. Motorbikes, TV sets, and radio-cassettes have not yet become necessities here because inhabitants have no opportunity to use them.

The six well-to-do households here correspond to a middle-income household in the three other villages we studied. Families are considered rich if they have enough food (even if they mix rice with other cereals) and more domestic animals than other families (two or three buffaloes, one or two horses, two or three pigs, and some dozen chickens and ducks), and a bigger stilt-house than others.

The pillar of a big stilt-house has a circumference of over 60 centimetres. A house with a tiled roof is seen as a sign of wealth and elegance; in Po Lung there are only four such houses. Wealth and style are expressed in the money spent on constructing such a house. The house of Mr Sanh is an example. In order to tile the roof of his five-room house by the end of 1994, Mr Sanh had to buy tiles worth as much as 2.6 million dong. The tiles were produced in the Huong Canh centre of Vinh Phu province. Mr Sanh had to buy them from a merchant on the outskirts of Bac Quang district and hire a motor vehicle to transport them. In addition, he hired thirty people and ten horses to carry the tiles to the building site. The journey took three days to complete.

Mr Tai Seo Dau stands out among the rich families. How does his family pull ahead of his counterparts? He has eight family members of whom three are labourers; he has rice-fields large enough for 10 kilograms of rice seed and also patches of hilly maize land large enough for 3 kilograms of seed; and 3,000 cassava plants. Even so, this family has only sufficient cereals to mix with rice for eating or for animal husbandry. He harvests only about 500 kilograms of paddy per year. However, to make up for the deficiency, he concentrates on animal husbandry and does other jobs as well. His household has eight buffaloes (two of them calves), two horses, two goats, and two

196 PROFIT AND POVERTY IN RURAL VIETNAM

pigs. He usually buys young animals of medium weight; these will grow up more quickly and are more likely to survive.When they are well grown, he sells them and buys new young animals to replace them.

In 1994, he was able to buy an additional 2 tons of paddy from the sale of a buffalo, a pig, chickens, cassava, and firewood. He also rents buffaloes to other farmers for tilling their land. At present, he has five rental buffaloes, four of them for households in Po Lo commune, and one for households in Po Lung village. Each year, the person who rents the buffaloes pays him 1.2 quintals of paddy per animal. Now and then he hires labour to dig ponds, and to line the garden and canal bank with stones. According to his rough calculations, he had a total revenue of about 3 million dong in 1994, excluding the animals not yet sold. At present, he is the sole owner of a hydroelectric station. Thanks to the availability of electricity he has bought electric fans and radio-casette recorders for family use.

How does the Dau family get along without possessing much land or labourers? The secret lies in the way production is organized. Mr Dau is 40. He enlisted in the army for four years, from 1978 to 1982. Thus, he came into contact with many farmers and learned better ways of doing things. He has devised a scheme to maximize his benefits by using the labour of his family in an effective and rational manner. He uses only the labour of his son (15) and daughter (13) to develop the animal husbandry. Moreover, he learned how to diversify his business by renting buffaloes to other farmers. Actually, he has only to use part of his funds for buying buffaloes. The people who rent the buffaloes have to feed them and still have to pay him the rent in paddy. Thus, his family possesses eight buffaloes but feeds only three. Compared to other well-off families, the Dau family has much less labour. For instance, Mr Dung has eight labourers, whereas Mr Sanh has seven.

What is common to all the well-to-do families, is that nearly all the heads are either former soldiers or village cadres and thus have been able to meet and learn from people from the larger society.

The poor households in the village suffer from a serious shortage of food. They eat only maize and cassava for two to three months a year. Several households do not even have cassava. The village has nine such households, of which two are Han. We visited most of them. The poor live in dilapidated dwellings and nothing worth more than 5,000 dong can be found in them. Mr Sai Sao Lin had to cut down trees in his forest garden to sell firewood. If the poor beg for firewood, the owners of forest gardens let them collect dry twigs. A poor household can collect one bundle of firewood per day worth 5,000 dong, while the price of rice in early 1995 was nearly 4,000 dong per kilogram.

The poor have even gone into hill gardens of other people to beg for cassava, or to hire themselves out as labourers, or they have borrowed money from their relatives far and near as well as from wealthier villagers.

Interview with Mr Vinh

Mr Sai Chung Vinh (28) welcomed us to his newly built house on stilts. It was so skilfully crafted that it looked luxurious and enjoyed a tremendous view over the valley and the mountains. Mrs Sai Gia Luong (25) sat with their first-born, a month-old daughter, on her lap. She wore a blue ethnic dress. The scenery was irresistible. But there was hardly any furniture; what was even worse was that they had nothing to eat.

Mr Vinh's mother has been a widow since 1994. She lives nearby. She has six adult children. The eldest son has moved to another commune, and a married daughter lives outside Vinh Quang commune.

Mr Vinh and his wife have rice land for 13.6 kilograms of seeds. They share the terraces with a large family (mother, brother, sister,

Figure 46: Mr Vinh and his month-old daughter [RL].

198 PROFIT AND POVERTY IN RURAL VIETNAM

and her family). "We have worked on them for generations", Mr Vinh says. In 1994 the rice crop was 600 kilograms. Mr Vinh and his wife were short of food for about six months, and had only two meals per day. They had some cassava.

Sometimes Mr Vinh cuts fuelwood for sale on the shore along the river. In addition, he owns 0.2 hectares of bamboo forest; it was planted long ago when he was still a small child. He would also like to sign a contract with the forest enterprise. There has been no discussion about it so far.

A cock crows outside while Mr Vinh discusses his finances. The family has two pigs; Mr Vinh is considering borrowing money to buy buffaloes, goats, horses.

Q: What comes first?

A: Buffaloes. A small buffalo costs 1.2 million dong. A female buffalo could breed and I could earn money.

Q: Do you have grazing land?

A: No, we do not. Only a small area for growing fodder for the pigs.

[Futile plans! We change topic.]

Q: Has Doi Moi meant any improvement?

A: Life is almost the same.

Q: How do your conditions compare to other households in the hamlet?

A: Our conditions are worse.

Q: Compared to your father?

A: We are both poor. If there is no rain we will not find anything to eat. We are poor even though we work hard. There is no water in the fields. When we plant sugar-cane or cassava, with no rain it will soon die. Some years are favourable, some bad like this year. The rain is already late ...

Q: Have you ever considered moving to another commune?

A: Where should we move? I have only four years of education. My wife has not been to school at all. We do not speak Vietnamese. I would just be an outsider, a foreigner with no roots. All my relationships are here in Po Lung. Here everyone knows my family and they know who I am. My ancestors are buried in Po Lung. Who would support my aging mother? How could I leave my brother or my sister and her family?

Outside Po Lung Mr Vinh has no assets; in his village there are some very important ones.

POVERTY AND ENVIRONMENTAL DEGRADATION   199

Four of the poor families were evacuated during the war between China and Vietnam and returned in the 1990s. It was their change of domicile that destabilized their livelihoods. Another reason for poverty and hunger is old age without family support or misfortune, such as the death of breadwinners or domestic animals. Mr Sai Sao Lin owed 130 kilograms of paddy to other people, a debt almost equivalent to his total paddy harvest for 1994.

THIRTEEN

Customary and Modern Approaches to Forest Protection

NATURAL RESOURCES IN DANGER

The people of Po Lung are in a quandary: the natural resources are mostly exhausted. The forests have been heavily damaged. As regards the natural environment, Po Lung's location near the district centre and not far from the arterial road has been a disadvantage. It is not only Po Lung, but also nearly all areas along the road leading to the district centre that have experienced forest destruction. The ravages caused by the border war between China and Vietnam have not yet been calculated.

Forest exhaustion has exerted a direct impact on the life of the population. The forest is a treasure trove for hunting and collecting, by which means people can supplement their ordinary incomes to surmount the difficulties encountered between harvests. Now all these products seem to be almost exhausted. Centella and amaranth are the only wild vegetables still found in the forest. Bamboo shoot was common in all the mountain regions, but now it only grows in a number of forest gardens. In the 1970s, hungry people might go into the forest to dig for oppositifolius yam, an edible yam frequently found in the forest. One day of digging might yield about 20 kilograms. At present, it is impossible to find any of them even after a thorough search. Hunting is no longer practised by Po Lung villagers, although they retain six rifles. Rarely is a gunshot heard as the game birds are extremely scarce.

APPROACHES TO FOREST PROTECTION   201

We have the impression that the people of Po Lung are standing at the crossroads: down one road lies the loss of ecological balance, and down the other, the need to restore it.

Annual commitment to the forbidden forest

Customs and customary laws still play a significant role in the social life of Po Lung villagers. These practices are not written down, but are reaffirmed every year in rites and rituals forming part of the offerings and worship in the forbidden forest. On the thirtieth of each lunar January people engage in solemn celebration in the forest, which lies at the far end of the village and covers more than 1 hectare.

It is called the forbidden forest because it is forbidden to let cattle graze there and the destruction of vegetation is strictly prohibited. Exploitation of the vegetation was absolutely forbidden until ten years ago. Then the village administration allowed people to cut a number of trees to build public utilities, for instance classrooms.

According to Nung belief, the forbidden forest is the abode of local gods who protect the villagers, and of several other spirits as well. The ceremony is organized annually to solicit the gods' blessings on the entire village population. They pray for a bumper harvest, happy life, and avoidance of disease. However, the people themselves still take on commitments of mutual aid and assistance, and of forest and harvest protection.

The organizer of the ceremony is the most venerable man in the village. Each household, whether Nung or Han, must contribute 10 kilograms of paddy. The paddy is used to buy a piglet and a chicken. On the day of worship, the household heads gather in the forbidden forest. Up to now, not only the households of Po Lung village, but also of Dong Diu village participate in this ceremony.

In offering sacrifices to the gods, the most venerable man burns joss-sticks from each household head. He prays not only to the local gods and spirits but also to the king of the La Chi people to bless the village population. The old man will stand before the altar and behind him stand all the household heads. After the offerings, all participants sit around the venerable man who will recall the agreements of the people and exhort all households to abide strictly by the collective agreement. The elements of this consensus are discussed below.

Mutual assistance with funerals

The convention clearly stipulates that when there is a death in a family, other households will help the bereaved family to organize the funeral. When paying respect to the deceased, each household should bring with them a chicken of 500 to 600 grams, one glutinous rice cake, six cans of rice (equivalent to 2.5 kilograms), two cans of soya bean, one

202   PROFIT AND POVERTY IN RURAL VIETNAM

bottle of alcohol and one bundle of joss-sticks. Also, household members should participate in the funeral affairs if they are asked. To help the head of the bereaved family with his ceremonial tasks relating to the cult of the deceased, the village administration would charge three persons with the following tasks:

- receiving and measuring the offerings from different families, when they come to pay their respects to the deceased
- directing the funeral affairs such as grave-digging, coffin-carrying, meal-cooking
- serving meals to the visitors.

Protection of natural resources

According to custom, village families are not allowed to fell trees or burn forest land for growing secondary crops. Cattle are forbidden to graze near headwaters or wells.

It is strictly forbidden to let cattle graze on secondary crop lands belonging to people. Compensation has to be paid to the landowner for damages caused by cattle. Custom stipulates that a family whose cattle destroys other people's crops for the third time are fully responsible for the damage and the victims have the right to kill the beast. Its flesh is to be divided equally between the owner of the land and the owner of the cattle.

Provision of forest protection was introduced in recent years after successive patches of forest and forest land were destroyed and a sense of private ownership of the forest began to evolve among the population. In addition to the prohibition of tree felling in forest lands belonging to other people, there is still an interdict on collecting or eating bamboo shoots on such forest lands. Violations incur a fine of 5 kilograms of paddy per bamboo shoot.

We asked Mr San whether any person had violated the customary regulations in past years. So far no one had violated them. After reaffirming the customary provisions and exchanging ideas, the people will eat together as a sign of solidarity. The meal is set out on large banana leaves on the ground, and is shared by groups of seven to eight people. While they eat and drink, they talk about their respective families, their villages, the crops, and the weather. In short, they get to know one another better.

These customs and regulations not only cover Po Lung and Dong Diu villages, but also a larger area of Po Lo commune. In fact, the conventions have become a general rule for the whole commune.

The future of Po Lung village is uncertain. In spite of that, the village has undergone several changes for the better in recent years. Nevertheless, for villagers in Po Lung the concept of the market economy

APPROACHES TO FOREST PROTECTION 203

is still incomprehensible. What they really want is to rid themselves of poverty and hunger, and nothing more. That is their aspiration. In the past few years the district and village administrations have tried to find appropriate solutions to the problems of a harsh climate and dry land. The first objective is to find better kinds of plants in order to secure a higher income for the people.

New varieties of seed are introduced to Po Lung through two channels: by the state through the district agricultural service, and by people on their own initiative. In pursuit of high yields and better resistance to pests, the villagers have searched for new rice strains. Such was the case with the experimental Chinese rice strain. In 1993 a villager visited a relative in China and brought home the Chinese rice strain. When people saw that it gave a high yield (70–80 kilograms of rice per kilogram of seeds against 60–70 kilograms of the black summer rice), cultivation of the Chinese rice spread to scores of households.

Sugar-cane was planted in Po Lung in the 1970s. Canes were brought into the village by the Don Diu agricultural cooperative. At that time, under the subsidized system, nobody was responsible for this experimental planting and it ended in a failure. This variety of sugar-cane ceased to be planted after two or three years. Since 1994 five households have begun to grow it again. Two of them borrowed money from Project 327 for experimental sugar-cane cultivation.

Since early 1995, Po Lung village has grown two kinds of fruit, apricot and plum originating from Tam Hoa Chuong, a place famous for its fruit. The trees are sponsored by Hoang Su Phi forest enterprise, which is the main district organ responsible for Project 327. As regards the tree-planting technique, the managerial board of the enterprise employed officials from the district agricultural promotion service to give guidance to the peasants. Pamphlets were distributed to every household, and saplings were given free. Every registered household had to accept at least twenty saplings. Each household head who attended a training course was granted an allowance of 8,000 dong. When we visited the participants, we observed that a high portion of planted saplings had survived, at several places as much as 100 per cent.

The changes in choice of plants have been slow but steady. Like many other ethnic communities, the villagers in Po Lung adopt new techniques and new seeds and saplings by following in the footsteps of progressive farmers, because they want to avoid risks. This has meant that the change of crops has taken time to progress.

Management of forest and forest land

The land relationship regarding forest and forest land in Po Lung village is problematic. Some minor problems need to be analysed to help the reader to understand this issue better.

204   PROFIT AND POVERTY IN RURAL VIETNAM

Contrary to what we saw in Lam Tien and Phuc Tam villages, in Po Lung the number of households with a forest garden is small. Less than half of the eighteen households interviewed had inherited a forest garden from their forefathers. Frankly, the Nung have no custom for incorporating natural forest into their forest gardens like the Tay. To date all eighteen Nung households have been entrusted with the use of forest and forest land.

The household of Mr Ren Van Sang has received the largest area, 10 hectares. As with fields, the difference in size between allocated forest lands is considerable; however, only one conflict dating back to 1992 was reported. The land in question had belonged to Mr Qui for a long time. When the formalities for distributing forest and forest land were completed, Mr Ngan argued that the land near his house belonged to him. The local authority gave it to Mr Qui because Mr Ngan already had 6 hectares of forest and forest land, and Mr Qui had none.

Thus, the process of entrusting forest and forest land to the peasants took place smoothly. The ownership of all existing forest gardens was legalized. In addition to forest gardens, the households are given forest and forest land to manage and use. By and large, the exhausted forest and forest lands regenerate fairly quickly once they are entrusted to households. However, this is the protected forest at the source of the Chay River, and the interviewees found it hard to say anything about their rights and obligations regarding the forest with which they were entrusted.

Unlike Lam Tien and Phuc Tam, in Po Lung there are more than 4 hectares that still belong to the village. Here exploitation is banned, and local people have complied strictly. This part of the forest is used for religious purposes by the Po Lung people. Moreover, they have used the wood for social purposes, such as schools or houses for the needy. Clearly, the five rights (inheritance, lease, transfer, change of purpose, and mortgage of land) do not apply to the forest and to the forest land-users of Po Lung. None of the eighteen households has any intention of selling the forest. Only one household wanted to buy part of the forest if someone else wanted to sell. When we asked members from other households if they wanted to buy more forest and forest land, they laughed and replied that they wanted neither to buy nor sell.

HOANG SU PHI FOREST ENTERPRISE

In 1977 Hoang Su Phi forest enterprise was established and given the task of organizing the afforestation in four communes in the district, Vinh Quang among them. No borders of the forest enterprise area were drawn, and there was no target set. According to the director, Mr Van, the afforestation was casual and without design.

APPROACHES TO FOREST PROTECTION 205

The period between 1977 and 1981 saw agricultural degradation in Vietnam. At the same time, there was fighting along the northern border with China. Thus, the afforestation undertaken by the forest enterprise was negligible.

Until 1993, Hoang Su Phi forest enterprise applied work link contracts for growing, tending, and protecting. Unlike Tan Thanh and Chiem Hoa, investment sharing or joint venture contracts were not yet adopted. Moreover, the enterprise is located in a forest protection area at the source of Chay River, the river with the hydroelectric station at Thac Ba. Thus, strict management of the grown forest was difficult to maintain. By 1994, after about ten years of afforestation, the mature pine area covered approximately 200 hectares. Link contracts did not require the workers to be responsible for the final result of production. Therefore, the low rate of planting bare land is understandable.

Besides, since these areas are protected forest, the task of the enterprise was afforestation and not commercial forestry. The capital for afforestation came from the state budget. The forest enterprise itself had no responsibility for the final results. Afforestation depended on the budget: the rate of success was not vital for and did not benefit the enterprise. Thus, the mode of management of capital was itself a cause of the slow recovery of the bare land.

Currently, the strategic target for economic development in Hoang Su Phi district is to concentrate on three key plants: pine, tea, and soya bean. Some families obtained pine seeds from Po Lo commune and brought them to the village for experimental planting. After that, many persons followed suit. Soya beans were first planted in Po Lung some five or six years ago. In 1994 nearly all households planted soya beans and pine.

Pine was originally introduced by Hoang Su Phi forest enterprise. After a period of experimentation, the enterprise concluded that this kind of tree was suitable for planting in Po Lung. The reason for choosing pine is that it provides valuable resin.

Doi Moi initiated a new period in the forestry. The enterprises could now sign contracts with farmers. The director and deputy director of the forest enterprise briefed us enthusiastically about these significant changes in the management of afforestation. The enterprise still receives its income from the state, not the market. However, it is not subsidized any more. The enterprise grows forests and the state has to pay for them. If a farmer's household creates 1 hectare of forest, the enterprise receives 60,000 dong. The pay to farmers varies with location: a farmer earns a total of more than 2 million dong over four years for afforestation of 1 hectare of land. In 1990, 811 hectares were allocated to farmers. In the same year, the remaining areas were contracted to the farmers.

206 PROFIT AND POVERTY IN RURAL VIETNAM

The first protected forest programme, *Song Chay*, was supervised by the forest and agricultural department of the district. The forest enterprise was only the administrator. However, since Project 327 came into being in 1993, the enterprise supervises and administers the programme again.

The protected forest programme aims at saving the environment. The estimated erosion of the hills and mountains here is 2–3 centimetres per year. Since 1990, about 300 farmer households carry out various conservation projects and thereby gain extra income. The highest income is 1 million dong per year, but that involves much hard work. The average is 400,000–500,000 dong. The lowest is 200,000 dong. The peasants plant the free seedlings they obtain.

Cooperation between the local people and the enterprise is good. Since 1993 and the introduction of Project 327, the relationship has become even closer. The enterprise advises the peasants on tending and gardening, and it pays them state money for what they produce. Technical workers from the enterprise visit the peasants to advise them. They distribute information and invite the farmers to visit the enterprise. Mr Khien, a Tay, one of the eight technical workers and the head of a service group, explains:

> I am responsible for sixteen communes. The remotest is 50 kilometres away. In the beginning, all work was done through the communes, villages, and hamlets. Since 1994, we have signed direct contracts with the farmers and 104 families signed them during the first year. I believe that contracts make people more responsible.
>
> Each land unit is about one-half to 3 hectares; the size depends on the number of labourers. Whole families take part in planting trees. Most of them can cope, but not all. The state invests in pine and tea plantations on soil that is not good for food crops. The forest enterprise supports poor families with investments, but other farmers have to cope on their own. So far twenty-three families have tea plantations. We encounter some problems because 70 per cent of the people cannot read or write and Communication is hard. We have to demonstrate things by actions.

The peasants sign contracts for 5 hectares for cultivation on bare hills and unused land. They also sign contracts to tend and protect afforested areas of 20 hectares. It takes fourteen years for the forest to mature, then it stands for decades. The farmers are not allowed to cut the trees. They are not producing raw materials like most other forest enterprises in the lowlands, but are growing protected forest to save the environment. After they have completed this task, the forest enterprise will probably be dismantled, the director says. However, there is still much to do.

APPROACHES TO FOREST PROTECTION 207

Q: It is common for poor people to sell firewood on the market. Will this still be permitted?

A: People are allowed to cut dry branches. They can cut in the non-protected forest and in the forest allocated to them. However, illegal cutting has to be settled by the communal authorities. They support us. In addition, people can collect and sell resin. In fact, eighty-eight households are at present involved in collecting resin.

Mr Thanh, a Nung, is the head of another service group for technical advice and resin production. He often visits the communes:

My duty is to assist farmers to produce 19 tonnes of resin. I am responsible for four communes, the most distant being 18 kilometres away. Each commune sets up its own goals about how many hectares of forest it is going to plant and tend, and how many tonnes of resin they will produce. I work with commune and village leaders as well as directly with the families.

Because almost all households in Po Lung live far from the forest land, only the household of Mr Lui Khai Minh has entered into a joint venture with the forest enterprise to collect resin for the latter. Since 1994, Mr Minh's household collects the resin from 800 pine trees and delivers 1,440 kilograms of resin to the enterprise. Mr Minh is paid 1,000 dong per kilogram of pine resin. A technical cadre from the enterprise, Mr To Tan Son, visited the pine garden to instruct those people intending to grow pine. He showed them the best way to cut the pine tree to harvest more resin and urged learners that they would receive 100,000 dong as a reward if they signed contracts to collect resin from 1,000 pine trees.

Joint venture in afforestation

In Po Lung, the joint venture with the forest enterprise to plant new trees got under way in 1995. So far, five households have registered for the afforestation venture. Additionally, six households had contracts to protect forest, including natural and planted forest. The payment for 1 hectare of afforested land is 49,000 dong per year, and 40,300 for natural forest. Five of the six households chose to protect natural forest.

The household of Mr Vang San Diu received the largest area (8.3 hectares) and the smallest was given to Mr Lu Seo Thi (1.3 hectares). Mr Luu Khay Pha contracted to protect 2 hectares of pine forest. Besides the payment for protection, he will collect pine resin for sale. The total area of forest that households in Po Lung village have contracted to protect is 22.5 hectares. This forest area is still under the management of the forest enterprise. In addition to paying for the

208 PROFIT AND POVERTY IN RURAL VIETNAM

contracted area, households in Po Lung also have the long-term right to use forest and forest land, as in other mountainous regions.

The main forest planting workforce is now the peasant households and not the forestry workers. The level of incentive (according to the 1995 prices) is given in Table 11.

Table 11: Incentive payment rates given to peasant household by Hoang Su Phi forest enterprise, 1995

Activity	Year	Payment (dong per hectare)
growing and tending	1st	991,000 dong per hectare (= ca. 280 kg of rice, local price)
tending and protecting	2nd	550,000
	3rd	583,000
	4th	134,000
protection	5th–50th	40,000 (= over 10 kg of rice)

In regard to the land relationships, it is necessary to clarify the rights of farmers respecting the forest in terms of the above method and level of payment.

Afforestation in Hoang Su Phi is to protect nature and not for commercial reasons. The forest is not for wood or fuel, but to improve the conditions in a huge area and, more concretely, to conserve the Chay River water source, and the water power needed for the Thac Ba hydroelectric station. Obviously, the protection of the environment through afforestation is difficult to measure, since it concerns the preservation of a threatened ecology.

Is it possible for farmers to earn their living by growing protected forests? In the immediate future, if each household plants a few hectares, they will be able to make a living. But when the bare land available for afforestration runs out, and protection supplants cultivation, the prospects will change. Instead of 280 kilograms of rice for planting 1 hectare, people will receive only 10 kilograms of rice for protecting the same amount of land. Is it possible for the farmers to plant enough land to ensure a living wage?

Not even the above-mentioned method of contracting makes the farmer responsible for the final results of his work. With this form of contracting, if the forest is for commercial purposes, the farmers will receive 100 per cent payment for their work and surplus as defined in

APPROACHES TO FOREST PROTECTION 209

the contract. For protected forests, even if growth is excellent, they will receive only the fixed payments stipulated.

In considering ownership of forest land in Hoang Su Phi, it is apparent that farmers' households do not enjoy the five rights to the protected forest. Is it possible for the contract form to cover bare land and hills? To be honest, we believe that to be unlikely. It is imperative that a study be made into how to improve the way of contracting and entrusting land to farmers, so that the planting of protected forests is effective in all respects.

During our stay in Po Lung, we realized that the farmers' households do not have a clear sense of their long-term rights when they receive seedlings from the forest enterprise. We are not sure that the local authorities have clearly explained the farmers' rights to them when they plant protected forests.

From a rural economist's point of view, the study of the forest land relationship in Hoang Su Phi should have the following objective: to demarcate the area of protected forest needed to safeguard and restore the water source of the Chay River and to improve the environment. Clearly, the solution of land relationships is unlikely to restore the forest. However, resolving land relationships is a critical priority in converting agricultural farmers into forestry farmers. Detailed and concrete solutions for implementing the 1993 Land Law over protected forests would be different from those for the forests of Chiem Hoa, Vinh Hao and Tan Thanh that provide raw material to paper factories.

FOURTEEN

An Unequal Struggle for a Better Future

THE WORKFORCE

When nine forestry enterprises were hurriedly set up in the north in 1977, there was neither a master-plan for afforestation nor a feasibility study. Hoang Su Phi forest enterprise was one such creation. The state assigned it two main tasks: to protect the environment and to defend the border. The enterprise is one of five that have survived. The others were dismantled in the early 1980s as hurriedly as they were set up.

Hoang Su Phi forest enterprise was the first and only one in the district. All forest land was owned by the state. The enterprise reached an agreement with local people about planting trees on land that was not used for agriculture. In 1977, the state target was 32.2 hectares of planted forest.

The policies encouraged people to move from Vinh Phu. The peak year was 1978, when 600 workers left Vinh Phu province and 100 local people were recruited. They were single men and women between 17 and 25 years of age. The workers were organized in seven brigades, four of them in remote border areas.

By 1981, these activities were slowing down. More than 200 workers were sent to Vinh Hao forest enterprise. Five brigades, including those in the remote areas, were disbanded. A new brigade was formed by workers from these five brigades.

Workers who remained at Hoang Su Phi testify about the worst years of their lives: "The hardest years were 1977 and 1978, in the beginning when we worked near the border." From the start there were more male than female workers: about 60 per cent were men.

AN UNEQUAL STRUGGLE FOR A BETTER FUTURE   211

According to the director, young men wanted to leave their families and become public employees, while young women wanted to get married. After two years, many female workers went back to their home areas.

In the period between 1977 and 1984, all workers had stable jobs. In 1983, the enterprise was awarded the third-class Labour Order. From 1983 to 1985 young Nung locals were recruited as workers. However, from 1985 to 1990, the enterprise faced extreme difficulties. It did not receive any support from the state. No investment capital meant no regular work. From 1986 to 1989 the workers were left to survive on their own. Petty trading in tea and sticky rice kept them alive. They bought and sold goods from the market for a small profit. About twenty workers applied for termination of their work contracts and returned to their native areas to become farmers. Others had nowhere to go. They too remember their worst years:

> In the late 1980s and early 1990s, we did not have enough work and received no payment for several years. I had to rear pigs and hens. I became involved in petty trade. I bought hens, rice and soya beans from the local farmers and sold them at the Sunday market. We could only have two meals a day. We ate cassava.

> The worst years were in 1987 and 1988. There were no jobs. I did petty trading. I worked as a daily labourer, for example on road work.

In 1989 there were only 140 employees left. Most of the workers had returned to Vinh Phu. The improvements that have since taken place do not affect all workers equally:

> The most difficult years were between 1989 and 1991. We lacked food for five months and had to eat cassava. Even in 1994 we were short of food for four months.

The remaining thirty-three employees

In 1994 the remaining three production brigades were dismantled. In 1995 there were only thirty-three employees left: twenty men and thirteen women, none of them over 40. The majority of the thirty children were of school age.

Eighteen employees have married within the enterprise; thus, one can talk about enterprise endogamy. Endogamy is deeply rooted in Vietnames culture. Village endogamy is linked to the custom of making rigid distinctions between insiders and outsiders. It prevails among the contemporary families. The different types of marital alliances among the eighteen married employees are set out in Table 12 overleaf.

212 PROFIT AND POVERTY IN RURAL VIETNAM

Table 12: Categorization of marital alliances within the Hoang Su Phi forest enterprise, 1995

Type of marital alliance	No.
(a) Marriages within enterprise	
Both husband and wife are forestry workers	3 couples
Female forestry workers married to technical workers/members of service groups	3 couples
Female forestry workers married to the director and deputy director	2 couples
Male forestry worker married to the cook	1 couple
(b) Marriages outside enterprise	
Male forestry workers married to a cook, hamlet teacher or teacher-training student	3 couples
Male technical adviser married to an assistant doctor	1 couple
Female forestry worker married to a farmer	1 couple
Unmarried (one a single mother)	5 persons

We visited fifteen households, excluding the unmarried and childless workers, most of whom are young and do not yet have their own households. The fifteen households interviewed contained twenty-five employees, no less than thirteen of whom had been employed from the beginning in 1977 and 1978. The other eleven were recruited between 1983 and 1985. One worker was a latecomer from 1993.

With one exception, all those recruited between 1983 and 1985 are Nung, while the 1977–78 group is more diverse ethnically: Kinh, Nung, Tay, Hoa, and La Chi. About half the workers are from local ethnic groups. Typically, several people in the 1977–78 group have seven years of schooling, some even ten years or more. Generally, those recruited between 1983 and 1985 are younger, less educated, and poorer. The Nung workers have rarely more than three or four years of schooling. Four workers are illiterate.

The living conditions of the forestry workers

While the older workers encountered hardships due to the border war with China, the latecomers arrived when the forest enterprise had com-

AN UNEQUAL STRUGGLE FOR A BETTER FUTURE   213

pletely lost its ability to provide work and salaries to its employees. Some of those who endured the early years at the border remember how deprived they felt. Some also tell of hardships in the late 1980s and early 1990s, of all their efforts to be able to buy rice, and how they did anything to support their families. Since the Vietnamese regard cassava as fodder, they look down upon it as food for humans.

All six latecoming Nung households were short of food for two, three, and up to five or seven months per year during the worst years. Some workers had to survive on bare cassava and maize.

The workers started to move out of the collectives after 1990. At present, most families have private houses, while four families and the single workers still live in collective houses. No doubt the workers were impatient to move into private houses. They built or bought small houses with two rooms. Those who could afford them chose wooden walls, tile roofs, and cement floors, while others had to be content with clay walls, roofs of palm leaves and earthen floors. They hardly settled in before they planned to upgrade or expand the house. Mr Sep explains:

> We need to build a large house. Every evening people from the neighbourhood come to watch TV in our small house. They do not leave before 10 o'clock. This disturbs the children's school-work and prevents my wife from sleeping. The enterprise has a large cinema-like TV room, but its location in the valley means reception is not as good as here, higher up.

A couple bought a Nung-style stilt-house with 2,000 square metres of land in 1990. The thin walls are made of split bamboo. The roof is thatched. A kitchen has been added to the open basement. The clay walls have cracked. We sit and talk on low boards on the rough earthen floor in the dark kitchen. Daylight from the open door illuminates the room. Nearby is an open well with good water. The yard is littered with rubbish, and covered by brown palm leaves and logs. Two small pigs root about. Mrs Lien explains: "We intend to build a new house, that is why the logs lie in the yard. In October we will borrow some money from the enterprise."

We have just talked about the hard years when they did not have enough jobs, no pay, and not enough to eat. We ask: whether Has Doi Moi has meant any improvements. "Yes, investment loans for the poor", came the reply.

Since the workers have built their houses relatively recently, they have only just started gardening. In most cases the plot is small. Boundary issues are not yet solved, so the basis for the household economy is rather weak. For example, a Nung family has invested 8 million dong in a large house. They are now short of rice and doomed to eat cassava half the year. Yet they have a garden (without approved

214   PROFIT AND POVERTY IN RURAL VIETNAM

borders). They have lately planted fifty plum and ten apricot trees. They are also digging a fishpond.

The director regrets that due to limited access to capital the enterprise can only assist employees with loans of 1–2 million dong. The workers pay it back when they are able, and there is no interest. However, workers have been able to buy timber and logs at a lower price, and some of them have got construction materials free of charge. Some say they paid the market price and got higher quality. Friends and workmates assisted them in building their houses. No doubt, the housing standard has improved, and will apparently continue to do so.

Productive and reproductive health

Malaria is rampant in the district and the major killer. According to the deputy head of the public health centre of Hoang Su Phi, malaria was eliminated in the early 1960s, but after the liberation of the south, soldiers returned with the disease and spread it again. The government has provided the centre with DDT and has instructed people to use mosquito nets. Due to the hard living conditions, the poor cannot always afford them. The province has provided medicines and in 1991 the centre established a six-member team to fight malaria.

In 1994, the team set up a blood-testing centre. Malaria was found in twenty communes. Of 2,132 patients who attended the centre from twenty communes, 481 were identified as malaria cases. The total prevalence of malaria is unknown. Among forestry workers it appears high. Of the twenty-five employees interviewed, fourteen stated that they suffered or had suffered from malaria. The frequency was high among workers recruited locally between 1983 and 1985 and later (nine out of ten). However, one-third (five out of fifteen) of the workers who arrived in the late 1970s were also affected. Some had suffered from malaria attacks for years before they were cured; others had had access to medicine at an early stage.

> I have suffered from malaria since my childhood. I got it when I was 7 or 8 years old. It became serious when I was between 16 and 18. I had a high fever and it lasted for a long time. I took some medicine from the drug store dispensary. There are more medicines available now compared to previous years. Fortunately, I have not had malaria in the last few years. (Nung interviewee [29])

> I got malaria when I was 14 years old. I took medicine and now I rarely suffer from it. Late last year was the last time. We have mosquito nets, but owing to the hot weather we do not always use them. (Nung interviewee [30])

Some years ago, health workers still had to encourage the general public to use drugs. People did not believe in them. Today people perceive

AN UNEQUAL STRUGGLE FOR A BETTER FUTURE   215

drugs to be effective. They go to the commune's health stations for services. When they are seriously ill they attend the district centre.

Besides malaria, goitre is common, and nearly 50 per cent of the children in the district suffer from malnutrition. The Women's Union has recently provided food for malnourished children in four communes.

Q: How do you reach people in the remote settlements?

A: There are one or two healthworkers in each commune. They have a meeting here every month. It gives them an opportunity to collect medicines. They use horses for transport.

Q: Do people use traditional medicine?

A: Only some families know how to treat particular illnesses. The medicines are family secrets, mysteries. The Tay teach their daughters about medicine. Among the Nung and the Dao the daughters learn about abortion medicines. They are secret and are only used in special cases.

"When the weather changes"

Some occupational diseases are common. Nearly half of the forestry workers we met complained about backache and aching joints. Usually they feel the pain "when the weather changes". Knees and legs are especially at risk because of the walking up steep hillsides:

> I have problems with my joints because of walking long distances uphill. I have been examined by a doctor who twice gave me acupuncture. It made me feel better. I do not consider retirement yet, but if I cannot walk ... (Nung interviewee [36])

> The joints in my knees ache, sometimes also my back. I bought some traditional medicine in a wine bottle. I press it on my knees. It is not for drinking. No, I have never in my life been checked by a doctor. (Nung interviewee [38])

Mrs Loi is a victim of a work accident:

> In 1981 I was injured while working on the roads. Dynamite was used to blast the mountain, and a stone hit my head. I lost consciousness and was brought to the clinic. They kept me for a month. The stone, as large as a tea cup, hit the top of my skull and cracked the bone. Whenever the weather changes, I suffer from headaches. It happens once or twice a year and lasts for several days. Sometimes I lose consciousness and cannot work any longer. (Kinh interviewee [36])

We asked her if she had received any compensation. She replied, "Almost no money. I received some sugar. A box of milk."

The new insurance system has been in effect since 1994. The workers do not complain about the free treatment. Things have become so

216 PROFIT AND POVERTY IN RURAL VIETNAM

much better. There are more drugs available. The fact that the forest enterprise is located close to the district centre gives the employees easy access to health services, compared to those in remote communes.

No more than two children

One cause of poverty and hunger in Po Lung village is population growth. People of 30 have almost five children on average. People aged 40 or more mostly have grandchildren. Family planning has only been carried out extensively since 1993. People in Hoang Su Phi district in general face the challenge of either checking population growth or self-annihilation through poverty and hunger. The campaign for family planning is gaining in scope.

In 1992, the family planning programme was intensified in Hoang Su Phi. The birth rate in 1992 was 3.8. In 1994 it had decreased to 2.7. The party's goal is to reduce the birth rate to 1.7 for the whole country by 2000. The target for Ha Giang province is currently 2.2 and for Hoang Su Phi 2.4. Thirteen communes in Hoang Su Phi district have their own population boards. In the remaining fourteen communes such boards will be established.

One of the main tasks of the Women's Union is to promote family planning. The Union has local branches in all twenty-seven communes, and five to seven work groups have also been set up. The representatives of the Hoang Su Phi Women's Union regard it as their key task to persuade women to adopt family planning. The couples have the choice between four kinds of contraceptives: IUDs, condoms, pills, and sterilization.

In 1994, 1,297 women began to use contraception. Sterilization was introduced in early 1994. In total, 614 men and eighteen women were sterilized in that year. The first four cases were women.

Q: Are there any incentives, any kind of "bonus", for those who undergo sterilization?

A: Each person who has been sterilized receives 170,000 dong. The Women's Union gave the first four women a gift of 1 kilogram of sugar, a box of milk and a thermos flask. Parents with three or four children are encouraged to be sterilized. In fact one father had only a daughter ... Most of them come voluntarily.

Q: Not all of them?

A: Those who are already sterilized act as good examples to others. In the first quarter of 1995 an additional 210 women applied for contraceptives and fifty-one people were sterilized.

According to the figure given at the public health centre there were some twenty abortions in 1993.

AN UNEQUAL STRUGGLE FOR A BETTER FUTURE   217

Q: Does the Women's Union persuade women who expect their fifth or sixth child to undergo an abortion?

A: We do try to persuade women who are expecting their fourth or fifth child. Some years ago we paid a bonus for abortions, but we do not have the money for that any more. It is a hindrance that some women cannot come here because of the distance. It is 60 kilometres by foot from the most remote places.

Q: Do the parents pay fines for more than three children? If so, how much?

A: Since 1992, a young couple should have only two children. The fines are 50 or 100 kilograms of rice for each additional child. The amount depends on the commune. The parents have to pay the same amount yearly until the child is 18 years old.

Q: Do grandparents accept the limit of two children?

A: Generally speaking, the older generation agrees. They remember what it was like to have ten siblings.

Most female forestry workers had already adopted family planning two to three years before 1992, the official start of the campaign in Hoang Su Phi. Most of them have an IUD. There are few complaints about side-effects, although some women feel that they are "not as strong as they were before the IUD". However, they are not sure about the reason for this. It could also be due to hard work and increasing age.

By and large, the responsibility for fertility control lies with the women. We met only two exceptions. One couple uses the rhythm method which requires cooperation between the spouses. The poorest of the males, a farmer married to a forestry worker, was sterilized in 1994. His wife has had an IUD for seven years without any complications. However, 170,000 dong is a lot of money for a hungry man.

Most of the forest enterprise families have two or three children. Compared to the workers' parental families, their own families are much smaller. The previous generation had five children on average.

Forest services and resin collection

Since 1995, forestry workers' families are regarded as farmers. They can have land allocated to them or they can sign contracts with the enterprise. However, at the moment no workers are being allocated land, because they are engaged in the nursery and in providing services to farmers. Nor are long-term contracts being offered. Instead, there are only small contracts for work at the nursery: caring for seedlings and producing plastic tubes for them, besides contracts for tending and protecting 1 or 2 hectares of forest. The largest protection areas,

5 and 10 hectares, were contracted to two workers remaining in the collective house 8 or 9 kilometres from the enterprise.

Currently seventeen workers are busy with the seedlings. That is the total workforce for the foreseeable future. When nursery production began in 1977 there were three big nurseries. Today only one remains. In 1977 they produced 150,000 seedlings. The present output depends on how much the state invests. The seedlings are not for sale, only for afforestation. So far there are no forest *trais*, though some might emerge with Swedish aid, Mr Van guesses.

> The workers will have enough work for the next year. We plan to cultivate 800,000 seedlings for the next year. The enterprise sells seeds and plastic tubes to the workers at the following prices: seeds for 20,000 dong per kilograms; tubes for 15,000 per kilogram; fertilizers for 35,000 per 1,500 seedlings; insecticides for 40,000 per 1,500 seedlings.

The workers can purchase tubes, fertilizers, etc. on the open market or from the enterprise. One or two months after they sign the contract, they are provided with 20 per cent of the above investments by the enterprise. The remaining 80 per cent they will receive when they hand over the seedlings.

Thus the workers sell back tree plants to the enterprise. After five or six months, the enterprise pays 195 dong per seedling. After one

Figure 47: The workers are engaged in the nursery caring for pine seedlings [EL].

AN UNEQUAL STRUGGLE FOR A BETTER FUTURE   219

year they will pay the workers (and farmers) after assessing the results. The workers complain about the delays in payment:

> While we are waiting for the salaries, the families face difficulties. How can we manage our households? When I finish they make an assessment of the results and I get paid for it all. In my opinion they should pay it every year so that we can manage our daily lives. It would be even better if we received money every month.

> It is good that the work can be done effectively and we can earn much money. Our problem is that we have to wait for the payment.

The director is aware of the complaints:

> We can give them some money in advance. Beyond that they have to wait for the state money as we do, too: the 20 per cent advance depends on available money.

Today, the forest enterprise has three main tasks; to plant forest, to cultivate seedlings and plants, and to collect resin. In the past, the main task was afforestation. However, if the workers perform only forest services, they cannot support their families. For a time, collecting resin was supplementary income, now it has become part of the work. Before the introduction of the Project 327, no attention was paid to forest production. Things have changed, explains Director Van, and he continues:

> So far, almost all our capital comes from the state. Last year we got 35 tonnes of resin, worth 70 million dong. It is 10 per cent of our total budget. In 1995, resin is expected to cover 30 per cent of the budget. The state is not going to reduce its budget in this area, so we will have extra income. The 70 million will be used to pay the workers and improve their living conditions. The very first year we had no income from resin. In the coming years, I hope to be able to sell the processed resin. We intend to have a workshop here to process resin.

While we are talking, we ask him for his opinion of the logging ban in Tuyen Quang. "Large issues are for big men, and not for local directors. This issue belongs to the provincial and central levels."

Family and the state as guarantors of subsistence rights

In comparing their life to the life of their parents, workers typically used access to cash and food as yardsticks:

> My life is somewhat better than that of my my parents, since farmers have no money. We live a better life. My parents based everything on farming, while we are two state employees. (Mr Giang, 36, Nung)

220   PROFIT AND POVERTY IN RURAL VIETNAM

> Our life is better. We have salaries. My life is better. My parents do not have enough rice. (Mr Minh, 30, Nung)

> Our life is better nowadays. We eat meat now and then during the week. (Mr Thanh, 37, Nung)

Nevertheless, those fathers who did have non-farming occupations (carpenter, road worker, or cadre) or who owned buffaloes and horses, were rated as having a better life. Furthermore, a few individuals thought that their living conditions were almost the same as those of their parents. The significance of these subjective comparisons is difficult to assess, for we do not know if the workers compare the present to the situation faced by their elderly parents or to their own childhood recollections. However it is a perception shared by many workers that life has improved compared to the previous generation.

The forestry workers have been able to progress out of the drudgeries of peasant life. Instead of family and native community, the state guaranteed the subsistence of its employees. When the state failed to keep its promises, wage-earners were pushed back towards subsistence and its coping strategies. According to Scott (1976), fear of famine has given rise to what is called the "subsistence ethic" in most precapitalist societies. It rests on social arrangements like patterns of reciprocity, enforced generosity, communal land and work-sharing. The cohesiveness of the home village, the strength of the bonds between generations, and the celebration of common ancestors in Vietnam are all institutions safeguarding people's security. Although the forest workers have moved from their villages into the state sector, they have not severed their family bonds. Since most parents of the workers in Hoang Su Phi forest enterprise are poorer than their children, they can only provide assistance in periods of hardship:

> We can borrow something from my parents-in-law if we are in a very bad way. Four years ago, when my wife had just had a child, we borrowed about 10 kilograms of rice. (Mr Sinh, 29, Nung)

> My parents provided us with 30 kilograms of rice last year when we built our house. (Mr Phuong, 37, La Chi)

> Our parents are poor. They only support us with their labour, nothing else. (Mr Khien, 37, Tay)

Generally, parental families live in difficult conditions themselves and need assistance from their children, especially their sons:

> Our families are not able to help us. It is rather that I assist my parents with honey, alcohol and money. (Mr Thao, 32, Kinh)

Exchange of gifts is a way to reconfirm mutuality. Even when the gifts pass in only one direction, they express ever-lasting concern

AN UNEQUAL STRUGGLE FOR A BETTER FUTURE   221

between the generations. Several of the older generation are already dead, and some parents are widows and cared for by a child or a stepchild:

> My father is dead. You see, I have two mothers. My mother who gave birth to me lives here in our house. She has only me. My second mother [stepmother] had three children by my father. (Mr Van, 35, Kinh)

> My parents are both dead. I look after my second mother [stepmother]. She is ill and cannot walk anymore. (Mrs Mai, 30, Nung)

According to Pham Van Bich (1997),

> the continuous importance of kinship outside the nuclear family derives from the fact that kinship bonds provide the only means of support and service, which they cannot obtain elsewhere.

However, since the 1990s more credit is available. Especially in 1994 and 1995, the employees have been able to borrow between 1 and 3 million dong on a three-year term from the enterprise. The money has been used for livestock, fishponds, houses, and goods like TV sets and motorbikes. Some of the poorest households hesitate to borrow money, fearing that they will not be able to repay it. A few have incurred debts to relatives and friends. We have encountered no trace of usury. The forest enterprise does not charge interest.

When we asked about the most urgent needs, the answers were often very down-to-earth: enough food; enough work for the whole year; strong household-based economy. The recurrent word is "stable": stable life, stable working conditions, stable subsistence. According to Scott (1976), peasants are security-oriented and less keen to take the risks that attend efforts to maximize gain. While engaging in petty trade, workers buy soya beans, sticky rice, etc., from the peasants at the Sunday market and resell it for a small profit during the week. What surprised us was the "calculation" the peasants make: they sacrifice profit to the workers, but still sell their products to them. Considerations of security in having regular business relationships and deriving some benefit are more cogent than maximizing profit. Following Scott (1976), we can speak of the priority of subsistence concerns over profitability. Why not call this a concern about sustainability?

Those who do well, and those who still fear for their subsistence

The majority of forestry workers have seen their living conditions improve. They describe the impact of Doi Moi as follows:

> The working conditions are better. I have enough work. I can do what I like, petty trade, etc. I can borrow money to raise pigs. I have a fishpond now. (Mr Sinh, 29, Nung)

222   PROFIT AND POVERTY IN RURAL VIETNAM

There is more freedom in general and more business deals in particular. Contracts work better. Now there is work to do. (Mrs Hoa, 37, Kinh)

Things have changed. We have enough jobs and good health. We receive money in an immediate way. If we work hard we are paid for it. (Mr Ngoan, 38, Kinh)

1995 is our best year. (Mrs Lien, 38, Nung)

The salaries are not high and food is expensive, However, there have been some improvements in the last years. (Mr Phuong, 37, La Chi)

Life has not changed much. (Mr Son, 37, Tay)

The distribution of the gradual improvements has been uneven. Technical advisers have the highest salaries (300,000–400,000 dong a month). Some of them have a wife whose earnings are at the same level (assistant doctor, cook). Even a teacher contributes a regular income. We can add trading, distilling of alcohol, collecting resin, investing in fruit gardens, pigs, and fishponds, as other sources of income. Somehow, the years when the workers had to fend for themselves have evoked their spirit of enterprise. Households with the highest incomes earn up to 10 million dong. That is about half of what the wealthiest households in Brigade 481 make in a year.

Yet there are households that do not earn more than 3 million dong. By selecting the three poorest households, one ends up with Ms Luc, a single mother with a daughter. Her story sounds familiar: she cohabited with a fellow forestry worker. They separated because their parents did not agree to the marriage, claiming that the two lived too far from their native homes. The father of Luc's child left the enterprise and married a woman more acceptable to his parents. Luc's earnings in 1994 were less than 2 million dong, while she owes between 3 and 4 million to her brothers.

Mrs Mai and Mr Minh live under severe conditions. They have two small children and an old "second mother" [stepmother] to care for. The timing of events was bad for them. They became forestry workers when there was no work; now that there is work they are tied down with small children. They earned slightly more than 3 million in 1994. If they can cope in the next few years, they may be able to prosper.

There is less hope for another Nung couple. Mr Giang is a poor farmer, and being poor in Hoang Su Phi means very poor indeed. Mrs Lien, a forestry worker, earned less than 3 million dong in 1994. The year before her income was less than 1 million. Mrs Lien suffers repeatedly from malaria. They have three children aged from 5 to 14.

"ALL HAVE TO EAT RICE": RELEGATION OF EDUCATION

There is a saying in Vietnam, "All have to eat rice", which means that ensuring there is food on the table must have the highest priority: education is of lesser importance. But how will it affect the children and their prospects when Vietnam becomes integrated into the global economy and the relative isolation of Hoang Su Phi is breached? How can the children of ethnic minorities scattered across roadless land take part in the process of building modern Vietnamese society? Who will have a say in setting the terms of modernity – the party, the technocrats, national and foreign investors, other groups with vested interests like the army, grassroots movements, intellectuals, student activists? Most dialogue between the ethnic majority and the minorities requires a common language and literacy.

We asked locally recruited forest workers about their own school experiences and their hopes for their children:

> I went to school when I was 15 years old. At that time I began to learn Vietnamese. I passed four grades, thus I can read and write. Lien, my wife, spent only one year at school. Since she could not speak Vietnamese, she cannot read and write. (Mr Giang, 36, Nung)

> I was 15 when I went to school. I am literate. I can read, write, and calculate. As a son of a cadre I had some advantages. I could choose to go to school. My brothers also went to school, but not my sisters. (Mr Sinh, 29, Nung)

> At 8 I went to school and stayed there for four years. Since I could not speak Vietnamese, I only learned to read but not to write. My wife could speak Vietnamese. After five years in school she reads and writes well. We talk Nung in the family. (Mr Minh, 30, Nung)

Mr Tiep has succeeded in education. He is an exception among the Nung at the enterprise. "I went for one year in pre-school and seven grades in school. At the first grade I learned to speak Vietnamese." He also has three years of training at the vocational school in forestry in Tuyen Quang. At 36 he still wants to qualify by attending a professional training course and by learning foreign languages.

What, then, do the forestry workers hope for their children's future?

> I would like my sons to become teachers or state employees. (Mr Sinh, 29, Nung)

> I want them to go to school. They speak both Vietnamese and Nung. (Mr Dau, 40, Nung)

> Our sons do rather well at school. We hope that they will get stable jobs in future. (Mr Ngoan, 38, Kinh)

Figure 48: "Our children do rather well at school. We hope that they will get stable jobs in the future." [RL]

> We would like our children to become teachers or state employees. It all depends on their abilities. However, people here are regarded as less clever and we parents are not able to support our children in their studies. (Mr Giang, 36, Nung)

It appears that the children of the Nung, Tay, and La Chi forestry workers are bilingual. According to the parents, this is due to social mixing in the collective quarters:

> The children speak both languages equally well, but generally they use Vietnamese. They first learned Vietnamese; Nung was their second language. They grew up in a collective house where everyone spoke Vietnamese. (Mr Tiep, 36, Nung)

The closeness to the centre and the command of Vietnamese makes it possible for Nung children to be better educated than their parents. The parents do not have to pay school fees, only contributions to the

Figures 49 and 50: The village school and one of its two classes [RL].

maintenance of the school. These total 20,000–30,000 dong per year for each child. The school staff and the parents meet and agree on the amount.

Interviews with village teachers
How to prevent modernization from working against the children of the poor? What will happen to ethnic people whose thinking is alien

226   PROFIT AND POVERTY IN RURAL VIETNAM

to the logic of profit-making? Do minority cultures risk being annihilated? We wanted to explore these larger issues in a concrete context.

We met a few primary school teachers who are married to employees of the forest enterprise. Mrs Tram works at a village school. She herself went to school for ten years and studied for two years at the junior teacher training school.

> Since December 1991, I have taught at the local primary school. We can see the roof of the school high up on the hills. It takes me fifty minutes to walk there.

The school starts at 7 am. For two years her husband has looked after their little son while Tram works.

> There are thirty pupils in the class. There is only one class altogether. The pupils are between 8 and 15 years old. They are all beginners. I teach the same curriculum to all of them. Some of the pupils can speak Vietnamese, some cannot. People here belong to the Dao ethnic group. I teach them Vietnamese.

> *Q: For how many years do they go to school?*

> A: Generally only one year, but if they still have a poor understanding they have to attend one more year. They do not continue their education. However, if the local authorities open another class, I can teach them. It is reported that another class will be opened in autumn 1995.

> *Q: What do the pupils learn in one year?*

> A: They learn to read and write Vietnamese, and how to calculate; how to add, divide, and multiply. They go to school five days a week, three hours per day. I guess that about 10 per cent of the children in the commune do not go to school at all.

> *Q: What kind of problems do you face as a teacher?*

> A: The salary is late, sometimes by a month or more; sometimes it is paid on time. I run short of money. My work involves a lot of walking, 4 to 5 kilometres per day, uphill and downhill.

Tram likes her job. Her monthly salary is 280,000 dong. She also raises pigs and cultivates cassava and maize.

> *Q: You are Nung. Do you face any problems in teaching Dao pupils?*

> A: Yes, not knowing the Dao language makes it difficult. It would be more effective if I spoke their language.

> *Q: Do you have any discipline problems?*

> A: No, the pupils are good. They like to go to school. I meet their parents six to seven times a year. I also see them all on November 20, teachers' day. They offer me gifts then.

AN UNEQUAL STRUGGLE FOR A BETTER FUTURE   227

Q: Do the parents pay any contribution to the school?

A: No, except when the roof of the school is damaged or the building needs to be repaired. Then the parents come and provide labour. The pupils have to buy exercise books and pens, but they get the textbooks free.

Q: Do the teachers have staff meetings?

A: The teachers in the commune meet once a month, usually on the day when they receive their salaries. We also discuss common problems and experiences.

Q: For example?

A: We discuss the delay in our salaries. We try to find the best way to explain Vietnamese words. We talk about each teacher's plan and curriculum.

The next teacher to be interviewed, Mrs Su, has passed seven grades and a two-year course at the teachers' training school in Ha Giang. Now she works at a primary school 5 kilometres from the forest enterprise. She has to stay at the school five days a week because of the distance. She goes home by foot at the weekend. The road is very steep.

Q: Which class do you teach?

A: I have a Grade 5 class. The ages of the pupils vary between 13 and 20. There are eighteen pupils in my class and six classes in the school.

Q: What is the ethnic background of your pupils?

A: They are Tay, Nung, and La Chi. The majority are Tay, followed by Nung. They speak Vietnamese very well. I love being a teacher. I enjoy teaching the Vietnamese language and reading books and poems. I teach four lessons over three hours a day.

Q: What kind of problems do the pupils face?

A: There are not enough tables or desks, not even for the teachers. The pupils have to stand for a very long time. Some pupils have to write while standing up. The roof of the school is damaged. We have to stop working when it rains.

There are nine girls and nine boys in my class. When the school year began, there were twenty-two. Some have left because their families needed their labour. Most of those were girls. Dropping out is common. From 10 to 30 per cent of the pupils leave during the school year. By and large, good pupils drop out. Most of the oldest are forced to stay at home and work in the household. In the mountainous area, parents have to sign a paper agreeing to keep their child in school. Otherways they have to pay a fine.

Q: Do the parents pay any contribution to the school?

Figure 51: Mrs Su, a teacher, is married to an employee at the forest enterprise. They are both Kinh [RL].

A: They do not pay money, but they donate workdays. On one occasion they gave roofing materials.

Q: Do you use any punishment?

A: We tell the pupils to stop disturbing the lesson. If they do not stop, they have to do manual work, for example, cleaning the school. But the pupil might then not come to school any more. Learning here is different from other places. Parents are often not able to help their children with homework. And, as we say, "all have to eat rice". This means that producing food has the highest priority. Education comes lower down.

Interview with Mr Ngu, head of district education office

Mr Ngu, the head of the education and training office of the district, supplied the figures on education set out in Table 13.

Table 13: Teacher/pupil statistics for Hoang Su Phi district, 1995

Type of school	No. of pupils
primary school	4,755
junior secondary school	187
senior secondary school	32

AN UNEQUAL STRUGGLE FOR A BETTER FUTURE   229

About one-third of teachers are Kinh from the delta. They are bilingual in Vietnamese and usually Nung. Half of the local teachers speak four languages: Nung, Dao, H'Mong, and Vietnamese. The rest can speak Vietnamese and Nung. The majority of the teachers are Tay, Kinh or Nung. Roughly two-thirds of the teachers are women.

The district is short of teachers for junior secondary education and so it has not been possible to open classes in the communes. Only one class has been opened recently 15 kilometres from the centre.

There is also a boarding school with 270 pupils. It covers all levels, from primary to secondary school. Furthermore, forty people study at the adult education centre which trains cadres at the commune level as well as primary school teachers.

According to Mr Ngu the main difficulties are these:

- The long distances to the schools: children have to walk up to 9 kilometres.
- There are 6,250 children from 6 to 14 years who do not attend school.
- The schools have no tables or desks. Much of what has been made locally is inferior.
- Three ethnic groups face special difficulties. The Phu La have been evacuated. They have newly returned and find themselves in a transitional state. The Pha Then live in remote areas far from the roads. The Cao Lan have their settlements on the highest mountain range.
- The commune- and village-level schools are very different. The main difference is in the quality of the teachers. At the commune level the teachers have completed twelve years of school and two years of teacher training. At village level, the teachers have nine years of school plus one year of teacher training in the district. This system has undergone changes over time.
- The life of the teachers is extremely difficult. They have no supplementary incomes. The highest salary is 535,000 per month, the lowest is 252,000 dong. In the last decade, teachers used to enjoy an allowance of 1 per cent of their salaries each year. They also received a mountain allowance. Now these two allowances have been dropped. Moreover, teachers were provided with money for 2 litres of fuel for the lamps. They no longer get that either.

There have been policy changes in education since the late 1980s. According to Mr Ngu things have not improved. However, the state is reconsidering the above benefits.

The development of the commune- and village-level schools
Since we wanted to be briefed on the development of the education and its underlying philosophy over time, we went to Mr Lu Van Pao.

230   PROFIT AND POVERTY IN RURAL VIETNAM

He had started to work in the educational field in the district in 1964. He is newly retired from his last position as headmaster of the district teacher training college. He meets us with a grandchild in his arms. His house is close to a deep ravine. There is a dovecote outside the house. We enter a large high room. On the walls hang art reproductions, among them a sophisticated portrait of a Western woman, distinctly unlike the posters of the beauties that the airline companies plaster all over the country. Close to a bed stands a bookshelf. I notice an electric fan and a TV set on the table.

Mr Pao begins by dividing the last decades into three periods:

1) *Illiteracy elimination, 1964–68.* The conditions in the country were difficult, but local people wanted to educate themselves. The Ministry of Education sent more than twenty people to the district. They had to assist local authorities in training local teachers and in teaching at schools in the communes. At that time about fifty local people who could read and write volunteered to teach in the schools. The target groups were from those aged 12 to 45 in literacy classes and those under 12 in the ordinary schools. In 1965–66 almost all communes had a school, either an old or newly established. Some good results were achieved.

2) *1969–79.* [Mr Pao lights the water pipe and exhales billows of smoke.] Those twenty teachers gradually withdrew from here. The fifty volunteers either went on to further teaching or stopped working. At that point the communes only had temporary schools. Now they decided to build major schools in the communes. More classes were opened and the schools were fitted out. The quality of the education improved markedly over the initial period. However, enrolment of pupils declined because the small temporary village schools disappeared. We were short of teachers. We could not continue all the literacy classes. The remote, upland classes were dissolved. It was wartime. Still, in the second period we invested in those classes that we could maintain. We did our best to improve the quality of education.

3) *1980 up to the present.* The campaign against illiteracy continued. Textbooks were revised. From this period on the development of education has been stable. The teachers are qualified and well trained.

Mr Pao has been describing the formal system of education and neglects part of the harsh reality. The time has come to confront him with what the teachers at the village schools have told us. We ask him to comment on the differences between commune- and village-level schools.

AN UNEQUAL STRUGGLE FOR A BETTER FUTURE   231

My opinion is not very objective, I am afraid. I have struggled for a good education at the commune level. Teachers at this level have access to five or six colleagues, discussions, and books. They can exchange experiences. Those who teach at village level do not have the same conditions. There are only one or two teachers. They have to spend part of their time talking to local people and working together with them. In terms of time, they lose a lot.

The commune-level schools are part of the formal system. In my opinion, the communal schools have an important role to play. I consider them to be the backbone of education. Sometimes, the villages have to adjust their education to prevailing conditions. However, they have to consult the district-level authorities. Those who teach at village level have to live far from their families and sacrifice the good life. That might affect them.

The two kinds of schools have different structures. All pupils are equal and welcome at commune-level schools. However, we have to open village schools for the small children. They have to start at village level.

Q: What about the age distribution at the village schools?

A: We open this kind of school because we want to give all equal access to education. We cannot invest more on small remote populations. Still, there are several options for those pupils: they can continue at the commune level and some are chosen and sent to the boarding school. We are short of teachers. We should train teachers and open new classes.

Q: What are the main obstacles to creating equal access to education in Hoang Su Phi district?

A: According to my experience as a teacher over thirty years they are the following:

- transport and communication is underdeveloped
- the population is scattered
- living conditions in the uplands are very poor and people have to choose between food and literacy
- lack of teaching staff and of qualified teachers. Well-trained teachers do not want to work in remote areas
- lack of teachers in teacher training colleges.

Cultural diversity and equal access to education

Our interview with Mr Lu Van Pao changed direction:

Q: You did not mention cultural diversity as an obstacle?

A: I did not mention teaching difficulties as obstacles. However, it is an obstacle.

Figure 52: Dao mother with her child [EL].

Q: What is your opinion of Vietnamization, bilingualism and cultural diversity?

A: I think that every minority has their own way of living, their customs. At the same time that they have to preserve their cultures, they have to learn Vietnamese. Vietnamese is a necessary common language for common writing, and common documents. Those who live near the district centre communicate with people who speak Vietnamese. Tay and Nung are good at learning. The Ca Lao and La Chi are among those who face the greatest difficulties. They live scattered and far away. The H'Mong, too, live high up and dispersed.

Q: Is there any support for the mother tongue in the present education?

A: When we teach Vietnamese we also use other languages. For example, when I explain the word "cup" in Vietnamese I also use the word "cup" in the other languages. You know, I used to be headmaster of the boarding school. During the war against China, 150 students left Hoang Su Phi. The boarding school had to be evacuated for ten chaotic years. It moved from place to place. That is how I came to have a command of several minority languages.

Figure 53: H'Mong mother with her child. Will the children of the ethnic minorities have more education than their parents? [RL]

Mr Pao is a local Nung. He is fluent in Nung, Dao, H'Mong and Vietnamese, and he claims that he understands all the local languages.

The parents of Mr Pao could neither read nor write. Pao was able to attend a commune school since his parents lived in the district centre. He mentions that two of his brothers joined the army against the French. Today, Mr Pao is a father of six children; two daughters are teachers, and a son is a student at a teacher training college. His wife is a retired teacher. She is a Kinh. As a supplementary income she engages in petty trade from a clay hut alongside the roadside. Her goods are on display on a wooden bed outside the small shop – or, perhaps one should say, the bed *is* the shop.

The old Vietnamese respect for learning and scholarship is here transformed and modernized so as to make education available to all citizens. There is a strong credo in favour of equal access to education. As elsewhere, the future prospects of children are stratified. There are

234 PROFIT AND POVERTY IN RURAL VIETNAM

children who do not attend school at all, and others who go to village schools but have teachers who may or may not speak their mother tongue.

Centrally located children have access to commune schools, and some children are chosen for boarding schools or schools in bigger towns where well-qualified teachers like to work. The introduction of centralized commune schools favoured many children, but they deprived others of the little to which they had access. The children of employees of Hoang Su Phi have reasonably good prospects compared to the previous generation as well as to the children of Po Lung village, not to mention all the children on the periphery of the uplands.

ECOLOGY, ETHNICITY AND EDUCATION

By now we are familiar with some recurrent patterns of change: after years of deprivation, delayed salaries or default of payment, ravaged forests, and a state unable to keep its promises, the party adopted a gradual transformation by privatization, by return and redistribution of state-owned land, and by defining new roles for the local farmers and forestry workers.

In spite of the common features, nowhere (with the exception of area II in Vinh Hao) was the poverty as appalling, the malaria as rampant, the workers as neglected, the nature as damaged as in this case. The recovery brought by Doi Moi came late, the current practices still bear risks and uncertainities, which are particular for the *forest conservation* and the *cultural diversity* of the region.

Allocation of forest is not a universal panacea

Po Lung mountain village offers breathtaking views. The visitor falls silent before the grandeur of the landscape. The green banks of the stream at the bottom of the valley, the traces of human labour on the terraced hills, the farthest mountains merging with the sky. But the beauty is deceptive. What we learned from Po Lung village caused us to worry about the environment. This was the first time we had witnessed the environmental hazards caused by deforestation. Before coming here we were unable to imagine how most of the slopes could be bare in such a high and remote area. After working with commune and forest enterprise officials, Mr Hoang Ngoc Chuong and Mr Van respectively, we identified the main causes of deforestation:

- to satisfy demand for timber, lumber, and fuelwood in the lowland regions
- to supply the fuelwood for local demand (in the mountainous region the kitchen fire burns all day and night)

AN UNEQUAL STRUGGLE FOR A BETTER FUTURE   235

- to supply military barracks
- to clear land for swidden cultivation of food.

Nobody had told us about the predicament of the ownerless forest. This was something almost contrary to the ideas of many researchers. They tend to believe that the cause of deforestation is that the forest has no real owners to manage and protect it. Especially since the 1993 Land Law, everyone has assumed that deforestation resulted from collective ownership of forests and forest land. Now everyone hopes that the transfer of forest and forest land to the farmers will basically resolve that calamity. In other words, deforestation can be halted and the forest restored by solving the land relationship. Before coming to Hoang Su Phi, as a rural economist, Mr Ang shared this idea.

What are the real causes of deforestation? We concluded from the interviews with Hoang Su Phi officials that the three first causes are still existing, while only the fourth has been eliminated. Indeed, the other three causes are now even more acute than before because demand for wood is increasing as socioeconomic development accelerates. The three sources of demand will not decrease by entrusting forest and forest land to farmers. Thus, the implementation of the Land Law of 1993 in Hoang Su Phi has not ended or reduced the impact of deforestation. According to Mr Ang, the transfer of forest and forest land to households for long-term use only changes the manner in which the imbalance between supply and demand is tackled.

There is one major change in the local inhabitants' supply of and demand for food. Previously local people deforested indiscriminately for swidden cultivation, but nowadays they do it in that part of forest that they enjoy the right to use. This has encouraged them to find ways to increase soil fertility, and to plant crops under the forest canopy in a way that partly reduces the devastation of the natural forest.

According to the chief of Po Lung village, Mr Ren San Dung, the exhausted forest has become more vigorous after some years of care by households. Whereas both sides of the lane from the village to the district centre were once bare, now trees are beginning to grow. It is a regenerated forest of low economic value, but even this vegetation is better than bare land.

In brief, resolving land relationships by entrusting land and forest land to farmers has merely allowed everyone to manage and use a plot of forest and to reduce random deforestation. Further study is needed about whether all the poor managers of forest and forest land who lack food, can now live by forestry alone. Thus, unlike the protection of forests that produce pulpwood, and unlike land for rice cultivation, entrusting forest and forest land to households in the protected forest of Hoang Su Phi is not a universal panacea and it is not the only solution for the preservation of the forest.

236   PROFIT AND POVERTY IN RURAL VIETNAM

Where minorities are a majority

The Nung living in Po Lung village still follow their customs. Very few people have lived and worked outside the region and few speak Vietnamese. The level of education is low. But in the midst of hunger and illiteracy the villagers maintain the dignity, hospitality and moral order of an old civilization. By and large, the concept of market economy is alien and unintelligible for them.

With up to ten different ethnic groups, Hoang Su Phi district is a good example of a unique form of ethnic settlement in Vietnam, a pattern that has important implications:

> Many ideas about indigenous participation are virtually impossible to implement in the context of such diversity. The use of minority languages in primary schools presents almost unsolvable problems when a single classroom holds speakers of several languages. The presence within the same locale of so many ethnicities makes it difficult to meet aspirations of self-rule. (Rambo and Cuc 1996)

In order to make themselves heard within and outside their community and region, the ethnic minorities have to achieve bilingualism, which means Vietnamization. They need the command of a common language to enable children with different cultural origins to succeed in school. But, how to carry out Vietnamization measures without forcing children to renounce their ethnic identities? How to respect ethnic bonds while at the same time enabling the young to adopt and explore influences from a multi-ethnic environment and a global communications network?

Regrettably, Vietnamese awareness of ethnic issues focuses mainly on poverty and environmental degradation. However urgent these issues, they should not supplant issues of culture. The latter may look secondary from an economic perspective, but are often closely related to the success or failure of the chosen policies. It is worth considering how particular combinations of tradition and modernity, continuity and change, can support reforms. The ignorant and unimaginative attitudes of the majorities have often doomed indigenous people to the margins, to be seen as remnants or obstacles, fit only to perish, or to satisfy tourist demand for the exotic, as has happened in northern Thailand, where some of the same ethnic groups are spread.

We have explored how the school system is prepared to handle the challenge of multi-ethnic education. The policies appear inadequate when confronted with the complexity of the ethnic issue. Education is a keyword in the discussions of the ethnic issue. Yet education is not a magic wand, not a universal panacea, for coming to grips with cultural diversity and eliminating poverty. It appears that serious dysfunctions within the education system need to be addressed.

FIFTEEN

Summary: The Impact of Doi Moi

BACKGROUND

Doi Moi can be understood as a dismantling of the Vietnamese revolution, a stepwise deconstruction of the collectivistic, state-controlled model of modernization, and a simultaneous introduction of a market model of economic development. The adherents of each model share the goal, yet their means to achieve it originates from opposite interests and ideologies. We have tried to follow up what these contemporary transformations have meant for farmers in four villages and workers in four adjacent forestry brigades.

The villages we visited offer a perfect image of the ecology of the northern mountain region, though they are not alike. With the exception of Po Lung, the villages lie in the valley. We had to cover long distances up hill and down dale to reach Po Lung and Area II of Khuoi Nieng. Except for these two, the places we visited are not far from a market or district town. Phuc Tam was established long ago, but Lam Tien, Khuoi Nieng, and Po Lung were founded about one hundred years ago.

When visiting these four villages, one can encounter five ethnic groups, i.e. Kinh, Tay, Nung, Dao and Han. Almost every village has at least two ethnic groups. On average there are fifty to sixty families in lowland villages and twenty to thirty in northern mountain villages. The four villages under study are fairly typical mountain villages.

By evoking an image of the villages, we hope that readers have grasped some basic information about them before considering the crux of this book, namely the impact of the state's renovation policies. Our ambition was not to encompass the whole problem on a regional

238   PROFIT AND POVERTY IN RURAL VIETNAM

scale, but only to add to understanding by citing concrete cases. The road to awareness is always through concrete examples.

AGRICULTURAL GROWTH AND COMMODIFICATION

Changes in the wet-rice land relationship

Over the past half a century, the land issue has been a crucial problem for the agricultural development of Vietnam. The revolutionary changes in the land relationship since the 1950s can be divided into the following periods:

- *Land reform 1953–57.* Peasants became owners of small-scale wet-rice land. This type of ownership unshackled production and agriculture achieved a relatively high growth rate.
- *1960s–80s collectivization.* The peasants supported the Communist Party of Vietnam, and thus assented to cooperativization and collective ownership of wet-rice land. Farmers who had recently become masters of their own land then became cooperative members. In this period agriculture developed slowly. Food shortages were not eliminated.
- *Post-1989 redistribution of land.* After 1989, wet-rice land was redistributed to farmers' households. It began with the gradual and partial transfer of production links to households and progressed to a complete transfer of rice cultivation to the farmers. Agricultural production tied by collective production relationships has been released. The growth rate has increased in proportion to the farmers' wet-rice land ownership: more than 2.4 per cent from 1981 to 1988, and more than 4.1 per cent from 1989 to 1993. Food shortages among peasants that have existed for centuries have been eliminated.

The impact of Doi Moi on the wet-rice land relationship in different localities has been similar although variations are found in their steps and methods of implementing reforms. Although the settlement of land affects the vital interests of millions of farmers, the socio-economic situation has remained stable, thanks to the dynamism and ingenuity of the local leadership. This is indispensable to high and durable agricultural growth.

Despite successful implementation of Doi Moi on wet-rice land, disputes have occurred. Where the commodity economy flourishes, disputes are more serious. The severity of land issues is greatest in Phuc Tam and least in Po Lung. In Phuc Tam, the goods and money have infiltrated deeply. If the commercialization of land is the condition for shifting from a subsistence economy, Phuc Tam has begun that shift. The concentration of land here will take place rapidly.

SUMMARY: THE IMPACT OF DOI MOI 239

In Po Lung, the educational level is low. Villagers' conception of rights is undeveloped. They did not seem to know or care if the size of the land they received was bigger or smaller than the local average; they felt no envy. Furthermore, we saw no households that exercised any of the five rights defined in the 1993 Land Law. The level of dispute in Lam Tien and Khuoi Nieng villages was at an intermediate level.

Doubled and trebled rice yields

In the 1970s the state of Vietnam had decided that the mountain region should be self-sufficient in food. This was in the period when the economy was entirely subsidized by the state. In order to produce food, forests were heavily destroyed to make way for cultivation. Intensive farming was not practicable and ever more extensive cultivation areas were needed to secure a greater rice output to attain self-sufficiency. Other products of economic value, such as industrial crops, medicinal plants and herbs, and other forest products, were not yet in demand for the market.

Since the inception of the state's renovation policy, a new vitality exists in the mountain region. Farmers in the valleys with extensive wet-rice fields began to practise intensive multi-cropping. In Lam Tien and Phuc Tam the rice yield has doubled and even trebled compared to the pre-renovation period. In Khuoi Nieng people have striven to grow more and more cassava. They have created products of commodity value from their orchards and by husbandry, and have earned additional income through trading and business activities in order to get enough money for food. Food is abundant in markets brought there by merchants from the plains, the Red River, or the Mekong River delta. Access to food allows people to expand into other activities.

From subsistence to commodification

The market economy has flourished in the villages (with the exception of Khuoi Nieng Area II and Po Lung). This is evidenced by the abundance of local articles produced for sale. Only a decade ago many daily necessities were rationed; now they are displayed in shops and stalls right in the village. The goods are supplied not only by private merchants who bring them from other localities, but also by the inhabitants themselves, who fetch goods from other places and sell them directly to the villagers. This is a novelty in the lives of mountain people, who were not used to undertaking commercial activities.

In former times people would give or lend necessities to one another and there was no question of buying or selling them. This was

Figure 54: Only a decade ago many daily necessities were rationed. Now they are displayed in shops and stalls along the roads [RL].

done only with regard to community outsiders, and on the market. It is worth noting that several inhabitants of villages like Phuc Tam and Khuoi Nieng have even attached themselves to the regional merchant networks, that is to say, they have gone beyond the village sphere for commercial purposes.

Commodities of some value are chiefly produced by the people of the valley, the area for local specialities like the oranges of Lam Tien and Khuoi Nieng. A number of farm products formerly used for family consumption only, or sold as an adjunct to self-sufficiency, are now produced for sale and business deals. A number of families in Lam Tien, Phuc Tam, and Khuoi Nieng breed pigs and goats, and vast areas are cultivated with cassava for sale. Production of goods for sale has now been assumed by households with the ability to do so. The same tendency finds expression in the establishment of *trai*s, chiefly intended for commodity production.

As a result of the market economy, the labour of the inhabitants has become a commodity. Hired labour is commonplace in nearly all the villages under study, although each village has its own peculiarities. In Lam Tien people usually hire labourers from another locality; in Phuc Tham the Tay desire to work only for the Kinh; and in Khuoi Nieng people hire labourers no matter what their family lineage. This is a remarkable change for people of the northern mountain region of Vietnam.

SUMMARY: THE IMPACT OF DOI MOI   241

VILLAGE ADMINISTRATION AND RENOVATION

The village organization restored

Economic changes naturally entail social ones. This is seen in the impact of the village organization on people's lives. In traditional society, the village constitutes a unit of residence for mountain people, who have separate territories, separate social organizations, and distinct beliefs, including the cult of the house spirits. The village's role was replaced by the cooperative during the period of state subsidization and central planning. In recent years, the village organization has been restored to its former status, including the revival of the title of village head. He is the head of an administrative subdivision of a commune and holds the highest authority in the village. This is the very foundation for the consolidation of the community culture and a community mentality.

The agricultural cooperative continues to exist in three of our four villages, but it has changed. In earlier times, the cooperative assumed administrative functions such as land management, tax collection, mobilization of labourers, and even military conscription besides production. Now the command function of the cooperative has disappeared. Instead, the cooperative provides technical advice and sees to irrigation and drainage. In Lam Tien even these functions were entrusted to the village administration.

Limitations of renovation

The largest effect of the renovation policy on rural areas in Vietnam in general, including the mountain regions in the north, is to hand over to peasants the right to what they produce and create awareness of the market economy. These two aspects are linked and mutually enforcing. If peasants are handed over the right to use land and to be masters of what they produce, but the state obstructs the marketing of those products, the family economy will remain within the framework of self-sufficiency. On the contrary, if peasants are allowed to sell their products freely, but have to operate within a centralized economy, they will have no products for sale or exchange.

However, with regard to the peasants in the mountain region, there is nothing unusual in handing production over to the households, since their forefathers already had such a right. What is novel here is integration into the market economy. This requires knowledge. It gives rise to an increased division of labour and social stratification. These characteristics are unfamiliar to the majority of inhabitants in the remote mountain villages, although there are some places in the highlands where people participate in commodity economy. There must also exist favourable conditions for the production of local

242   PROFIT AND POVERTY IN RURAL VIETNAM

specialities such as the excellent tea in some communes of Hoang Su Phi district.

In our opinion, renovation has had little impact on the highlands. The situation in Po Lung mountain village and Area II of Khuoi Nieng village are telling examples. The inhabitants face difficult challenges, while financial aid from the state and other sources is inadequate. If due attention is not paid to their particular situation, they will not adapt to the market economy. This would be tantamount to abandoning them to the challenge of a competitive economy and to poverty-stricken living conditions.

FOREST AND FOREST LAND

If the impact of Doi Moi on the wet-rice land relationships is agricultural growth and social stability, there are problems in the forest and the forest land relationship which demand further study. For years forest and forest land were owned by the state and the people. In the pre-Doi Moi period, state forest enterprises were assigned the task of exploiting the natural forest. This resulted in the reduction of Vietnam's forest land from 14.5 million hectares in 1945 to 9.3 million hectares in 1994.

Thus, deforestation was not only due to the absence of a real owner of the forest (as many people maintain), but also to misjudgments made in defining the tasks of the state forest enterprises. However, if the main task was to replenish forest resources, effectiveness could not be great because of the lack of clear ownership.

The four state forest enterprises we examined were all established in the 1960s and 1970s, and they all received vast land areas which were far greater than they were able to manage and control. Considerable forest destruction took place, especially as the divergent interests of local people and the state forestry were never resolved.

When the state no longer provided capital to the forestry, the enterprises had to generate their own incomes. For example, in 1985 Chiem Hoa forest enterprise started to sell planks to the delta. In exchange, it received foodstuffs and other consumer goods for its workers. The state targets and the unofficial targets existed side by side. In 1987 the deputy director had expressed his worries that they were "harvesting too much and planting too little ".

Eventually, the Tuyen Quang province authorities banned logging which came to a halt. Since 1992 the enterprises have had to restrict exploitation and renew the forest resources. The barren hills, poor soil, and the threatened water sources in the vicinity of Hoang Su Phi forest enterprise bear witness to the urgency of restoring ravaged vegetation.

SUMMARY: THE IMPACT OF DOI MOI

The forest brigades

Being a forest worker in northern Vietnam meant that the state took care of employment, work distribution, remuneration, housing, school and health services until about 1990. Prevailing ideology dictated that all economic activities should be run either collectively or by the state. Private business was not allowed in principle.

Workers were organized in production units called brigades, a kind of total institution. A brigade had buildings for administration (housing the brigade leader's office), a consulting room, nursery, and kindergarten. It had a leader and a board of representatives from the mass organizations. The board consisted of party members.

Workers lived in long rows of collective houses, with a group of workers or a family to each room. The houses were crowded and every sound was public. They were often basic and dilapidated.

The brigade as a forestry or agricultural production unit can be understood as an effort to overcome strong rural family traditions adhering to Confucian virtues and a tight community cohesion that were seen as obstacles to social progress. Peasant families in the Red River delta adhered to blood and marital ties, to the authority of old men, hierarchy, and the subordination of women. The socialist revolution aimed at liberating the forces of production, that is family members, the young and women, from the subordination of family and kinship, first, by instituting new and more equitable family laws, second, by setting up brigades, where solidarity between colleagues and citizens would replace ties of blood. Customary rites and celebrations that reinforced family cohesion were restricted and counteracted by the party.

Typically, the members of the forest brigades were young; few were over 40. Thus, the older generation was missing and teenagers were rare. Some 60–70 per cent of forestry workers were women, most of them mothers with small children. While the image of the forestry worker is a strong male, young mothers with children around them were typical foresters. This was not an intended result of recruitment policies, but the men were in the army and often they looked for other kinds of work.

The remote locations deprived many women of the chance to get married. Single motherhood was accepted if a woman reached 30 without being able to marry. The father had to remain anonymous to prevent the reappearance of concubinage. Female workers fell into four categories: unmarried women with or without children; married women with husbands present or absent. Many of the husbands worked elsewhere and visited their families occasionally. In the everyday life of the brigade, single mothers and wives with absent husbands faced the same hardships.

244   PROFIT AND POVERTY IN RURAL VIETNAM

Although cooperatives reflected the age composition of the local populations and the excess of women was much smaller, the relationships between generations and genders were redefined in the organization and remuneration of work, as well as in decision-making.

Both workers in agricultural cooperatives and in the state forestry faced extreme poverty. What worried the forestry workers most when we met them in 1987 and 1989, was the insecure food supply. They received only 70 per cent of their rice ration and the deliveries were often irregular. Salaries were delayed for months and sometimes there was not enough work. Poverty was appalling. Generally, the mid-1980s and early 1990s were some of the worst years.

INTEGRATION OF FORESTRY AND FARMING

At the beginning, the three forest enterprises (Tan Thanh, Chiem Hoa and Vinh Hao) managed 27,000–39,000 hectares of forest and forest land, but the areas were gradually limited to 5,000–10,000 hectares. The rest was returned to the communes and then allotted to local farmers. By comparison, in 1990 Hoang Su Phi forest enterprise received a masterplan to re-establish 34,100 hectares of forestry for environmental protection only.

The reduction of state forest land made the control of swidden cultivation more efficient. Another advantage was that the rest of the land was allocated or contracted to local people who did not destroy the forest.

Tan Thanh forest enterprise started to sign contracts with farmers from 1988. The contracts took different forms over time. In the period between 1990 and 1993 Chiem Hoa, Vinh Hao, and Hoang Su Phi forest enterprises allocated or contracted land to local farmers, who then became involved in forestry. The changes in the forest relationship have had a marked social impact. They have turned local farmers into forestry workers, and forestry workers into farmers. Agriculture and forestry have been integrated. This is a promising development for the restoration of forest resources in Vietnam.

It has also contributed to improved relationships between forestry workers and farmers, hitherto restricted and strained. There are new elements of collaboration. As both the state enterprises and the cooperatives have formally transferred the education and health services to local districts, both workers and farmers now receive services at the same spot.

Initially, under Doi Moi much forest and forest land was allocated to the households of farmers and workers. This is a precondition for restoring forest and forest land. Nevertheless, our visits to four forestry enterprises revealed that forest allocation is not a magic wand

SUMMARY: THE IMPACT OF DOI MOI   245

to restore forest resources. Afforestation requires big capital; that is why forest generally recovers in a natural way.

After forest land is allocated to households, they need to be assisted with capital in order to survive commercially. This is relatively feasible in areas with supplies of raw material. However, for people who live in Hoang Su Phi and grow conservation forest to restore a degraded environment, living by forestry alone seems impossible, except during the initial four to five-year period of replanting and tending saplings. So far there is no long-term prospect. Further studies are needed into creating capital to protect and sustain forests for ecological reasons.

Reduction of workforce

The forestry enterprises had provided a large number of people with jobs while the state subsidized their produce. With the advent of Doi Moi, the enterprises had to get rid of their surplus employees. Table 14 gives an idea of the decreasing numbers of employees:

Table 14: Number of forestry enterprise employees, pre-1987 to 1994–95

Forestry enterprise	Pre-1987	1987	1994–95
Tan Thanh	–	838	230
Chiem Hoa	1,500	1,323	323
Vinh Hao	250	730	200
Hoang Su Phi	700	140	33

Many workers had reached the full retirement age, while others retired because of ill health. However, the most prevalent reason for retirement has been Regulation 176, that was in force from October 1989 to December 1991. It offered workers an opportunity to leave with a lump-sum payment, and gave enterprises the opportunity to shed superfluous workers. In fact, the enterprises reduced their labour force by up to 40 per cent under Regulation 176, although the reduction had already started and still continues.

A common household strategy for couples has been for one spouse to leave under Regulation 176 while the other continues as a forestry worker. Another common solution was for people to return to the delta by using the favourable loans opened up through Doi Moi. The proportion of those who return to the delta and those who remain in the brigades varies between enterprises and brigades. Seventeen out of forty-three retired workers in Minh Dan brigade left for the delta,

246   PROFIT AND POVERTY IN RURAL VIETNAM

as did eleven out of seventy Brigade 481 workers during the 1987–93 period. Generally, most retired workers at Vinh Hao and Hoang Su Phi returned to their native lands. Vinh Hao Brigade 5 is an exception.

FAMILY ECONOMY AND LIVING CONDITIONS

Years before official policy sanctioned and later supported privatization of social life by letting the workers build their own houses and have their own gardens, some families had already made these moves of necessity. As early as 1987 Tan Thanh forest enterprise provided its workers time to cultivate land and raise pigs to achieve self-sufficiency in food.

The logging ban in Tuyen Quang made workers' living conditions extremely precarious and this encouraged each enterprise to find temporary alternatives for the survival of their workers. Even Chiem Hoa forest enterprise with less access to agricultural land than Tan Thanh, simply had to find land for its workers. In 1993, it lent 2,000–5,000 square metres of wasteland per household. It was lent because of the prevailing critical conditions.

The first stage in an expanding family economy was a plot for a private house with a garden. The families grew rice, cassava, peanuts, soya beans, and fruit for their own consumption or for sale on the local market. Often, workers could also cultivate hill-rice between the newly planted forest rows. Breeding pigs was (and is) a common way to save money for future investments. Many households have fishponds and consume or sell the fish. They have gardens with orange trees, and even orange *trais*, which are recent innovations and considered to be lucrative.

Even the poor have access to credits for small investments. The interest rates are low (about 2 per cent) or non-existent. We found no cases of usury.

Salaries from forestry work and incomes from the family economy in the rich and average families of Minh Dan Brigade and Brigade 5, Vinh Hao, were of equal value. Salary and the revenues from the family economy each amount to half the total income. The combination of forestry and farming will become increasingly important in future.

Chiem Hoa forest enterprise has less land. Thus, the workers in Brigade 481 have taken advantage of their location along a district road. They have involved themselves in diverse business activities like buying rice when it is cheap and selling it when the price goes up; raising pigs and chickens; firing bricks and tiles; distilling alcohol; breeding and selling fish; growing fruit trees, cinnamon, and lemon grass; offering services like rice husking and rice plucking; catching snakes for restaurants in Hanoi and China. A similar enterprising spirit prevails in Khuoi Nieng village, Area I, which is located near the

SUMMARY: THE IMPACT OF DOI MOI   247

Hanoi–Ha Giang highway. Rich farmers in Khuoi Nieng counted their incomes in hundreds of millions of dong, while wealthy people elsewhere earned 20–30 million dong per year.

Besides the changes in material conditions, the workers emphasized the importance of being masters of their own lives and work. By 1994, the workers' relationship to their employer had become more limited and more task-oriented. The brigade had lost its character as a total institution. Workers had moved out from collectives and built their own houses.

The gender imbalance prevails to some extent, but the brigades are more family-like. Many absent husbands have rejoined their families.

Indeed, a dramatic deconstruction and reconstruction of values has taken place in a historic process, where young daughters and sons of large and poor delta farmer families were recruited as state employees. They faced misery and disillusion, and are now caught in a new wave of modernization by the market.

Most explanations of the failure of the state and the cooperatives refer to economic causes, financial crises, the bankruptcy of the state, shortages of food, etc. There is less analysis of how the workers and cooperative members have resisted or reacted to those parts of the socialist order that oppose the core values of the pre-revolutionary family and community relationships.

Winners and losers of a dismantled revolution

In the period of state subsidization, nearly all people faced the same situation. They lived in poverty and strained circumstances and there were not many wealthy households. In all four villages, it is now easy to find households that have become rich during the change in the land relationship. Now that profound social stratification is taking place, the differences between rich and poor are being accentuated. According to local criteria, people are wealthy when they have enough food, a brick-and-tile house, a motorbike, TV set, radio-cassette, five to seven head of cattle, and four or five pigs. Further, they have accumulated funds for investments.

The rich have made their fortune by various means. Most of them originate from poor families. They used to be cadres and soldiers who left their families to join the resistance forces or they were officials in the administration. These people had an opportunity to learn how to do business.

Brigade 481 serves as an example of ongoing social differentiation among forestry employees. Though it should be mentioned that we do not know what has happened to all those workers who already had left the brigades.

Figure 55: A well-off family [EL].

The key to economic success is diversification and the ingenuity to find and combine many different sources of income. The second major asset is labour. In regard to forestry workers, this is first and foremost family labour, although hired labour is becoming more widespread and soon may be used by the wealthy forest-*trai* households.

In present conditions, the winning households have the following assets:

- they are healthy and able couples in a stable marriage; that means two pairs of productive hands
- they no longer have small children
- they have a family and kin network for mutual support in crises and for investments
- they are locally well-rooted insiders

Some people are losers for structural reasons. They are victims of war and destruction, of global crises as well as national ones. They were

Figure 56: A poor family with a sick child [EL].

guinea pigs for an enforced ideology and an unsustainable political economy. They were not able to recover after the hardships of the "lost decades". The timing of life events went wrong for them.

The poor in the villages have nothing of value. Poor households have often met with misfortune or recurrent diseases; they have many children, or have had a profligate or even alcoholic family head. Their members have to hire out their labour to those who can pay. Nowadays, the poor among forestry workers have enough food. They eat three meals a day and live in temporary houses of wood and bamboo. Most of their children attend school. However, they lack investment capital and assets such as fishponds and cattle; they do not possess the luxuries like TV sets, etc.

The poorest of the poor are the single mothers still living in the collective houses. They eat food of inferior quality and have only two meals a day. There are twenty such single mothers in the whole Chiem Hoa forest enterprise. The trade union subsidizes them. The poor lack some of those assets that the rich have at their disposal:

250   PROFIT AND POVERTY IN RURAL VIETNAM

- *labour:* they have only one pair of hands in a situation where the number of productive hands counts
- *health:* the family has a sick member
- *family support:* they come from poor families and cannot count on assistance for investments or in need
- *food:* they do not eat well and lack the energy to switch to other kinds of work when forestry fails to provide jobs
- *flexibility:* some workers are imprisoned by the past, and unable to see new options.

The community spirit, which still prevails in the northern region, has meant that the opposition between rich and poor is not yet acute. Nevertheless, people are concerned about increased stratification. How can one find a reasonable balance between two policy options: on the one hand collective ownership, which results in chronic food shortage and uniform poverty and, on the other hand, household owner- ship of land, which results in common access to food but a widening gap between rich and poor?

Social services and family support
While the forestry enterprise and the agricultural cooperative were earlier responsible for all kinds of social services, the state has with- drawn from its role as the provider of social security.

Today, employees pay fees amounting to 15 per cent of their monthly salary into a health insurance fund, out of which the enterprise pays 10 per cent and the employee 5 per cent. The insurance covers only the employee and not the family. Children pay insurance fees at school, but immunization of small children, and campaigns against malaria and malnutrition among children continue free of charge.

Several workers who have been ill complain about the treatment they received at clinics and hospitals. They feel discriminated against as insured patients, compared to private patients who pay cash. How- ever, there are lots of drugs on the market, and people try to cure themselves.

On the other hand, the population and family planning programme that for years existed on paper only, has now been put into action. In late 1988, the government of Vietnam specified financial and work penalties for couples who have more than two children. The policy of two children is now supported by sanctions and incentives, varying from place to place. The Women's Union plays a major role in en- couraging women to use contraceptives. In Lam Tien a couple with a third child is fined 50 kilograms of paddy. The fine has been applied since 1992. In Phuc Tam, the use of contraceptives is still limited.

SUMMARY: THE IMPACT OF DOI MOI 251

There is no mention of sanctions, and the emphasis is on persuading people to practise birth control.

The family planning programme in Hoang Su Phi district became active in 1992. The fine for each additional child varies from 50 to 100 kilograms of rice, the amount depending on the commune. The parents have to pay the same amount annually until the child is 18 years old. Sterilization was introduced in 1994. A total of 614 men and four women were sterilized that year in Hoang Su Phi district. Those who agree to be sterilized receive an incentive of 170,000 dong (about US$15). Family planning services generally reached employees of the forest enter-prises some years earlier. In remote places, like Po Lung village, family planning has been carried out extensively only since 1993. The decrease in the number of children from five or six to two will, in the long term, transform the lives of women and affect the gender system.

The control of the brigade boards and mass organizations is still strong in one brigade, while it was almost non-existent in another. In Brigade 5 workers feel deprived of forums for their complaints. The breakdown of the previous order has caused discontent and anxiety. Some workers feel themselves to have been the victim of arbitrary treatment when the mass organizations no longer protected their interests. One should not forget that the role of mass organizations has been both repressive and supportive.

In line with the new economic policy, workers take an increasing responsibility for their lives outside contracted forest work. Many workers, and women in particular, worry that the state is less supportive than before. Seemingly, people look for a suitable balance between being their own masters and state intervention. Yet, Doi Moi has been followed by the celebration of ancestors and a common genealogy in family gatherings, and by the revival of rites such as weddings and funerals. Hundreds of participants pay contributions to a family fund which can be used for social support, investments, scholarships, etc. It seems that people look for security in family bonds.

In the villages of northern Vietnam the basic unit is the family and the household, not the individual. The rural Vietnamese did not change from production collective to individual identity, but moved from enforced identification with the brigade to re-emphasizing family as the basic economic unit, and family network as the source of social security. Both men and women identify strongly with what is good for the family, and tend to see themselves more as custodians of the common family interest than as self-interested individuals.

Consequently, migrant single mothers find themselves in a process of enforced individuation at not being identified with a male head of household (husband, father, son, brother, or even a brother-in-law) but just as a separate female person. Readers have surely understood

252   PROFIT AND POVERTY IN RURAL VIETNAM

that the Vietnamese team members approach the heads of households. Hardly any recognized female heads of the households exist. When a previous research team conducted a study of female-headed households, it raised such a confusion and protest in Hanoi that the label of the study had to be changed to "Women without a husband in the house". There seems to be a social logic in the male line of descent, the exclusive role of the sons in the cult of ancestors, and the headship of the family that cannot be taken over by women.

Anyhow, villagers in the north tend to identify with their families to the extent of having a "family identity". Therefore, a person who lacks family identity cannot be fully recognized and risks becoming socially marginalized. Unfortunately, the single mothers' struggle for basic survival leaves them with little chance to assert female autonomy as a viable option.

THE STATE AND ETHNICITY

According to Brown (1994) ethnicity can be defined "as an ideology which individuals employ to resolve the insecurities arising from the power structure within which they are located". Brown's focus is on the state and the state's influence on socioeconomic disparities and the advantages that accrue to those possessing a particular language and cultural identity.

Moreover, the state promulgates the national identity that defines the ideological parameters within which ethnic consciousness and mobilization of ethnic interests are bound to develop and operate. Although ethnicity is influenced by the state, it is never determined by it; and, as Brown adds, the state's attempts to influence ethnicity are always problematic (Brown 1994: 2, 4).

One can speculate about the existence of forces that might have silenced the expression of ethnic interest in Vietnam. One has been the common external enemies. The Kinh and the ethnic minorities have been united in their common struggle against the French colonialism, the US army, and the war at the Chinese border. Another force is the strong socialist ideology that disregards ethnicity at the expense of class-conflict. Doi Moi has created a new situation.

According to Brown, ethnicity as an ideology,

> constitutes a situationally generated form of political consciousness in that it is a response to environmental factors which may potentially attach to any cultural aggregate, but that it also has sufficient psychological power to act as an important causal factor in politics. (ibid.: 31)

These two sides of ethnicity are expressed in the distinction between a primordial and a situational approach. Intrinsic to primordial

SUMMARY: THE IMPACT OF DOI MOI   253

ethnicity is its character as a psychological and political kinship myth (ibid.: 258). "The kinship myth, then, is a foundation myth of common ancestry, origin, migration or history, which gives specific and dramatic meaning to the ethnic ideology" (ibid.: 7). We have described the strong bonds of family and kinship among the Kinh majority as well as the ethnic people we met. It has been said that the Vietnamese fought in a heroic and self-sacrificing way against the French and the US more to defend their families and communities, than for the sake of the nation. Ethnic consciousness undoubtedly constitutes an emotionally powerful ideological response to external threats, not least to the patterns of insecurities generated by the power of the state.

We have described the instrumental strength of the mutual family support, community-based institutions of work exchange and solidarity amongst male age associations. We have also shown the vulnerability of those who slip through the mesh of such networks.

The family, the community and the age associations are all collectivistic. Yet, both the models of modernization, the market model as well as the collective model, have been hostile against primordial units (bonds of blood and obligations, native community), in their efforts to liberate the self-interest of the individual from the class-interest of the oppressed. Would it be possible to find a workable compromise between the pure versions of those models and the interests of families? Is there a way to back up the voluntariness of long-standing commitments between people?

We know little about the conflicts and encounters that occur between different ethnic groups in the Vietnamese mountain region in the north. We became aware that some groups have been (and are) regarded as security risks since they are spread on both sides of the border between Vietnam and China. We also learned that Tay people are regarded as equals, or nearly so, by the Kinh, while the general attitude towards the minorities appears somewhat "superior" or "colonial". However, the whole issue has been newly awakened (1990s). There is a great need for research and political dialogue. This need was recognized by central authorities who look for direction.

We have compared the impact of Doi Moi on the main ethnic groups in the four villages. The 2 million Kinh migrants in the northern region have brought about economic and cultural Vietnamization of the region. The ethnic patterns vary widely in all the cases we studied. While the Kinh are usually overrepresented in wealthy households, there are significant exceptions. The Dao in Khoi Nieng accumulate wealth and expand. Although the Kinh are economically stronger in Phuc Tam, the Tay dominate culturally and they are the sociopolitical leaders. In Hoang Su Phi, the Kinh are a tiny minority.

Figure 57: Young Dao woman [RL].

Socioeconomic changes entail cultural ones, although cultural change assumes a specific character and differs from economic change. In recent years changes have been rapid. However, it would not be fair to dismiss all the achievements of the preceding period. As we witnessed in the villages, changes in material culture, such as housing, dress, eating and drinking are the easiest to effect. These changes mean acceptance of some Kinh cultural features, that is Vietnamization. Interestingly, while some material aspects of culture are derived from the Kinh, the Kinh align themselves with the spiritual beliefs and customs of local ethnic minorities. For instance, in Lam Tien and Phuc Tam the Kinh have largely accepted the custom of mutual aid and assistance for funerals and housing construction associated with the Tay and Dao. In Khuoi Nieng, the Kinh practise the Dao cult of house spirits. This may mean that the Kinh know how to behave properly towards other ethnic groups within the same village.

Figure 58: Dao youth. Note from Figs. 57 and 58 that there are several sub-groups of Dao with clear cultural distinctions, not least in the way they dress [RL].

In general, cultural and spiritual factors are rather slow to change. Nevertheless, in the past few years, because of (a) the urgency of eradicating famine and reducing poverty, (b) the extent of environmental destruction, and (c) the strong impact of the law and of information, communication, and education campaigns, old ideas have undergone fundamental change. A good example is the momentum achieved by the population control and family planning programmes.

In places like Lam Tien and Phuc Tam, and in all four forest enterprises, television has become a common feature of life each evening. There are not enough television sets in the village, but owing to the community spirit, persons of one household are welcome to watch television in another household. Television programmes attract a large audience both as a recreational activity and as an educational resource on science and technology, not to mention personal financial advance-

Figures 59 and 60: All children are eager to learn [RL].

ment. In Khuoi Nieng there is not yet a receiver, so the village cannot pick up TV signals from the central station. However, Brigade 5 at Vinh Hao forest enterprise has a parabola antenna, so the villagers go there. The TV audience is mainly composed of children and adolescents.

Radio sets and radio-cassette recorders are quite common as people can now afford them. These changes are easy to see. There is also a deeper change, that is a modification of traditional culture.

SUMMARY: THE IMPACT OF DOI MOI 257

The multi-ethnic state and education

It is a matter of regret that village education has not kept in step with the economic changes. The populations of Lam Tien, Khuoi Nieng, and Po Lung villages are unaware of this matter. The peasants are more eager to enrich themselves than attend to their children's schooling. One place where there is strong economic development is Area I in Khuoi Nieng village, but education there is negligible. The Dao majority in the village have only one pupil in grade 4 of primary school. By and large forestry workers are more aware of their children's need of education.

There are indications of a widening gap in the next generation. The introduction of tuition fees after primary school, the demands by all schools for contributions for different purposes, and the cost for extra lessons after school hours, have made education more and more expensive. In addition, the need for helping hands on farms etc. means that many rural households cannot dispense with their children and adolescents. As a Vietnamese saying puts it, "all have to eat rice." For the poor, food has a higher priority than literacy.

While the Tay children in Lam Tien leave school at an early age, the Kinh children excel in education. In Phuc Tam the Tay children progress, while the Kinh pupils lag behind. What is true of children of the poor is even truer of poor children from ethnic groups with limited access to education. Poor minority children are especially vulnerable for the following reasons:

- Many of them do not speak Vietnamese.
- The methods of teaching do not reflect the special needs and aptitudes of minority children.
- They do not have access to extra lessons.
- Parents are unable to help them with their school work.
- They may suffer from malnutrition.
- Many of them live far from communal schools.
- Transport and communication are underdeveloped.
- Well-trained teachers do not want to work in remote areas.

The children need a command of the national language, but functional Vietnamization has to be achieved without forcing children to renounce their ethnic identities. They need to be able to adapt and explore cultural artefacts and influences within an environment of cultural diversity and new global communication networks. There is also need for education about other ethnic groups for children of the majority, as well as the general public in Vietnam.

Epilogue

The transformation of Vietnam proceeds. While the socialist model has fallen into disrepute, the market model triumphs. It has provided food, consumer goods, and purchasing power; it has done away with obstacles for trade and exchange; it has allotted land, and promoted general wealth. The obvious gains tend to mask the costs: tensions and contradictions, losers and excluded groups. The mass poverty that prevailed before Doi Moi makes the emphasis on economic and material progress understandable. We have reported improvements in terms of economic diversification, income and commodification, but this does not tell the whole story: there are important issues we have left out.

However, we have explored the usage of mutual support within family, community, the brigades, and the revolution. Yet, the logic of economic development tends to substitute relationships of reciprocity by economic ones. The villagers in Lam Tien hesitated to use hired labour. Did they feel it degrading? Money depersonalizes human relationships; it takes away other obligations. Paying makes you free, that is one reason why economic exchange brings with it "a decomposing of the social tissue and a disintegrating of ties of solidarity" (N'Dione *et al.*, 1997: 373). Economy has to be tamed by social and moral values, and undue collectivistic meddling has to be restrained by economic options. In this manner social reciprocity becomes an indispensable value in the prevention of processes where winners are separated from the losers.

References

Barry, Kathleen (ed.) (1996) Vietnam's Women in Transition, London: MacMillan; New York: St. Martin Press.

Brown, David (1994) *The State and Ethnic Politics in South-East Asia*, London and New York: Routledge.

Colloquium on "Women, Employment and Family". Mimeo. Hanoi, 1983.

Fforde, Adam and Stefan de Vylder (1996) *From Plan to Market; The Economic Transition in Vietnam*, Colorado and Oxford: Westview Press.

Gammeltoft, Tine Mette (1997) "Women's Bodies, Women's Worries, Health and Family Planning in a Vietnamese Commune", PhD thesis, Institute of Anthropology, University of Copenhagen

Hy Van Luong (1992) *Revolution in the Village. Tradition and Transformation in North Vietnam, 1925–1988*, Honolulu: University of Hawaii Press.

Huard, Pierre and Maurice Durand (1954) *Connaissance du Vietnam*, Hanoi: École Française d'Extreme Orient.

Larsson, Katarina and Lars-Erik Birgegård (1985) *Living Conditions of the Forestry Workers at Bai Bang Pulp and Paper Mill*, Stockholm: SIDA.

Law on Land [approved by the legislature IX of the National Assembly of SRV] (1993) Hanoi: Vietnam Trade Information Centre.

Liljeström, Rita (1987) *The Living Conditions of the Forestry Workers with Particular Attention to Women*, Part 2, Stockholm: SIDA.

Liljeström, Rita and Tuong Lai (1991) *Sociological Studies on the Vietnamese Family*, Hanoi: Social Sciences Publishing House.

260 PROFIT AND POVERTY IN RURAL VIETNAM

Liljeström, Rita, Adam Fforde and Bo Ohlsson (1987) *The Living Conditions of the Forestry Workers Associated with the Bai Bang Project*, Main Report, Stockholm: SIDA.

Liljeström, Rita, Adam Fforde and Bo Ohlsson (1988) *Migrants by Necessity*, SIDA Evaluation Report No 1/88, SIDA, Stockholm.

Lindskog, Eva (1989) *Final Report of the Forestry Workers' Living Conditions Programme, Vinh Phu Pulp and Paper Mill Project*, Scanmanagement, Bai Bang, Project report.

Lindskog, Eva (1993) *Participatory Rural Appraisal for TFAP: People's Participation in the Design of a Small-Scale Rural Development Project in Tin Yen District, Quang Ninh Province, Vietnam*, Rome: FAO.

Ljunggren, Börje (ed), (1993) *The Challenge of Reform in Indochina*, Cambridge, Mass: Harvard Institute for International Development.

N'Dione, Emmanuel Seni, Philippe de Leener, Jean Pierre Perier, Mamadou Ndiaye and Pierre Jacolin "Reinventing the Present: The Chodak Experience in Senegal" (1997) in Majid, Rahnema and Victoria Bawtree (eds) *The Post-Development Reader*, Zed Books; London and New Jersey: Dhaka: University Press Ltd; Halifax, Nova Scotia: Fernwood Publishing; David Philip, Cape Town: David Philip.

Nhung bien noi ve kinh te - van hoa o cac tinh mien nui phia bac (1993) [Economic and Cultural Changes in the Mountainous Provinces of the North], Hanoi: Nha xuat ban khoa hoc xa hoi.

Norlund, Irene, Carolyn L. Gates and Vu Cao Dam (eds) (1995) *Vietnam in a Changing World*, London: Curzon Press.

O'Harrow, Stephen (1995) "Vietnamese Women and Confucianism: Creating Spaces from Patriarchy", in Wazir Jahan Karim (ed.), *Male and Female in Developing Southeast Asia*, Oxford/Washington DC: Berg Publishers.

Pham Bich San (1995) "Social Implications of the Economic Renovation in Vietnam", Paper presented at the seminar on Doi Moi in Vietnam, September 1995, Stockholm.

Pham Cao Duong (1985) *Vietnamese Peasants under French Domination 1861–1945*, Berkeley: Center for South and Southeast Asia Studies, University of California.

Phan Huy Le, Tu Chi, Nguyen Duc Nghinh, Duong Kinh Quoc, Cao Van Bien, Phan Dai Doan, Huy Vu, To Lan, Mguyen Khac Tung,

REFERENCES   261

Nguyen Danh Nhiet, Chuong Than, Phan Xuan Nam, Nguyen Sinh (1993) *The Traditional Village in Vietnam* , Hanoi: The Gioi Publishers.

Pham Van Bich (1997) "Changes of Vietnamese Family in the Red River Delta", forthcoming PhD thesis, Institute of Sociology, Göteborg University.

Rambo, Terry A. and Le Trong Cuc (1996) *Development Trends in Vietnam's Northern Mountain Region*, Report to SIDA

Rubin, Susanne (1987) Fieldnotes from Chiem Hoa, Memo.

Scott, James (1976) *The Moral Economy of the Peasant*, New Haven, Conn.: Yale University Press.

Turley, William and Marc Selden (eds), (1993) *Reinventing Vietnamese Socialism, Doi Moi in Comparative Perspective*, Colorado and Oxford: Westview Press.

Index

ancestors 77, 251
  cult of 52–53
  worship of 53

animal husbandry 34, 86–87, 192–3, 195, 201

associations
  "fellow villagers" 90
  housing construction 90–91, 254
  of (male) age groups 22, 253
  of village elders 41,79
  Tung Khoa 22,90

Bai Bang Paper and Pulp Mill 95, 152, 162, 171–172

bananas 192

banks 60, 87, 163. *See also* loans

bilingualism 93, 223–224, 226, 229, 232, 236

Brigade 481 3, 76–130 *passim*, 158, 222, 246–247

brigades 75, 127, 243. *See also* forestry enterprise; state; trade union
  as production unit 75, 104–106, 243
  embrace workers' whole lives 75–76
  population of 103, 113

buffalo. *See* animal husbandry

Cao Lan 77, 229

cash-crops 61, 155, 163. *See also* bananas; cassava; oranges; rice; tea; *trais*

cassava 105, 125, 139–140, 145–146, 149, 188, 191

cattle. *See* animal husbandry

Chiem Hoa (forest enterprise) 3, 76–130 *passim*, 242–246

child labour. *See* poor households

children 22, 47–48, 55–57, 66–68, 88, 103, 117–118. *See also* education; family; family planning; single mothers

China
  1979 border war. *See* Sino–Vietnamese war
  migration from. *See* ethnic minorities

Co Lao 134

collectivization 8, 18, 75, 188, 190, 238

commodity economy 33–34, 84–88, 127–128, 134, 144, 147, 238–241, 258. *See also* subsistence economy

264 PROFIT AND POVERTY IN RURAL VIETNAM

Communist Party 64, 75, 104, 115, 171, 174, 243
local cell 41, 166–168

contract system 9, 25, 29, 44, 62, 79–80, 136–138

contracts 24–25, 63, 159–160, 205–7, 211, 222, 244
for agriculture. *See* work links
forest land 43–45, 97–98, 153–154, 206, 217–218
forest protection 97–98, 115, 120, 206, 217–218
investment 205
joint venture 44–45, 205, 207–209
tree-nursery 125, 217–218

cooperatives 8–9, 18, 24, 25–26, 60, 76, 78–80, 84, 102, 127, 136, 151, 241, 244
management of 8
decline of 25, 40,

cultivation. *See also* bananas; cash crops; cassava; oranges; rice; tea; *trais*
slash and burn 17–18, 97, 101, 139, 147, 149
swidden 24, 101, 235, 244

Dao 17, 32–33, 58, 77, 134–135, 145, 148, 178, 253
migration 135, 148
change in culture 148

Decree 100 8–9, 24, 44, 80. *See also* contract system

diversification 119–122, 128, 248, 258. *See also* commodity economy

Doi Moi 1, 29, 101, 109, 169, 205, 237, 258
effects of 14, 51, 70, 127, 133–134, 167–168, 170–172, 174, 242

improvements from 198, 213

economy. *See* commodity economy; diversification; subsistence economy

education 72, 103, 157–158, 244. *See also* school teachers; state
aspirations 224
difficulties 150, 166, 229–230, 236, 257
drop-out rate 68–69, 92–93, 184
fees 69, 126–127
illiteracy 179, 230
importance of 126
multi-ethnic 68–70, 23, 231–232, 236, 257
of lesser importance 223–228, 231, 257
parents' involvement in 126
policy changes 229
standard of 68–69, 92–93, 184
state provision of. *See* state
traditional respect for learning 233

environmental degradation 178–179, 205, 236

ethnic minorities 3–7, 17–24, 72, 76–77, 134–136, 144, 151–152, 154, 178, 181–182, 229, 236, 237, 253. *See also* Co Lao, Dao; Han; H'Mong; Hoa; La Chi; Nung; Pha Then; Phu La; Tay
(functional) Vietnamization 232, 257
migration 135, 148, 183
regarded as security risks 253
relationship with Kinh. *See* Kinh

INDEX 265

family. *See also* ancestors; marriage
economy 60–62, 65, 72, 113, 141, 163, 165, 168, 241, 246–247
filial obligations 53,
remaining at home after marriage 22, 187
size 20–21
structure 20–22, 48–50
support 62, 88–89, 123, 130, 220–221, 250, 253

family planning 65–66, 89, 109, 111, 182, 184–185, 216–217, 250–251, 255

fish farming 146

five rights 11, 83–84, 99, 190, 204, 209, 239
not understood 209
not explained 209

food
shortages 29, 46–47, 101, 105, 123, 127, 149, 158, 167–168, 178, 188, 198, 250. *See also* hunger
subsidized prices 20, 62, 157, 239. *See also* state

forest and forest land 42, 98–100, 203–204

forest enterprises 18, 242. *See also* Chiem Hog; Hoang Su Phi; Tan Thanh; Vinh Hao
contracts. *See* contracts
reorganization 62–65

forest gardens 27–28, 71, 152–153, 204

forests
aforestation 153, 204–205, 208, 210
constraints on development 161–162

deforestation 59, 110, 161, 200, 242
forbidden ~ (religious protection) 201
logging bans 60, 63, 72, 96, 112–113, 115, 119, 122, 124, 162, 172, 219, 242, 246
protection of 109, 152, 154, 161, 202–203, 205–209; ~ difficult 114
versus farming (conflict of interest) 99–100, 109

funeral customs 94, 147, 201–202, 251, 254

genealogy 22, 77, 251. *See also* ancestors

gift-giving 22–24, 220

goats. *See* animal husbandry

goitre 67, 215. *See also* health

gold mining 121, 146

Han 183

health. *See also* goitre; malaria; malnutrition
care 157–158, 163, 244, 250
responsibility for. *See* state
ill ~ 51–52, 63, 116, 125. *See also* retirement
insurance. *See* social insurance

H'Mong 77, 134, 178, 180

Hoa 134

Hoang Su Phi (forest enterprise) 3, 177, 204–235 *passim*, 244–246

horses. *See* animal husbandry

houses
collective 162
Dao 148
Kinh 37–38

266 PROFIT AND POVERTY IN RURAL VIETNAM

shift from communal to own 45, 114, 119, 159
state building grants 160
Tay 37–38
stilt 37–38, 148, 183, 194–195

household structure. *See* family

hunger 24, 188, 199, 216. *See also* food shortages

intermarriage. *See* Kinh-minorities relationship

illiteracy. *See* education

illness. *See* health

joint ventures. *See* contracts

Khuoi Nieng (village) 3, 133–174 *passim*, 237

Kinh 17, 19–20, 27, 30–31, 94, 128, 134–135
adoption of local customs and beliefs 93–94, 254
Kinh-minorities relationship 20, 93–94
migration 7, 20, 31, 72, 77–78, 101, 135, 253. *See also* migrant workers
mixed marriages 23–24, 114

kindergarten 55, 72, 106, 158

La Chi 134, 201, 224, 227

labour. *See also* migrant workers
demand for 163, 250. *See also* work, shortage of; unemployment
exchange of 87, 147, 253
hired 33, 61, 71, 87–88, 133, 142, 146–148, 155, 161, 194, 240, 258
rates 87, 208

labourers, day 164, 211. See also labour: hired

Land Law 1988 2, 9–10

Land Law 1993 2, 11–12, 24, 27, 71, 77, 81–84, 99–101, 138, 153, 188, 190, 209, 235, 239

Lam Tien (village) 3, 18–20, 24–28, 29–41 *passim*, 66, 68, 70, 237

land. *See also* land allocation
collectivization. *See* collectivization
conflicts 10, 18, 24, 71, 77, 99–100. *See also* land allocation
erosion 206
forest ~ . *See* forest and forest land
management system 42–43
reform period (1953–57) 238
transfers 43, 238

land allocation 25–27, 43, 80–83, 144, 152–154, 234–235
complaints about 26, 136
conflicts over 26, 81–82, 138–139, 152–153, 238
norms for 26–27, 188

language barrier 183–184, 257. *See also* bilingualism

loans
by Women's Union to women 216–217
common funds 90
for new enterprises 58, 60, 87, 90, 121–122, 164, 213–214, 246
positive results 118
relocation 51, 245
to women 89–90, 216–217
unpaid debts 123, 199
usury not found 221

maize 139

malaria 67, 150, 156, 165, 214–215, 234, 250

INDEX

malnutrition 67, 215, 250, 257. *See also* food: shortages

market economy. *See* commodity economy

marriage 88, 130. *See also* family
endogamy 180
mixed 23–24. *See also* Kinh: minorities; single mothers
outside enterprise 212
remaining at home after 22, 187
within enterprise 212

migrant workers 33–34, 103, 151, 251–252. *See also* Kinh: migration
keeping in touch 130
returning home 50–53, 109, 114, 115, 160, 246

migration
ethnic minorities 135, 148
Kinh. *See* Kinh: migration

Minh Dan
brigade 3, 17–72 *passim*
commune 17, 25, 37–38, 40, 43, 66, 72

mothers. *See* family; single mothers

mutual assistance 52–53, 58, 87, 120, 128–130, 146–148, 201–202, 254. *See also* associations; family: support; labour: exchange of

new economic zones 18, 151

Nung 77, 134, 136, 178, 180, 183–187, 201, 204, 213, 224, 227, 236
funerals. *See* funeral customs
marriage 185–187. *See also* marriage
migration 183

nursery 55, 67, 103, 106

oranges 140, 146. *See also* cash crops; *trais*
harvest 141
rising prices 140
storage 141

organizations
informal. *See* associations
official. *See* Communist Party; trade unions; Women's Union; Youth League

Po Lung (village) 3, 177–236 *passim*, 237

Phuc Tam (village) 3, 75–94 *passim*, 237

paddy. *See* rice

petty trading 85–88, 144–146, 211, 33

Pha Then 229

Phu La 229

pigs. *See* animal husbandry

poor households 118–119, 122–126, 133, 147, 163–164, 188, 196–197, 207, 222, 247–249
begging 150, 196
child labour 127
must hire out their labour. *See* labour: hired; labourers, day
reasons for becoming 40, 122–126
rich–poor differences. *See* rich and poor, differences between

population control. *See* family planning

poverty 47, 150, 178, 198, 216, 234, 236, 244
ethnic differences 39–40

production brigade. *See* brigades

private enterprise
  restricted 157
  resurgence 109, 239–240. *See
    also* commodity economy;
    petty trading; rice: trading

rice
  cultivation process 139. *See
    also* cultivation: slash-
    and-burn; ~ swidden
  trading in 85–86
  yields 7, 29–30, 62, 194, 239

Resolution 10 10–11, 25, 29,
  44, 79–81, 136, 138. *See
  also* contract system; work
  links

renovation policy. *See* Doi Moi

rich and poor, differences between 39–40, 71, 91–92,
  128, 133, 194–199, 246–
  247. *See also* poor households; wealthy house-holds

retirement 50–52, 109
  due to age 160
  due to sickness 51, 114, 245
  strategies of 51, 116–117, 245

Regulation 176 51, 245. *See
  also* retirement; work-force
  reductions

resin 205–207, 217, 219

rights. *See* five rights

schools. *See* education; school
  teachers; state: end of subsidized system

school teachers 225–230
  falling income 229
  tough working conditions 229
  variable quality 70, 257
  volunteer ~ 230

self-sufficiency. *See* subsistence economy

settlement programme 18, 148

shops, growth in 144–146. *See
  also* petty trading

sickness. *See* goitre; health;
  malaria; retirement

single mothers 47–48, 50, 53–
  58, 64, 111–112, 156, 163–
  164, 222, 243, 251–252
  identity of child's father con-
    cealed 56, 249
  lack of family support 164

Sino–Vietnamese war (1979)
  156, 183, 185, 190, 199–200,
  205, 212–213, 232. *See also*
  migration: ethnic minorities

social insurance 165, 215–216,
  250

state
  dominate role. *See* brigades
  end of subsidized system 59,
    64–65, 124, 158–161, 220,
    234, 253
  provides complete social secur-
    ity 76, 102, 157–158. *See
    also* social insurance

state forests. *See also* forest
  enterprises
  ownership transfers 43. *See
    also* land allocation
  regarded as ownerless 18, 42

subsistence economy 33–34,
  127, 144, 149, 155, 184, 221,
  238–240. *See also* cultivation;
  slash-and-burn; ~ swidden

"subsistence ethic" 220. *See
  also* mutual assistance; subsistence economy

INDEX

supplementary occupations 193–194

Tan Thanh (forest enterprise) 3, 17–72 *passim*

Tay 17–19, 22, 24, 27–28, 30–31, 76–78, 90–91, 103, 128, 134, 178, 224, 227, 253. *See also* families; forest gardens; funeral customs; houses; labour: exchange of;
culture and customs 88, 92–94
greater social role 92–94
migration 135. *See also* migration: ethnic minorities
peer associations 120. *See also* associations

tea 141

teachers. *See* school teachers

television 39, 255–256

trade unions 64–65, 105, 115, 124, 166–168, 171, 174

*trai*s (farms), orange 31–33, 57–58, 60–62, 70, 141, 163–164, 240. *See also* oranges
cultivation 32
expansion of 31

Tung Khoa. See associations

unemployment 115. *See also* retirement; work: shortage of; workforce reductions

unmarried mothers. *See* single mothers

village administration 40–41, 108–109, 241

village council 108

Vinh Hao (forest enterprise) 3, 151–174 *passim*

Vinh Phu Service Union 171–172

wages delayed 59, 106, 219, 244

work, shortage of. *See also* work-force: reductions 109–110, 129, 168

work-force reductions 160, 245–246. *See also* retirement

work links (eight) 8–10, 25, 79–80, 136, 188, 205

wealthy households 118–122, 133, 163, 191, 196, 247–248
increased use of hired labour. *See* labour: hired; labourers, day
reason for becoming 39–40
rich–poor differences. *See* rich and poor, differences between

women
dominate trading 180–181
loans to. *See* loans

Women's Union 41, 56, 64–65, 89–90, 105, 115, 124, 166–168, 171, 174, 184, 215–216, 250. *See also* loans

Youth League 11, 41, 105, 115, 167–168